Exotic Women

University of Pennsylvania Press
NEW CULTURAL STUDIES
Joan DeJean, Carroll Smith-Rosenberg, and Peter Stallybrass, Editors

A complete listing of the books in this series appears at the back of this volume

EXOTIC WOMEN

Literary Heroines
and Cultural Strategies
in Ancien Régime France

Julia V. Douthwaite

upp

University of Pennsylvania Press
Philadelphia

Library of Congress Cataloging-in-Publication Data
Douthwaite, Julia V.
    Exotic women: literary heroines and cultural strategies in Ancien Régime France /
Julia V. Douthwaite.
        p.   cm. — (New cultural studies series)
    Includes bibliographical references and index.
    ISBN 0-8122-3125-2 (cloth). — ISBN 0-8122-1357-2 (paper)
    1. French fiction—18th century—History and criticism.   2. French fiction—17th
century—History and criticism.   3. Women and literature—France—History—18th
century.   4. Women and literature—France—History—17th century.   5. Literature and
anthropology—France.   6. Exoticism in literature.   7. Heroines in literature.
I. Title.   II. Series.
PQ637.W64D38   1992
843'.509352042—dc20   92-2548
                                                                                         CIP

Contents

Illustrations

Acknowledgments

My first acknowledgment must certainly go to those who generously took the time to read this manuscript when it was still in its formative stages; I owe my greatest debt of thanks to Elizabeth Horan, Valerie Miner, Joan McGregor and Kirstie McClure. A Humanities Research Award from Arizona State University made it possible for me to complete the revisions and final draft. For their intellectual and emotional support, warmest thanks to Jayne Lewis, Kirk Read, Debora Schwartz, Carolyn Simmons, Mary Poteau-Tralie, and last but certainly not least, my husband, Richard Viglione, and my mother, Mary Somerville. Finally, I am grateful to Joan DeJean for believing in the project from the beginning.

Introduction

> **Unknown,** adj. It is not said of things that we do not know, because one does not say anything of what one does not know, but rather of things that one does know and the qualities that one expects to find.
>
> *Encyclopédie*

This study maps out stories of marginals, women inhabiting the borderlands of European society: literally in the figure of Mme de Lafayette's Zaïde, who is shipwrecked on the coast of Spain, and figuratively in the persons of Mme de Graffigny's Zilia, Abbé Prévost's Théophé and Mme de Monbart's Zulica, who are brought into France through no will of their own and forced into the margins of a new society. Some characters inhabit the hinterland of literary representation, so to speak, and make their impact on the textual universe indirectly (Montesquieu's Persian harem wives, La Dixmerie's Tahitian lover). What I hope to show is how the exotic woman's experience resonates with French cultural beliefs about foreign peoples in the late seventeenth and eighteenth centuries, and how this mirroring of literary and cultural conventions illuminates other changes in the ancien régime mentality.

Literary texts have meaning in the larger context of social and ethnographic thought. My analysis underscores the pertinence of the exotic novel as a vehicle of cultural translation or instrument of consciousness by framing literary readings with broader discussions of the politics of foreign contact in "anthropological" or travel writings and iconography. Assuming that all narratives, in the broadest sense of the term, are deployed between a narrator and an implied addressee, I present literary ways of "knowing the unknown" as analogous to pseudo-scientific strategies for "explaining the unknown" found in travel writings, and aesthetic modes of "showing the unknown" in book illustrations. While each medium—literary, ethnographic or pictorial—adheres to particular generic, racial or iconographic conventions, the topoi that consistently appear help identify the operative rules for representing exotic peoples in the late seventeenth and eighteenth centuries.

As the *Encyclopédie* entry indicates, the unknown emerges from references to the known. Similarly, any depiction of an exotic Other duplicates, to a certain measure, self-representation. Indeed James Clifford has argued that "every version of an 'other,' wherever found, is also the construction of a 'self.' "[1] By imagining the unknown Other as an exotic woman, French writers—particularly women writers—devised a means to comment on and reinvent their own world. My focus on the history of the exotic woman, then, allows for and in fact demands a self-conscious consideration of French women's history. The story of an exotic woman's initiation into and conflicts with French society offers an ingenious vehicle to imagine unconventional ways of negotiating women's concerns within the boundaries of ancien régime culture.

In each of the novels studied, the exotic heroine's relationship to patriarchal authority—embodied in the person of a suitor, a priest, a male colonist, or a father figure—forms the central source of her conflict with European culture. These fictional scenarios of resistance to male authority parallel the contestatory attitudes toward such patriarchal institutions as the absolute monarchy and its satellite, the Catholic church, found in eighteenth-century social and political thought. By juxtaposing texts from different moments during the ancien régime (the 1670s, the periods 1721–1747 and 1770–1784), I hope to suggest the impact that the ideological shift from absolutism to liberalism may have had on women's lives. My analysis of women's plots thus ties literary production to the social realities that accompanied the shift from late seventeenth-century values of deference to political authority and acceptance of religious determinism to the development of a new "enlightened" attitude characterized by moral skepticism, bourgeois individualism, and eventually, republican patriotism.

Women did not necessarily come out ahead in the war of the *philosophes* against "gothic" beliefs and "despotic" institutions. In spite of the egalitarian discourse of "natural rights" supporters, the legal barriers to women's property ownership under the ancien régime excluded females from participation in the political life of the new state. Under the rubric of reform, many French women found themselves bound more tightly than ever to the private, domestic sphere of family life. The notion of an enlightened "citizen" put forth by French *philosophes* suffers from a narrowness of vision similar to the limited notion of a colonial "civilization" espoused by eighteenth-century statesmen and anthropological theorists. In this context both "citizen" and "civilization" designate abstract, prescriptive ideals that purport to improve upon existing conditions (in the

French nation or the exotic culture) from the top down or the outside in. The great *philosophe* Voltaire argued that the Enlightenment should begin with society's elite (*les grands*) before concerning itself with the masses, and even then it should take care to prevent the common folk from learning to read.[2] The influential parliamentarian Charles de Brosses called for French colonization of the "Austral Lands," envisioning a model colony that would offer civilization and technology in exchange for natural resources, but his major goal was to establish a French monopoly on the native economy and territory.[3] Neither the *philosophes'* appeals for citizens' rights nor the politicians' calls for expanding French civilization abroad paid much attention to the effects these reforms might have on individuals inhabiting the lower rungs of a civic or cultural order. My discussion of the conflicts involved in "civilizing" the exotic Other in imaginary communities ultimately brings to light analogous problems in the historical process of "citizen-izing" the female subject in the French national community.

Methodological Issues

Traditional scholarship on Enlightenment exoticism, beginning perhaps with the work of Gilbert Chinard, Pierre Martino and Geoffroy Atkinson, has long discussed the savage or exotic Other as a product of European *bricolage*.[4] I emphasize the impact of gender and colonial politics on literary, anthropological and pictorial representation in order to demonstrate that the rhetoric of exoticism is not only an outer-directed discourse aiming to control and dominate non-European peoples, but also an inner-directed discourse which masks the (male) controller's secret fears of losing power, as well as his sexual anxieties, self-loathing and apprehension of religious, class or national difference.[5] My study thus discusses the exotic heroine not just as a "subtype" of eighteenth-century literature, but as a highly charged symbol capable of unveiling some of the blind spots in Enlightenment thought (and in traditional accounts of Enlightenment history). While eighteenth-century thought is often commended for its progressive political and social theories and French society is idealized as a scintillating network of salons dominated by powerful women, my analyses show the limited validity of such concepts. Focusing on the representations of outsiders to the French norm reveals the underside of idealistic Enlightenment philosophy, illuminating such "blind spots" as (1) the problematic distribution of power and voice in European-authored fictions of cultural Otherness; (2) the social limitations of political liberalism; and (3) the essentialist principles hiding behind Enlightenment claims to cultural relativism.

My analyses stress the textual conflict between the occidental writer and the exotic subject by focusing on how meaning in fictional texts emerges from the play between those levels of fictional discourse that Gérard Genette has labeled *histoire,* the story or lived experience, and *récit,* the narration or telling.[6] The level of *histoire* includes the fictional story of the Other's entrance into European society and its historical context (as represented in the novel); the level of *récit* encompasses those strategies used in relating the narrator's (or the heroine's) thoughts and actions to the ideal imagined reader or *narrataire.* By examining how French authors project the fictional voice and narrative persona of the Other vis-à-vis the known script of the Self, I hope to show how exotic female characters were used to question such key concepts of Enlightenment thought as individual self-determination and rational objectivity.

In its juxtaposition of canonical works of French fiction, popular novels by women since neglected, "anthropological" writings and book illustrations, the present study constitutes a kind of "cross-cultural montage," a technique associated with the "new historicism." Represented by thinkers as diverse as Stephen Greenblatt, Michel Foucault and Stephen Gilman, the method currently known as new historicism draws on a broad variety of cultural texts to demonstrate that the relation between artistic and social production of meaning is more complicated than was supposed by old historicist and New Critical methodologies. In its attempt to re-figure the sociocultural field in which literary texts are produced, the new historicism "refuses to credit the positivist notion of the literary text as a simple reflection of an immanently knowable reality," Ellen Pollack explains, "on the same grounds that it refuses to privilege 'literature' as a mode of signifying that transcends historical contingencies."[7]

Self-consciously informed by the theoretical insights of cultural materialism, Marxism and cultural history, this method (as defined by Greenblatt) posits that the work of art is "the product of a negotiation between a creator or class of creators, equipped with a complex, communally shared repertoire of conventions, and the institutions and practices of society."[8] Literature must be understood in three interlocking ways: as a manifestation of the concrete behavior of its author, as itself the expression of the cultural codes by which behavior is shaped in a particular historical context and as a reflection upon those codes.[9] This effort to investigate the relations between literary texts, other modes of discourse, and contemporaneous social institutions opens criticism to different kinds of voices than those traditionally regarded as the objects of literary analysis. Ideally, such work would question the dictates of traditional literary canons as well as the presumed "objectivity" of nonfictional writing.

These revisionary theoretical assumptions, however, have not always been borne out in new historicist analyses. Critics have attacked this methodology for its tendency to represent culture as a monolithic entity constituted by totalizing, hegemonic ideologies. Greenblatt's notion of a "communally shared repertoire" of conventions, institutions and practices has been criticized as a vision of culture that reproduces the elite male values that have traditionally controlled cultural production. Furthermore, new historicists are guilty of a masculinist bias, charges Judith Lowder Newton.[10] They carry on as if their assumptions and practices had been produced exclusively by men, yet the work of feminist critics has had much to do with the development of this approach. Indeed, feminist historians have long been practicing the intertextual technique known as "cross-cultural montage" in their efforts to reconstruct the lives of individuals excluded from the master narratives of Western culture. Feminist literary historians have long called for a radical rethinking of literary canons, and pointed to the problematic ways in which literary and aesthetic value has been determined by historically specific social contexts. While the annals of new historicism have ignored the pioneering work of feminist scholars, feminism has contributed, and will continue to add, inestimable depth to such literary/historical enterprises in the future.

My study attempts to reconcile feminism and the new historicism by bringing recent theoretical debates on the politics of colonialism and gender to bear on the representation of exotic women in a variety of seventeenth- and eighteenth-century texts. My fascination with the literature and the historical contexts of early modern exoticism took root in the juncture between two aspects of late twentieth-century cultural criticism: the Western anthropologist's slow realization of some ethical complexities involved in representing non-European peoples and, within feminist literary criticism, the attempts to reshape women's engagement with the Western tradition by incorporating the writings of our foremothers into existent literary canons. My thematic focus on the non-European outsider complements my historical focus on neglected women writers: both topics highlight the processes that determine who may speak or contribute to the French cultural or literary "conversation."

From its origins, anthropology has built upon encounters between a sovereign European observer and a non-European native who occupies a lesser status and a distant place.[11] As recent work by cultural critics Talal Asad, Edward Said, James Clifford and José Rabasa has shown, the imbalance of power between anthropological observers and their "native informants" has always been a problematic issue, as has the Eurocentric bias of anthropological reportage.[12] For the exchange of anthropological information is necessarily predetermined by the European's choice of informant, the topic and wording of questions, and the observer's own cultural presuppositions. The politics of colonial domination (or the threat or memory of domination) further polarizes the relations between observer and observee, rendering the resultant analysis not only culturally but politically suspect. My readings of exotic fiction and travel writing aim to take account of such concerns by examining the sociopolitical context in which the works were produced and the vision of cross-cultural contact that they project. Since the Enlightenment is widely regarded as the formative moment for modern anthropological theory, I also consider the philosophical underpinnings of these early "anthropological" texts and compare their methods and assumptions with twentieth-century models.

As a feminist critic, I conceive the literary text as the product of an often unresolved dialectic between the artist and society, and the feminist critique as a polemic in which the significance of these conflicts is revealed in historical and critical contexts. This means moving away from holistic analyses of large-scale structural elements in literary history in order to appreciate the local conflicts engendered in individual authors and local discourses. By exploring the gaps between the prescriptive, functional representation of ideal female types and generic exotic peoples in eighteenth-century anthropological texts and the experiential representation of gender and cultural relations in private fictional lives, I hope to demonstrate the potency of fiction as a site of local conflict. Informed by the work of feminist historians Joan Landes and Joan Scott and literary historian Joan DeJean, my discussion of women's social history through literary analyses highlights the relevance of women's writing to their lives, particularly as regards the issues of education, marriage law and property ownership.[13] Instead of relegating women to a separate sphere apart from mainstream culture, this study stresses the interconnectedness of men's and women's roles in ancien régime society by comparing the male-female relationships found in novels by women with those of male-authored texts and by investigating what women and men took from each other (i.e., literary borrowings, influences). This emphasis on women's being-in-the-world is necessary to considering the shape of a female tradition in seventeenth- and eighteenth-century fiction, characterized by recognition of female precursors engaged in negotiating women's concerns in literature and what Nancy K. Miller terms a "feminist" narrative poetics.[14]

The chapters in this book form dialogic encounters between stories of foreign contact imagined by women and men authors. Each reading pair is framed by the novels' similarities in exotic origins, historical context and/or genre. In Chapter 1, I compare Marie-Madeleine de Lafayette's romance of a shipwrecked Greek princess and her Spanish suitor in *Zaïde* (1670) with Abbé Prévost's tragic story of a Greek harem slave and her amorous French master in *Histoire d'une Grecque moderne* (1740).[15] The dominant perspective in these fictions is that of the Self (male, European) who tries to decipher an opaque Other (female, oriental): their messages tell of romantic frustration and cultural dilemmas that are resolved, or at least contained, under the heavy hand of a patriarchal order. In Chapter 2, I contrast Charles Louis de Montesquieu's tale of an exotic visitor in Paris, the *Lettres persanes* (1721), with the feminocentric version created by Françoise de Graffigny in the *Lettres d'une Péruvienne* (1747). Within these novels the perspective shifts toward the representation of a foreigner trying to make out the rules of a strange world (France). While Graffigny bases her work on Montesquieu's model, she ingeniously rewrites the traditional heroine's plot by choosing a female protagonist from the New World, not the Old. Chapter 3 matches Nicolas Bricaire de La Dixmerie's account of a natural man's sojourn in France, *Le Sauvage de Taïti aux Français* (1770), with Marie-Josephine de Monbart's portrayal of a Tahitian woman's contact with Europe in the *Lettres taïtiennes* (1784). These fictions exemplify the polemical nature of pre-Revolutionary French literature: the visiting Tahitian not only criticizes French society, he or she also symbolizes a primitive culture at risk under European influence. The metaphoric figure of the Tahitian woman organizes notions of "free" sexuality, anti-colonial sentiment and Edenic natural resources interchangeably.

Each reading follows a similar itinerary: setting out from the exotic climes of the protagonist's cultural and literary heritage, then exploring the text, that is, a discussion of the exotic woman's function in the novel as a whole, and finally venturing into the ideological context of late seventeenth-century and eighteenth-century French society. The chapter subheadings titled "Contexts" and "In the Margins" announce the movement across this thematic topography and indicate the relations between fiction and broader issues of exotic representation. The analyses found under these subheadings describe how French travelers, natural historians, statesmen and artists conceptualized the exotic locales. To understand what a reader of 1747 might have associated with Peru, for example, or a reader of 1770 with Tahiti, I have gleaned ethnographic information from the many "cultural reference books" published during this era: universal dictionaries and histories of faraway lands, articles from the *Encyclopédie*, travel writings and voyage compendia. In order to imagine the horizon of expectations brought to these works by contemporary readers, I have drawn on other "exotic" texts of the time—plays and philosophical treatises on foreigners—as well as noted pertinent details of reception at the moment of the novel's publication (critics' reactions, publishing data, sequels). Seventeenth- and eighteenth-century book illustrations provide another invaluable clue to judge how period readers perceived the exoticism of these works.

Exoticism Defined: Early Anthropology and Aesthetics

The texts of seventeenth- and eighteenth-century anthropology embrace a broad spectrum of approaches in their representation of non-European peoples. Some modern critics contend that it is incorrect to consider such writings under the title of anthropology at all, given the idiosyncratic techniques and unsystematic reportage of the missionaries, merchants and sailors who constituted the majority of ethnographic observers during this period.[16] Even the works of the most learned and serious-minded commentators depict foreign locales and peoples in ways that seem highly anachronistic to the twentieth-century reader: their peculiar compilation of legend, hearsay and eyewitness observations hardly conforms to subsequent ideas of the "scientific." One could argue, as Margaret Hodgen does, that the writings of early anthropology manifest a stubborn or paralytic resistance to the wealth of ethnographic information that was available at the time.[17] Yet as an attempt to give meaning and order to the non-European world, these works would have made sense to the French reader; they would have inspired confidence in the writer's powers of synthesis. In the late seventeenth and eighteenth centuries, writing the Other is best understood as a mode of cultural consolidation, a way of imagining (and containing or appropriating) possible threats or models to the French ideal of a unified national community.

To avoid historical anachronism, let us define exoticism in eighteenth-century terms. For the twentieth-century reader, "literary exoticism" may conjure up fictions richly embellished with details of tropical flora and fauna, primitive rituals and religions. Such conceptualization of the exotic is a product of the nineteenth-century consolidation of anthropology, archaeology and sociology into scientific disciplines that structured the description of unfamiliar worlds. The exoticism of the ancien régime relies on an earlier tradition. Like Montaigne, who called for cultural relativism all the while idealizing the Brazilian Indian as the epitome of Greek classical values, eighteenth-century writers often seem torn between their progressive ideals and their traditional aesthetics. Eighteenth-century exoticism is anchored in the literary conventions and aesthetic norms of seventeenth-century classicism, which demanded that textual production meet such qualitative criteria as plausibility (*la vraisemblance*) and propriety (*la bienséance*). These standards of acceptability, rooted in an aristocratic, Eurocentric world view, covered aesthetics, morality and even stereotypes of gendered and national behavior. In the name of protecting French literature from any possible impropriety, the critic Mesnardière presented a list of "implausible" cultural types, including the courageous girl, the learned woman, the loyal Persian, the truthful Greek, and the uncivil Frenchman.[18]

During the eighteenth century, critics such as Fénelon began demanding greater attention to exotic detail in historical writings and condemning the portrayal of foreign personages who look, speak and act like the French.[19] These authors typically emphasized the importance of capturing the mores, customs and political systems of foreign nations. Natural and physical details such as the zoology, botany or architecture of foreign locales remain largely absent from French literature until much later, with Bernardin de Saint Pierre's *Paul et Virginie* (1787) and Chateaubriand's *Atala* (1801).

Seventeenth- and eighteenth-century book illustrations offer further insights into the meaning of exoticism in this period. As Philip Stewart has observed, "illustration" in this period covers a wide range of pictorial imagery, running from literalistic depiction to vague symbolization. While purporting to represent textual content, such images often did so only abstractly and symbolically.[20] An illustration represents a privileged interpretation of a literary or scientific text, whether oriented by the author's wishes or not; by fixing the possible meanings of the work, it influences the reader's understanding. But the illustrated book, then as now, is also an expensive item, a luxury product, and thus is predetermined to appeal to readers of a certain class and outlook. Although publishers became increasingly willing to invest in the illustration of literary and technical books during the eighteenth century, artists were bound by the logic of the marketplace to create images that conformed to the dominant taste of the well-to-do members of the reading public.[21]

In the classical age the aristocratic reading public demanded refined mannerisms in conversation, art and writing. Late seventeenth-century aesthetics, governed by the doctrine of *ut pictura poesis,* privileged imitation and artifice; their use of representation sought communication with an elite audience of initiates only.[22] The images in seventeenth-century book illustrations, then, draw on a repertoire of established "devices" (mythological characters, heraldic emblems, allegorical figures) and form easily identifiable codes of representation—easily identifiable, that is, to the knowledgeable reader. Since an objective of such art was to assure that the beholder grasped a certain understanding of the person or event pictured, the illustrator used only those elements that conformed to the ethics and aesthetics of a target audience that delighted in elaborate official ceremonies, scenes of European court life and grandiose Baroque architecture. So we find the "Peruvian" prince of Gomberville's *Polexandre* (ed. 1641) dressed as a European courtier in cape, knee breeches and dainty shoes in the midst of a "Mexican" setting that resembles the bucolic landscape of *L'Astrée* and countless other pastoral fictions of the early seventeenth century (Figure 8). However American he may or may not be, Gomberville's protagonist is clearly no savage; he is a nobleman of genteel habits, as witnessed by his gallant kneeling pose, suppliant gaze and respectful attitude toward the female figures in the scene—a noblewoman and her companion.

As the reading public grew and became a more heterogeneous mix of bourgeois and nobles, Parisians and provincials, the purpose of literary book illustration changed in eighteenth-century France.[23] Instead of aiming to transmit a specific message to a predetermined audience, the illustrator sought to touch the individual imagination in an increasingly diverse group of readers. In keeping with the late eighteenth-century novelist's desire to stir the reader's sentiments, illustrators designed their images to create an imaginary community between the reader, the characters, and the narrator on a personal, psychological level.[24] Some chose literal expositions of key scenes, complete with descriptive captions to direct the reader's understanding; others animated their pictures with fantastic images of magic, illusion and dream, aiming to make the reading process

verge on a state of reverie. One need only compare the sedate Europeanized scene illustrating Gomberville's *Polexandre* with the extravagant exotic
detail pictured in Gueulette's *Peruvian Tales* (ed. 1786), which features a
bejeweled, incandescent hand floating over the heads of two Peruvians
dressed in toga-like robes, one of whom occupies an ornate throne decorated with strange smiling heads (suns, in honor of the Incan Sun King)
(Figure 9). While Gomberville's illustration emphasizes the European sa-
voir-faire of the Peruvian courtier, the image in Gueulette's work associates Peruvians with the fabulous riches, strange cults and supernatural
events of a mythic land lost in time.

As befits the uncertain generic status of early anthropological writings, the images that illustrate travel accounts and ethnographic documents waver between the formal exposition of the technical illustration
and the expressivity of literary illustration. The picture of the Peruvians in
Prévost's *Histoire générale des voyages* (ed. 1773), for example, resembles a
graphic application of a sociological taxonomy (Figure 11). Its hierarchical,
numerically ordered presentation of the social types found in Peru gives
priority to the generic over the specific, the species over the individual,
and shows the necessary social order implied by the figures' race and class
standings. By imposing a linear, numerically structured interpretation
onto these figures, the illustration makes the human being a scientific object.[25] The images of North American natives in Raynal's *Histoire philosophique et politique des établissemens et du commerce des Européens dans les deux
Indes* (ed. 1776, 1781), on the other hand, feature vignettes of colonial life
which can be read as stories telling of the efforts toward peace and understanding between Europeans and Indians, though from two opposing perspectives: the Europeans enlightening the Indians and the Indians guiding
the Europeans (Figure 16, Figure 17). These graphic images resonate inter-
estingly with the instructional subtext of Prévost's and Raynal's works.
The illustration from Prévost's encyclopedic compendium of voyage literature exemplifies the scientific method of linear classification often deployed
in eighteenth-century natural history texts. The figures from Raynal's politically progressive *Histoire* enact two scenes from the master narrative of
European–non-European encounters: the story of the charitable European missionaries who intervene to "correct" the savages of their barbarian
ways, and the archetypal Thanksgiving story of the uncivilized persons
whose material and philosophical aid rescues the destitute European
settlers.

The novels of this study exemplify some dominant narratives of cultural encounter told under the ancien régime. But unlike the expansive fantasies of discovery and exploration in voyage literature, the novels are essentially French stories of foreign intrusion. Their settings are familiar, only their protagonists represent the "exotic." The heroes and heroines of these fictions are strangers transplanted to European soil, exotic in that they come from abroad; they interest French readers insofar as they, the characters, enter the domain of the known (the Occident, or more precisely, France). The novelists' dramatizations of the foreigners' encounters with French society draw on prevailing attitudes about "original" identity and the advisability or dangers of cross-cultural contact. Some characters remain untouched by European influences, others are destroyed by them; some strive to assimilate into French society, others struggle to retain their indigenous identity. The antagonism that marks the relations between the French hero and the oriental heroine in Prévost's *Histoire d'une Grecque moderne* suggests the uneasy relations between France and Turkey during the early eighteenth century, when France was establishing its authority (commercial and ideological) over the Levant. The tragic disruption that characterizes the meeting of Tahitian and European characters in La Dixmerie's and Monbart's novels (*Le Sauvage de Taïti aux Français* and *Lettres taïtiennes*) reflects the authors' fears that European schemes to develop trade and colonial posts on the islands were bound to destroy the Tahitians' unique society and annihilate one of the few remaining vestiges of unspoiled "nature."

Other novels dramatize the encounter of France and the exotic Other in ways that appear more informed by literary precedent or gender politics than cultural actuality. Graffigny's Peruvian heroine in the *Lettres d'une Péruvienne* hails from a long line of ingenuous foreign critics, including Marana's Turkish spy and Montesquieu's Persian philosophers. While the Peruvian ethnic identity has some bearing on the development of the heroine's plot, Graffigny's description of Peru conjures up an idealized primitive community rather than a devastated colonial territory. The exotic heroine's gender often does as much to motivate her plot as does her particular national origin. In Lafayette's *Zaïde*, the male narrator conflates Zaïde's foreignness with her femininity to justify his distrust and suspicion of her actions. The Tahitian heroine's rape at the hands of an Englishman in Monbart's *Lettres taïtiennes* translates into a powerful metaphor for the English devastation of her island home.

Exotic Heroines and French Women Writers

The recurring topos of the exotic heroine in the works of seventeenth- and eighteenth-century French women writers derives in part from the writers' doubly disadvantaged social identity in ancien régime society. As an outsider to the French system and a female in a patriarchal order, the foreign heroine's social estrangement corresponds to the woman novelist's marginal status as regards established men of letters. The position of women writers in France during this period was precarious; the very idea of a woman writing was considered by many to be inappropriate and unseemly. It is rumored that in 1728 Mme de Lambert feared for her honor when *L'Avis d'une mère à sa fille* was published in her name and without her consent, and that she went so far as to visit a bookstore in person and purchase every book published in her name so as to protect herself from further infamy.[26] On the other hand, writing was one of the few gainful activities in which a woman might earn an independent living and possibly receive public recognition. The plight of the foreign heroine in the French novel—her difficulty with the language and her long search for a place in French society—mirrors the plight of the woman novelist under the ancien régime, struggling to find a public identity and secure a decent living.

The importance of acquiring language and literacy in these novels suggests a significant intersection between women's literature and social history: access to education and learned language form the central obstacles to the heroine's full participation in society. Although the seventeenth and eighteenth centuries saw improvements in women's education, thanks to the efforts of the Catholic teaching orders (the Visitandines, the Ursulines, the Bénédictines), not to mention Mme de Maintenon's famous pedagogical institution of Saint-Cyr, the emphasis was largely on the practical arts necessary to form good wives—sewing, knitting, religion, rudimentary mathematics and writing.[27] Many women writers complained of the poor training they received and of the double standard that encouraged women to cultivate ignorance in order to protect themselves from the label of *femme savante* (learned woman). Even the most well-bred and educated women had problems with spelling, grammar and syntax and often had to rely on male friends or professional secretaries to correct their work before circulating it among the public. The acquisition of literacy and written language were thus major preoccupations for most women writers.

In a fictive context, such concerns translate into a sophisticated reflection on relations between knowledge, language and power. Like the writer whose future reputation and livelihood hinge on her ability to articulate her ideas in eloquent prose, the foreign heroine's plot is often conditioned by what Hélène Cixous terms her *venue à l'écriture,* literally the coming to writing or taking-on of a means of expression.[28] The heroines of Lafayette's *Zaïde,* Graffigny's *Lettres d'une Péruvienne* and Monbart's *Lettres taïtiennes* are all depicted as ignorant of the French language and must learn or be taught its rudiments before they can gain access to self-expression. Lafayette's heroine remains mute for the first half of *Zaïde,* while the hero (erroneously) speculates on her past and misinterprets her expressive gestures. The narrator's asides to the imagined reader (or *narrataire*), however, create a sense of complicity between the heroine, the narrator and the *narrataire,* and warn one to distrust the hero's warped judgment of Zaïde and to question the authority of his account. In the first-person narratives of Graffigny's and Monbart's works, the heroine must overcome her ignorance of French before the narration can even begin. Mastery of language signals the heroine's ascendancy to the status of writer, with the intelligence and self-determination necessary to control her own destiny.

The striking similarity between Graffigny's *Lettres d'une Péruvienne* and Monbart's *Lettres taïtiennes* (subtitled *Suite aux Lettres péruviennes* or "Sequel to the Peruvian Letters") suggests continuity in women's writings. The effort to create a female community in the male-dominated world of letters is evidenced by Monbart's acknowledgment of her female precursor as a model and her attempt to replicate Graffigny's strategies for women's empowerment in the *Lettres taïtiennes.* Both Graffigny and Monbart spent their literary careers in exile: the Lorraine Graffigny lived and wrote in Paris, while the Parisian-born Monbart spent most of her adult life in Germany. The story of an exotic heroine from a culture devastated by outside forces offered these authors an ideal pretext for analyzing their own sense of alienation and vulnerability in a foreign environment. Like the exilée, banished from her native home, the exotic heroine plays the role of the perennially misunderstood outsider, who never quite gets it right. The cultural problems confronting the simple, primitive heroines in Graffigny's and Monbart's works parallel some of the social problems plaguing the uneducated, legally dependent women of ancien régime France. In their portrayal of the heroines' uneasy conversion to the French language and struggles with the rules of "proper" behavior, these authors shed new light on the problems of "never quite getting it right" by raising the possibility that not the individual but the whole French system is wrong.

The story of a foreign woman's entrance into French society constitutes an exotic version of a well-known literary topos, the novel of "worldliness," in which an innocent, unknown young woman makes her début in Parisian society (as seen in the heroines of Villedieu's *Mémoires de la vie de Henriette-Sylvie de Molière*, 1671–74; Lafayette's *Princesse de Clèves*, 1678; Marivaux's *La Vie de Marianne*, 1731; and in the person of Cécile in Laclos's *Liaisons dangereuses*, 1782).[29] The ingénue symbolizes the mutable character par excellence, the blank slate in search of an identity. Thanks to her dependent status under ancien régime law, she has no formal name of her own, only those she inherits from others—her father, guardian or husband. What makes this moment in a girl's life so interesting is that it marks her entrance into womanhood, formally announcing her sexual availability and circulation in the public sphere. In "coming out" from the obscurity of her familial home into the public eye of the court or capital, the girl's social function becomes evident. A focus on this transitional period between the relative freedom of girlhood and the heavy responsibilities of womanhood allows a critique of the forces that delimited women's lives in ancien régime society, that is, the conflicting demands of familial heritage, paternal will, financial privilege (or lack thereof) and, lastly, individual choice. Casting a naïve, defenseless foreigner as an ingénue enabled writers to dramatically illustrate the irrationality beneath the complex logic of French social maneuvering and to expose the injustices of the dehumanizing process that forced individual women into predetermined social roles.

Fictions of worldliness dramatize the conflict between individual autonomy and societal obligation. The young woman in these tales is invariably accompanied or confronted by a symbolic guardian of the social order (a father, mother, priest or employer) who urges her to learn the rules of social intercourse and to accept the most advantageous position she can get. The advice proferred by these guardian figures invariably echoes the functional concept of female nature that dominated eighteenth-century thought: in reviewing the possibilities for the girl's future, they ask not "What is her potential?" or "What is she like?" but rather "What is she good for?" The girl's identity is thus dictated by the social and economic structure within which she is "good for" something, either as wife, worker or status symbol. Similar processes can be seen in accounts of an exotic woman's "coming out" in French society. Speculating on the possible roles the foreigner might assume in *le monde,* the benefactor/guardian reiterates the functional model, asking not "What unique cultural gifts does this person possess?" but rather "How can this person's background be best exploited within the bounds of my society?"

Power, Gender and the Exotic Novel

In contrast to the representation of exoticism in travel writing and anthropology, the novel appropriates and tries to undermine functional explanations of human nature in favor of a nuanced tableau of gender and cultural differences. The eighteenth-century novel participates in the bourgeois, scientific culture of the Enlightenment while nevertheless representing contestatory, oppositional points of view. As Mary Louise Pratt has argued, European travel writing tends to reify non-European peoples through descriptions positing the Western observer's omniscient authority and omnipresent vision.[30] Presented as a documentary reconstruction of foreign manners, the eighteenth-century travel account (typified by Prévost's gigantic compendium) purports to contain all the available knowledge on the Other "to form a complete system of modern history and geography representing the present state of all nations."[31] The European observer negates internal conflicts within a foreign society by describing the native population as a collective "they" whose activities take place not in a particular historical moment, but in a timeless present tense, implying that all "their" actions are merely repetitions of pre-given, unchanging customs. The novel, on the other hand, maintains a much more ambivalent relationship with authority. The eighteenth-century novelist's preoccupation with convincing the reader of the work's truthfulness is glaringly visible in the typical "editor's" prefatory claims of finding a "long-lost manuscript" or "translating" the letters of an anonymous, distinguished person. Novelistic time and action are similarly fragmented into discrete, localized events in an individual life. The popularity of epistolary and memoir forms attests to the reader's enjoyment of feeling privy to mutually conflicting sides of a story, a self-parodying account of actuality.

So while the travel account aims to be an eternally valid, informational discourse on geography, religion and political structures, the novel emphasizes the individual subject's experiential participation in concrete, historically situated events. In terms of iconographic differences, travel books generally feature pictures of standardized types or homogenized "native" groups practicing customary acts or rituals (as in the Peruvians of

Prévost's *Histoire générale des voyages*, Figure 11, or the dancing Tahitian girl of Cook's *Voyages*, Figure 15); novels are rather illustrated by vignettes of easily identifiable characters in key moments of their story (as in the illustrations to Prévost's *Histoire d'une Grecque moderne*, Figures 4 and 5, and Graffigny's *Lettres d'une Péruvienne*, Figures 12 and 13).

Although these fictions disrupt the conventional normalizing discourse of "anthropological" reportage, they nonetheless suffer from a kind of cultural bad faith because they claim to represent the Other, yet they are written by delegates of French culture.[32] I would suggest, however, that the emphasis on gender in the novel complicates the representation of cultural difference by signaling the internal conflicts within seemingly unified communities and evoking the psychological ramifications of European exploration and colonization abroad. Analyzing the interrelations of gendered and cultural conflict in fiction makes possible a new understanding of the mechanisms of power and knowledge in ancien régime France.

Of particular interest is the differential treatment of the exotic heroine in men's and women's writings. While the female body is the site of anxiety in all these works—either as a territory at risk of invasion or as an impenetrable barrier to male (European) desire—it obtains an almost fetishistic power in male-authored fictions. The male authors' lucid exposés of (male) European blindness to foreign cultures coexist, paradoxically, alongside their evident fascination with the "enigma" of exotic femininity. In the works of Montesquieu and Prévost the tantalizing sexuality of the exotic woman becomes a dangerous entity, symbolizing a sign or commodity traditionally exchanged at will among men that now threatens to take on a will of its own. This anxiety over the violation of sexual boundaries suggests the authors' fears of social change; concern for the body's apertures implies, as Mary Douglas points out, a "preoccupation with social exits and entrances, escape routes and invasion."[33] Dramas of sexual transgression may symbolize concern with the increasingly mobile circulation of individuals across such time-honored boundaries as class status, religious affiliation and familial bloodlines in the declining years of the ancien régime. The menacing irrationality of female sexuality is doubly related, in Montesquieu's and Prévost's works, to the economic threat of the bourgeoisie and to the cultural threat of the inscrutable, untrustworthy Muslim.

These relations between powerful and powerless, master and slave, so fundamental to the political stability of the ancien régime, are treated somewhat differently in female-authored novels. The confrontation between Montesquieu's volatile, dangerous Persian wives and Graffigny's noble, industrious Peruvian offers a telling example of the differences between male and female perspectives on the Other. The exotic heroines of women's novels exemplify loyalty, intelligence and moral decency. Ultimately their virtues are rewarded, although success demands a heavy toll on the woman's personal freedom, possibilities for sexual happiness and ethnic integrity. The heroines of men's novels represent morally questionable traits: infidelity, sexual precocity and guile. Their stories end with the hero restoring his control over the woman's dangerous passions and thereby maintaining the social order.

Such strategies for writing the Other in a French script reveal the authors' differential positions vis-à-vis the dominant ideology of French society. As I earlier suggested, the period from 1670 to 1784 was a tempestuous moment in French history, when the very cornerstones of the ancien régime—the monarchy, Catholicism and patriarchy—were undergoing a crisis of legitimation. One might read the exotic woman's intrusion on the norm as a literary means of representing the emergence of this new, unpredictable element of (non)belief in French thought. The author's treatment of the Other can thus be seen as a localized response to the conflicts dividing ancien régime society.

In depicting the exotic woman as a threat to be contained in the name of greater social ideals, Montesquieu and Prévost construct imaginary communities peopled by representatives of French political, social and economic concerns. The dénouements of these works insist on determining the Other's "civilization"; they aim at fixing the woman's allegiance to (or exclusion from) the civic order at any price. The imaginary communities of women's fiction evidence a preference for more provisional, domestic solutions to potentially political conflicts. The conciliatory attitude toward social and cultural conflict in Lafayette's and Graffigny's works, seen in their heroines' willingness to negotiate for a place in European society, reflects women's traditional exclusion from the official seats of power under French absolutism. Instead of tackling the problems arising from cross-cultural contact with the sweeping reforms or draconian measures of their male contemporaries, women-authored characters maneuver their way through the labyrinthine channels of power and knowledge to arrive at outcomes that, although satisfactory, involve significant compromises.

Products of the pre-Revolutionary culture, La Dixmerie's and Monbart's fictions witness the rise of a different mentality in the late years of the ancien régime, characterized by an idealization of "primitive" cultures and their "consensual" forms of political order. Both novels glorify Tahitian society as a moral model for the nascent republican order, which was imagined as a structure that would protect man's "natural rights" and universal freedoms. La Dixmerie concludes his work with an optimistic gesture—the Tahitian returning to serve his people as the ideal lawmaker— implying his belief in laws as guarantees against social and political disorder. Monbart, on the other hand, paints a much more somber picture; by the end of her *Lettres taïtiennes,* Tahiti is completely corrupted by European aggression and the Tahitian heroine—symbol of the islanders' bountiful nature, sexual freedoms and colonial potential—has no other recourse but to join her estranged lover in France. The mitigated hope for the future at the end of Monbart's fiction reflects a realization that even under the most "consensual," "egalitarian" political order, a woman does not have the means to influence her countrymen. Faced with the collective co-optation of the Tahitians by their English invaders, the best she can do is escape, and try to build a new home for herself and her husband in a land that represents the lesser of two colonial evils.

Anthropological Fictions and the Enlightenment

Greece, Turkey, Persia, Peru and Tahiti were among the most popular locales to capture the French imagination in the years 1670–1784, an epoch that spans a time of great social and political upheaval. As we move from the height of Louis XIV's absolute monarchy and the heyday of French classicism to the rise of the Enlightenment, and on to the tumultuous years of Louis XVI's reign, the progression of ideas parallels the changes in the intellectual climate. The classical concern for social and aesthetic unity and coherence gives way to the Enlightenment pursuit of a cultural and religious tolerance, and the late eighteenth-century demands for political and moral reform. My fictional locales take us from the French writer's contemplation of such "fallen" peoples as the modern Greeks and Persians, long bereft of their mighty empires and cultural brilliance, to the miserable Peruvians, robbed of their Inca splendor, before finally arriving at the unspoiled paradise of the Tahitians. In this movement from the Old World (Greece, Turkey and Persia) to the New World (Peru) and then to the untouched splendors of Tahiti, these novels depict an increasingly contentious message about the Europeans' supposedly superior social, moral and political order. By the time of the Revolution the foreign heroine becomes a figure used to demonstrate civilization's dangers, to question Eurocentrism, and to justify a cultural relativism.

By positing cultural relativism as the ultimate good, however, late eighteenth-century thinkers glossed over the thorny issues at stake in the representation of non-European cultures. Relativism and essentialism are merely two reflections of the same problem; both project the Self's ideas onto the blank slate of the Other. Essentialism posits that nations are always already complete, clearly defined and unchanging. Relativism implies that all nations are basically the same, incarnating different yet equal qualities of humanity, and that there are no real differences between peoples. Both attitudes condition a faulty appreciation of foreign cultures and our own, for both blind the observer to the unequal distribution of power and voice in a social group and obscure the presence of divisive conflicts in a community.

Modern anthropologists have often been reminded that their discipline is a "child of the Enlightenment," as E. E. Evans-Pritchard puts it, a science whose intellectual aspirations grew out of the ideas and ideals of the eighteenth-century *philosophes*. [34] Many would trace the twentieth-century anthropologist's concept of culture and "scientific" attitude toward cultural difference to the work of Enlightenment thinkers, yet the seminal issues of eighteenth-century theory created the very problems that have plagued the "science of man" in recent years. The Enlightenment concept of culture derives from the work of Locke, who argued that social orders are based not on innate truths but on environmental factors, and the work of Montesquieu, who attempted to demonstrate the functional laws linking a society's institutions to such material factors as geography and temperament. The "scientific" attitude of Enlightenment theorists derives from their call for "tolerance" in social and religious affairs.

These concepts were certainly useful innovations for the elaboration of anthropological theory, however one must keep in mind their sociopolitical context and their particular uses in the eighteenth century. While the *philosophes* demanded social and religious tolerance, they also idealized "reason" and rational change or "progress" as universal goods. Underlying these ideals is the belief that with reason applied correctly, the world's societies will eventually adopt the best (that is, the *philosophes'*) moral beliefs, institutions and scientific technical truths. The Enlightenment concepts of reason and progress are partisan; change is only "rational progress" to those who approve its social consequences.

My literary readings highlight some of the conflicts within the master narratives of European–non-European encounters and show that, for all their claims of disinterested scientific curiosity, the European anthropologists/observers were very much invested in their relations with the Other. The focus on exotic women reveals how gender conflict can be used to nuance or uncover the friction of cross-cultural encounters as well as to challenge such "enlightened" ideals as tolerance and progress. By examining the localized conflicts (between men and women, Christians and non-Christians, dominated and dominators) in fictional encounters of French and non-European peoples, I hope to revise the traditional interpretations of Enlightenment exoticism and anthropology. My analysis of the exotic texts of early modern France ultimately rejoins debates on the (mis)use of cultural Others which are very much alive today.

Notes

1. James Clifford, "Introduction: Partial Truths," in *Writing Culture: The Poetics and Politics of Ethnography,* ed. James Clifford and George E. Marcus (Berkeley and Los Angeles: University of California Press, 1986), 23.

2. Robert Darnton, *The Literary Underground of the Old Regime* (Cambridge, Mass.: Harvard University Press, 1982), 13.

3. For more on French colonial initiatives in the South Seas, see "Contexts: Anthropological Theories and Colonial Ambitions in the Austral Lands" in Chapter 3.

4. Gilbert Chinard, *L'Amérique et le rêve exotique dans la littérature française au XVIIe et au XVIIIe siècle* (1913; reprint, Geneva: Slatkine Reprints, 1970); Pierre Martino, *L'Orient dans la littérature française au XVIIe et au XVIIIe siècle* (1896; reprint, New York: Lenox Hill, "Burt Franklin," 1971); Geoffroy Atkinson, *Les Relations de voyages du XVIIe siècle et l'évolution des idées* (Paris: Edouard Champion, 1924).

5. Marianna Torgovnick's study of primitive rhetoric in the modern age, *Gone Primitive,* informs my concept of exoticism as an "outer-directed" and "inner-directed" discourse. See Torgovnick, *Gone Primitive: Savage Intellects, Modern Lives* (Chicago, Ill.: University of Chicago Press, 1990), 192–93.

6. This theoretical paradigm condenses the three-part model (*histoire, récit* and *narration*) that Genette develops in *Figures III* (Paris: Editions du Seuil, "Poétique," 1972), 71–76.

7. Ellen Pollack, "Feminism and the New Historicism: A Tale of Difference or the Same Old Story?" *The Eighteenth Century* 29, no. 3 (1988): 281–82.

8. Stephen Greenblatt, "Towards a Poetics of Culture," in *The New Historicism,* ed. H. Aram Veeser (New York: Routledge, 1989), 12.

9. Stephen Greenblatt, *Renaissance Self-Fashioning: From More to Shakespeare* (Chicago, Ill.: University of Chicago Press, 1980), 4.

10. Judith Lowder Newton, "History as Usual? Feminism and the 'New Historicism,'" in *The New Historicism,* ed. H. Aram Veeser (New York: Routledge, 1989), 152–55, 166.

11. Edward W. Said, "Representing the Colonized: Anthropology's Interlocutors," *Critical Inquiry* 15, no. 2 (Winter 1989): 211.

12. Talal Asad, "Introduction," and "Two European Images of Non-European Rule," in *Anthropology and the Colonial Encounter,* ed. Talal Asad (New York: Humanities Press, 1973), 9–19; 103–18; Edward W. Said, "Representing the Colonized"; James Clifford, "Introduction: Partial Truths," and *The Predicament of Culture: Twentieth-Century Ethnography, Literature and Art* (Cambridge, Mass.: Harvard University Press, 1988); José Rabasa, "Dialogue as Conquest: Mapping Spaces for Counter-Discourse," *Cultural Critique* 6 (Spring 1987): 131–59.

13. Joan B. Landes, *Women and the Public Sphere in the Age of the French Revolution* (Ithaca, N.Y.: Cornell University Press, 1988); Joan Wallach Scott, *Gender and the Politics of History* (New York: Columbia University Press, 1988); Joan DeJean, "Classical Reeducation: Decanonizing the Feminine," *Yale French Studies* 75 (1988): 26–39; and DeJean, "Lafayette's Ellipses: The Privileges of Anonymity," *PMLA* 99, no. 5 (October 1984): 884–902.

14. See Miller's definition of "feminist writing" in Nancy K. Miller, *Subject to Change: Reading Feminist Writing* (New York: Columbia University Press, 1988), 8.

15. While it may seem odd to consider Greece a "non-European" setting, the Greeks' long-time occupation by the Ottoman Empire and the "degeneration" of Greek culture under Turkish rule made seventeenth- and eighteenth-century French readers regard this nation as a stranger to the refined, enlightened world of European culture.

16. On the conceptual limitations of eighteenth-century anthropology, consult Gérard Leclerc, *Anthropologie et colonialisme: Essai sur l'histoire de l'africanisme* (Paris: Librairie Arthème Fayard, 1972), 11, 232–40.

17. Margaret Hodgen, *Early Anthropology in the Sixteenth and Seventeenth Centuries* (Philadelphia: University of Pennsylvania Press, 1964).

18. H.-J. Pilet de la Mesnardière, *La Poétique* (1640; reprint, Geneva: Slatkine Reprints, 1972), 137.

19. In Fénelon's appeal for accurate depiction of foreign mores (or *il costume*) before the Académie française in 1714, he stressed the need for details of foreign political structures in particular. See François de Salignac de la Mothe Fénelon, "Lettre à M. Dacier, Secrétaire-perpétuel de l'Académie française," in *Oeuvres de Fénelon* (Paris: Imprimerie de J.-A. Lebel, 1824), 21:232.

20. Philip Stewart, "On the 'Iconology' of Literary Illustration," in *Dilemmes du roman: Essays in Honor of Georges May,* ed. Catherine Lafarge (Saratoga, Cal.: Anma Libri and Co., 1989), 256.

21. Alain-Marie Bassy describes the effect that changing publishing practices and public tastes had on book illustrations in the late seventeenth and eighteenth centuries in "Le Texte et l'image," in *Histoire de l'édition française,* Vol. 2, *Le Livre triomphant 1660–1830,* ed. Roger Chartier, Henri-Jean Martin and Jean-Pierre Vivet (Paris: Promodis, 1984), 140–61.

22. For more on the doctrine of *ut pictura poesis,* see Erica Harth, *Ideology and Culture in Seventeenth-Century France* (Ithaca, N.Y.: Cornell University Press, 1983), 23–29.

23. On the diversification of the reading public in the years 1720–80, see Eric Walter, "Les Auteurs et le champ littéraire," in *Histoire de l'édition française,* Vol. 2, *Le Livre triomphant 1660–1830,* ed. Roger Chartier, Henri-Jean Martin and Jean-Pierre Vivet (Paris: Promodis, 1984), 390–91; and Roger Chartier and Daniel Roche, "Les Pratiques urbaines de l'imprimé," in the same volume, 403–29.

24. Bassy, "Le Texte et l'image," 154.

25. For more on the functions of scientific illustrations, see Alain-Marie Bassy, "Typographie, topographie, 'outopo-graphie': L'illustration scientifique et technique au XVIIIe siècle," in *Die Buchillustration im 18. Jahrhundert* (Heidelberg: Carl Winter, Universitätsverlag, 1980), 206–33.

26. Joseph de la Porte and J.-F. Lacroix, eds., *Histoire littéraire des femmes françaises* (Paris: Librairie Lacombe, 1769), 2:75.

27. Pedagogical offerings varied according to the child's region and class standing as well. Aristocratic girls of the Ile-de-France region received a fairly rigorous training in French, history and geography; lower-class girls from the distant provinces might only learn to sew and sign their name. For more on the history of women's education under the ancien régime consult Paul Rousselot, *Histoire de l'éducation des femmes* (1883; reprint, New York: Lenox Hill, "Burt Franklin," 1971); Georges Snyders, *La Pédagogie en France aux XVIIe et XVIIIe siècles* (Paris: Presses Universitaires de France, 1965); and Roger Chartier, Dominique Julia and Marie Madeleine Compère, *L'Education en France du XVIe au XVIIIe siècle* (Paris: S.E.D.E.S., 1979).

28. Hélène Cixous, Madeleine Gagnon and Annie Leclerc, *La Venue à l'écriture* (Paris: Union Générale d'Editions, 1977).

29. Peter Brooks calls these novels stories of "worldliness" in that they trace the individual's attempt to learn and internalize the operative rules of living in *le monde.* See Brooks, *The Novel of Worldliness* (Princeton, N.J.: Princeton University Press, 1969), 5.

30. Mary Louise Pratt, "Scratches on the Face of the Country; or, What Mr. Barrow Saw in the Land of the Bushmen," in *"Race," Writing and Difference,* ed. Henry Louis Gates, Jr. (Chicago, Ill.: University of Chicago Press, 1986), 139–53.

31. Antoine François, abbé Prévost, ed., *Histoire générale des voyages ou Nouvelle collection de toutes les relations de voyages par mer et par terre qui ont été publiées jusqu'à présent dans les différentes langues de toutes les Nations connues* (Amsterdam: E. Van Harrevelt and J. Changuion, 1773), 1:title page.

32. I will return to the issue of the European authors' cultural "bad faith" in the Conclusion.

33. Mary Douglas, *Natural Symbols* (New York: Pantheon Books, 1973), 70.

34. E. E. Evans-Pritchard, *Social Anthropology and Other Essays* (New York: The Free Press of Glencoe, 1962), 21.

1. From Romance Heroine to No Man's Heroine: East Meets West in Mme de Lafayette's *Zaïde* and Prévost's *Histoire d'une Grecque moderne*

> The unknown always disturbs man.
>
> Littré, *Dictionnaire de la langue française*

The Greek heroines of Lafayette's *Zaïde* and Prévost's *Histoire d'une Grecque moderne* reside in the margins between the Occident and the Orient. While Greeks were long thought of as the originators of occidental European civilization, after centuries of domination under the Muslim Ottoman Empire (beginning in 1453), they came to be associated with the Orient. The foreignness of Greeks for French readers was reinforced by the country's inaccessibility to European travelers; the "barbarian" peoples of the Balkans made overland passage out of the question, and the dangers of sea travel were almost as daunting.[1] Only in the early eighteenth century did French travelers begin to visit Greece with any regularity. Their accounts, however, merely reinforced the notion of Greek "degeneracy."

Travel writings and dictionaries of late seventeenth- and eighteenth-century France present an image of Greece tinged with nostalgia and regret; the Greek people are seen as the wretched, impoverished remnants of a once-great civilization and the victims of Turkish political oppression and social barbarism. The article "Greece" in *Le Grand vocabulaire françois* (1762–73) emphasizes the pathetic contrast between the Greece of Antiquity and the present day:

> this country which was once the haven of the sciences and the arts, which was embellished with so many flourishing cities, no longer offers to the eyes of the traveller but dilapidated cottages, heaps of ruins, and poor inhabitants who are buried in slavery, misery, ignorance and superstition.[2]

But the Greeks' misery also gave rise to less pitiable traits. The botanist Joseph Pitton de Tournefort, who visited Greece in 1700–1702, wrote that its inhabitants were "naturally argumentative," "only interested in money," "all thieves by profession," and that, in sum, "Nothing can escape the ignorance of the Greeks."[3]

Zaïde and *Histoire d'une Grecque moderne* present contrary accounts of the Greek character. The heroine and namesake of *Zaïde* is an honorable Christian woman, her Greekness serves only to emphasize her suffering and helplessness in the grips of a despotic Muslim father. Prévost's Greek heroine is much harder to define: her upbringing by an abusive father and prostitution to the Turks at an early age seem to indicate her moral degeneracy, yet her oft-repeated wish to convert to such "French" values as chastity and Christian morality suggests her innate goodness and potential for reform. Whether victim or villain, the heroines of both novels encounter European men who attempt to "save" them from their oriental fate. But before beginning their efforts at redemption, the heroes of these fictions must unravel the mysteries of oriental femininity.

The central narratives of *Zaïde* and *Histoire d'une Grecque moderne* are told in the words of a European man who equates the oriental woman with a tantalizing enigma that he must solve and an object-of-desire that he must possess. By paying close attention to the narrative devices used to depict the characters' personal perceptions and cultural expectations of *difference,* my analysis explores the ramifications of oriental "mystery" in European eyes. The textual and sexual conflicts between an occidental narrator and an oriental heroine come to light through a focus on the incongruities between the narrator's narrative or telling (his *récit* in Genette's terminology) and the characters' story or lived experience (their *histoire*). In keeping with its romance form, *Zaïde* presents the reader with a number of narrative voices, each reporting a different interpretation of reality in his or her own autobiographical "inset tale." The heroine herself does not speak until late in the novel, leaving the hero to speculate (obsessively and erroneously) about her "mysterious" past until he finally gains access to her person. But thanks to the other characters' *récits,* the reader can piece together the heroine's *histoire* and foresee the hero's chances of winning her heart. As the fictional memoirs of an aged Frenchman, *Histoire d'une Grecque moderne* offers the reader only one view of reality: the Frenchman's. Although he relates the heroine's words in his autobiographical *récit,* they are necessarily filtered through his peculiar vision of the past. Hence one has a hard time determining the true character of the Greek woman and the authenticity of her *histoire*.

The heroines' aura of mystery motivates the plots of both novels, inspiring the romance hero's quest for knowledge and the memorialist's searching hindsight reflections. Their dénouements, however, give evidence of the authors' very different conceptions of the Other's place in French society, as well as their opposing views on the legitimacy of that society itself. *Zaïde* ends with a reassuring scene of unity and reconciliation. The dissenter becomes a loyalist, the foreigner a family member, the Muslim a Christian, the object-of-desire a wife. Domestic unity and national security are restored and the legitimacy of the monarchical state is reinforced. *Histoire d'une Grecque moderne* ends with the tragic death of the oriental heroine: the mystery remains unresolved. The cultural assimilation enacted so smoothly in Lafayette's work here proves impossible; its failure manifests a glaring symbol of the unfounded authority of French values to "redeem" the oriental Other. By juxtaposing these two novels—written some seventy years apart—I hope to illustrate the changing mentality that marks the shift from classicism to Enlightenment and to chart the different fortunes of the exotic Greek heroine in a female-authored and male-authored text.

Contexts: Baroque Exoticism, Aesthetics and Fiction

Seventeenth-century French readers were quite interested in the Orient, yet their notion of Orientalism appears rather limited to the twentieth-century reader. The scholar Barthélemy d'Herbelot's voluminous *Bibliothèque orientale* or "universal dictionary" of the Orient quickly became a best seller upon its publication in 1697 and inspired a score of imitations and copies. In the preface to d'Herbelot's first edition, Antoine Galland, the future translator of the *Thousand and One Nights,* praises the author for satisfying one's expectations and making the Orient accessible to the French public.[4] D'Herbelot's guide to the mores, laws, usages and religion of Eastern peoples has been criticized by modern critics for this very reason, however. Edward Said condemns d'Herbelot for "taking the immense fecundity of the Orient and making it systematically, even alphabetically, knowable by Western laymen," and characterizes the *Bibliothèque orientale* as a simplified catalogue of oriental traits.[5] Indeed looking at these collections of cultural definitions, one is struck by the great variety of ethnicities considered under the single category of Oriental. As Galland explained in *Les Paroles remarquables des Orientaux* (1694), for the seventeenth-century reader "Oriental" signified "not only Arabs and Persians, but also Turks and Tartars, and almost all the peoples of Asia all the way to China, mahometans and pagans and idolaters."[6] This practice of cultural generalization was not considered an oversight, rather it was seen as the appropriate manner to deal with foreign peoples.

Just as the dramatists of the classical age represented human society on stage as an assortment of French "types" drawn from aristocratic experience (e.g., the master, the servant, the courtier, the lover), so seventeenth-century writers represented members of other cultures as exotic "types" drawn from a stock collection. Both French and foreign characters were expected to respect the norms of ancien régime society (as codified by royal censors and influential men of letters), that is, they were held accountable to the criteria of plausibility (*vraisemblance*) and propriety (*bienséance*). The detailed list of unacceptable types in critic Mesnardière's *Poétique* (1639) not only prohibits such anomalies of French character and class as the thoughtful valet and the erudite lady, it also rules out such implausible foreign characters as the Asian warrior, the subtle German, and the modest Spaniard.[7] The novelist Boisrobert similarly circumscribed the limits of exotic representation in *Histoire indienne* (1629) and reassured his readers that no untoward details of barbarous foreign mores would trouble their reading pleasure: "I make known the mores and ceremonies of peoples, at least those which can give some pleasure to readers, always avoiding those things which would shock their sensibilities and might displease them."[8]

The most radical message found in seventeenth-century cultural reference books is an appeal for a qualified relativism, an admission that strange other societies might have some affinities with French values. Galland prefaces his collection of oriental sayings with a request that the reader rethink the terms "barbarous" and "civilized" and judge "by the testimony of the Orientals themselves" whether these peoples "have any less intelligence and good sense than the other nations which are better known to us because of their proximity."[9] The extremely stylized representation of oriental characters in the popular fiction and drama of this period, however, gives credence to Said's claim that the primary result of early Orientalism was not so much to unsettle as to *confirm* the reader's beliefs in the archetypal difference of the oriental world (Said, *Orientalism*, 65).

This apparent lack of popular interest in bridging the gaps between France and other worlds seems paradoxical, especially given the many initiatives launched by King Louis XIV to expand French commerce and (to a lesser extent) colonialism overseas.[10] But if we recall that for many

Frenchmen "the foreigner" (*l'étranger*) was synonymous with Anne of Austria's much hated prime minister, the Italian Mazarin, this paradox makes more sense. Mazarin's policies provoked the mid-century confrontations of royalists and nobles and set off the bloody civil wars of La Fronde (1648–53). After years of debilitating in-fighting, destruction and death on French soil, it seems quite logical that the French would be less interested in reaching out to establish contacts in faraway, possibly barbarous locales than they would be in re-establishing a local, unified community at home.

One must remember that the reading public of seventeenth-century France was made up largely of aristocrats (and wealthy bourgeois aspiring to nobility) and that the French aristocracy perceived itself as a group threatened from above and from below. On the one hand, the aristocracy was menaced by the absolute monarchy of Louis XIV and his plans to extend royal control over areas that had once been the domain of the village nobleman. On the other hand, the nobility perceived a threat in the increasing prosperity and prestige of the bourgeoisie, which had by then begun purchasing the offices, property and even the titled names that previously had belonged to aristocratic families. This sense of threat and desire for reassurance emerges strikingly in contemporary fiction. As a medium written by and for the nobility, the novel could be expected to reinforce a conservative vision of historical continuity. Works such as *L'Astrée* (1607–27) explicitly reinforced the aristocrats' dreams of maintaining an elite, noble community in the midst of a changing world. The common rhetorical gestures of describing faraway locales in the clichéd formulas of pastoral, epic or romance and declaring a scene or person "indescribable" constitute other metaphorical nods of complicity from the writer to the reader, each tacitly committed to the idea that literature exists in the service of a shared set of aesthetic and moral standards.[11]

Marie-Madeleine de Lafayette's multifarious career as royal lady-in-waiting, salon habituée, court intriguante and novelist reveals her close connections to the aristocratic reading and writing elite. The form and content of *Zaïde* also bespeak its author's association with the dominant powers of the literary community: after all, the first edition of *Zaïde* was published with the influential critic Pierre-Daniel Huet's treatise "De l'origine des romans" as preface. While writing the novel, Lafayette reportedly called on her friend Jean Regnault de Segrais (well-known man of letters and secretary to the famous princess "La Grande Mademoiselle") to verify the work's formal perfection. *Zaïde* thus contains many of the key conventions of seventeenth-century fiction: the storyline begins *in medias res* and is repeatedly interrupted by inset tales that clutter the text with seemingly insignificant details of love affairs, battles and voyages. The primary plot follows the circular journey pattern of romance, marked by love, frustration and resolution. The hero's love-at-first-sight for an exotic unknown woman leads him into what John Lyons calls "an illusory world ruled by obstacle and misunderstanding" before he discovers her identity, wins her hand in marriage and makes the symbolic return to an idyllic world sealed by religious conversion and political unity.[12]

The historical underpinnings of *Zaïde*, subtitled *Histoire espagnole* ("A Spanish History"), indicate another link to reigning literary conventions. Many novelists of the Baroque age considered a historical background an essential component of literary production, though their vision of history often had more to do with fictional plausibility than antiquarian accuracy.[13] By anchoring their narratives with allusions to well-known markers of ancient history—famous personages, battles, conquests—authors could impart logic and coherence to otherwise wildly improbable fictional events.[14] The heroic adventure novels popularized by La Calprenède (*Cassandre*, 1664–67) and Georges de Scudéry (*Almahide ou l'esclave reine*, 1660–63) rely on highly stylized historical settings for much of their drama and interest. Indeed the plots of these works often seem lost in the innumerable descriptions of courageous military exploits, dashing adventures and royal pageantry that make up the bulk of the narrative.

Inspired by Pérez de Hita's popular, romanticized history of the Moors of Grenada (*Historia de las guerras civiles de Granada*, 1595; French translation, 1608), Lafayette's historical background underscores the affinities within the spirit of chivalry of Moorish and European contenders for the Spanish kingdom. Although they may be political enemies the Moors are no barbarians; aside from their religious practices, they resemble the Spaniards in their *politesse* and gallantry (a fact that makes their final conversion to the Spanish crown that much easier). In his "Spanish history," *Almahide*, Scudéry paints a similar picture of the Arab as a Europeanized figure, eminently acceptable for French taste. Stressing the great difference between the Moors and their unseemly neighbors, the Africans, Scudéry lays particular emphasis on the Moors' white skin.[15] "The generous character of this nation makes them magnificent and gallant, clean and superb in appearance, as much as one could be," he asserts, and thus creates the image of a known elegance, a foreign world made admirable in accordance with French codes of social refinement (Scudéry, *Almahide*, 1:79). In

Almahide as in *Zaïde* it is only the Moors' Muslim religion, coupled with their intermittent military aggression, which sets them apart from the courtly Spaniards.

But while Scudéry's "Spanish history" features countless details of battles, jousts, fiestas and noble spectacles, such fascination with military prowess and public ritual is significantly absent from *Zaïde*. Apart from a summary of ninth-century Spanish history at the novel's beginning and the briefly sketched battles between Moors and Spaniards in the middle, Lafayette's fiction is remarkably devoid of the grandiose actions and sumptuous detail demanded by her contemporaries. The central drama of *Zaïde* is neither heroic nor historical but psychological. The "official" history of ninth-century Hispano-Moorish conflict provides but a convenient stage upon which to dramatize the characters' "particular" histories of heartbreak and frustration. Instead of relying on historical determinism to motivate her fiction, Lafayette locates the causes of her characters' conduct in their psychological conflicts—between religious and societal obligations and individual desires. The Greek heroine's ambivalent attitude toward the hero comes from her resentment of societal rules on female subservience in marriage and fear of her father's reprisals; the Spanish hero's obsessive passion for the heroine is complicated by his conflicting political allegiances to his prince and his father, as well as his cynicism on female nature in general. While situated in a distant historical context, Lafayette's characters face very similar problems to those of the author's reading public: this shows their "universality."

Lafayette's emphasis on the characters' psychology presages the shift in literary style at the turn of the century, when novelists began conceiving their works as less artificial or *romanesque* and more akin to true, personal histories. The publication of *La Princesse de Clèves* (1678) was to give great impetus to this move toward interior dramas, but already in *Zaïde* one can see that the author took care to justify her characters' actions by depicting the inner workings of their consciences. Prévost's *Histoire d'une Grecque moderne* will mark a further stage in this development, given its first-person narration and notion of truth as one man's perception.

What interests me is the way Lafayette maps the conflict between the hero and the heroine onto the historical conflict between the Christian Spaniards and the Muslim Moors so as to stress the characters' sexual misunderstandings and familial problems over their cultural differences. The hero does not realize Zaïde's true identity (as daughter of a famous Moorish prince, arch-enemy of the king of Léon) until late in the book. He initially pursues her because of her beauty and melancholy mystery, perceiving her as an archetypal Woman—a disturbing, enigmatic being. The sexual tension of desire and suspicion which prods the hero into action is also prominently featured in the various subtexts (portraits, letters, inset tales) that add meaning to the romance plot. The inset tales all tell of difficult love, disagreements and cruelty between men and women. By emphasizing the essential similarity of the characters' experience, Lafayette reinforces the reader's sense that human nature is universally consistent. Whether Arab or European, all the persons in this book suffer from the same vices and passions. Their dilemmas grow out of the basic antagonism between the sexes, compounded by the conflicting demands of their religions and rulers. In her reduction of religious and political conflicts to conventions of behavior and belief, Lafayette suggests that one can transcend these differences, that reconciliation between one-time enemies *is* possible. But the tension between the sexes may not be so easy to resolve.

Zaïde, or the Unknown, Incomprehensible Object of Desire

Zaïde opens with a very brief résumé of the precarious political situation of the ninth-century Spanish kingdom of Léon, which was threatened from within by feudal factionalism and from without by Moorish domination. As the only son of one of the richest and most influential counts of Castile (who was then in open conflict with the king of Léon), Lafayette's hero Consalve is presented as a victim of the political crossfire between his king and his ambitious father—a situation similar to that of many young nobles during the French wars of La Fronde. After a cryptic reference to some "important reasons" that forced him to quit the royal court, Consalve leaves his home in search of a solitary exile in some faraway place. He loses his way and ends up in an obscure fishing village in Catalonia, where, physically and morally exhausted, he accepts the hospitality of a noble-looking stranger named Alphonse. It is in this melancholy setting that he comes across Zaïde, whose body is cast ashore one morning after a violent storm.

Describing his first encounter with this exotic-looking woman, the hero stresses her capacity for surprising him, fascinating him and disappointing his expectations. He first sees her as "something glittering in the sun," a radiant object of unknown nature, before he realizes that she is a shipwreck victim lying unconscious on the beach. On closer examination he discovers a magnificently dressed woman, whose beauty surpasses all others in his memory. He is so "dazzled" by her fair face and flashing black eyes, "surprised" by her delicate features and "enchanted" by her white neck that he imagines her descending from the realm of the gods to enter his life. When she finally awakens and speaks, however, she only creates more confusion: "she pronounced some words; he felt a gladness and a trouble. He came nearer to hear what she was saying; she spoke again, and he was surprised to hear her speak a language that was unknown to him."[16] In spite of the hero's considerable linguistic competence (fluency in Arabic, Italian and Spanish), her presence defies his powers of reason. Dressed in the Moorish style, yet ignorant of the Moorish tongue, she constitutes a dazzling enigma. After days of nursing her back to health and longing to make her understand him, Consalve is hopelessly smitten. The rest of the novel traces his attempts to discover her identity, make her love him and secure her as his own.

From the beginning, the heroine's place in this novel seems an alien territory, the unknown area to be charted and conquered by the hero. Although the volume bears her name, Zaïde inhabits the marginal space of seashore and boat, foreign lodgings and enemy palace, until she finally occupies the safe, neutral realm of wifehood. The heroine's ambiguous role in this "Spanish History" emerges strikingly in the frontispiece of P. Porter's translation (*Zayde, A Spanish History, or Romance*, 1678), which depicts Zaïde being rescued by the two men in front of Alphonse's house (Figure 1). The spatial arrangement of the picture emphasizes her intrusion on the norm. A thick black line delineates the beach upon which she lies, separating it from the land and its native society (represented by a Christian church surrounded by a small community and Alphonse's large European-style stone house) before extending out to sea, where three tall ships sail. Forming a large *U* encompassing Zaïde and the faraway ships, the line seems an iconographical suggestion of the woman's alterity, her links to other people, other places.

The presence of Alphonse, Consalve's host and confidant, further marginalizes Zaïde's place in the novelistic universe. In their conduct and their words, the two men create an exclusive, male-dominant community. Since Zaïde is foreign and unknown, Alphonse warns his friend to stay away from her; in his eyes she is a certain source of unhappiness, for Consalve cannot ever hope to possess her: "you are, without doubt, wretched to have placed your affection upon a person who in all likelihood you cannot marry."[17] Alphonse and Consalve exchange stories and maxims

Figure 1. Frontispiece of Segray [Lafayette], *Zayde, A Spanish History, or Romance*. Trans. P. Porter (London: William Cademan, 1678). Courtesy of the Bodleian Library, University of Oxford. (Shelfmark 8°.R.69.Art.)

throughout the novel, particularly on the subject of unhappy love and female treachery, and in all these narratives woman is the Enemy. Before the heroine pronounces a single word, Consalve casts aspersions on her character, representing the sleeping beauty as a Machiavellian temptress and steeling himself in advance against her sinister designs: "as soon as she is recovered, I will not look upon her charms any other way than as I would upon a thing of which she would make use of to betray more hearts, and make more men wretched. Great Gods! How many will she ruin? And how many has she already, perhaps, undone!"[18]

The heroine's enigmatic presence and linguistic strangeness form the basis for the many dramas of (mis)representation in Lafayette's work. The inset tales that help advance the central romance plot illustrate the great variety of psychological and social barriers which can hinder communication between men and women; they constitute a catalogue of sexual bad faith and misunderstanding. Even unimpeded communication becomes distorted and equivocal in this world, thanks to the characters' mutual distrust and emotional blindness, not to mention their differences in language, religion and political affiliation.

A rather pessimistic love story, *Zaïde* vividly portrays the symbolic "static" produced when representatives of two different worlds accidentally collide. Static—the interference or noise emitted when electrical particles collide in the atmosphere—proves a fitting metaphor for the problems that plague the lovers' attempts to communicate. Michel Serres describes the effect of static on human relations as an insurmountable obstacle to understanding: "we send out signals, gestures, and sounds indefinitely and uselessly. No one listens to anyone else. Everyone speaks; no one hears; direct or reciprocal communication is blocked."[19] Chronic misunderstanding recurs like a leitmotif in *Zaïde* and conveys an uneasy attitude toward the Other—be it foreign or female. Authentic communication, this novel seems to suggest, can only proceed between elements of Sameness. Just as static subsides only with the disappearance of electricity from the atmosphere, the friction of misunderstanding dissipates only when the heroine is naturalized and enters the hero's society at the end. (Yet the silence that enshrouds Zaïde's abrupt passage from father to husband at the "happy ending" hints at the heroine's ongoing alienation, even in the idyllic world of religious and political unity.)

Although she is unable to express herself in terms the hero can understand until late in the book, Lafayette's heroine nevertheless attempts to make herself understood through the nonverbal language of looks and gestures. The author's ideal reader (*narrataire*) is meant to grasp the meaning of these gestures with the help of the many clues written between the lines of her story. Zaïde's gaze, for example, is described as soft, obliging, "so charming," "so passionate." Subtle authorial interventions further supplement her silence. The author informs us, for example, that if it were not for Consalve's misguided apprehension of female duplicity he would realize her obvious affection: "If he had not been possessed with these thoughts, he would not have believed himself so unfortunate, nor would the actions of Zaïde persuade him that he was indifferent to her."[20] These asides announce the existence of a quiet yet consistent discourse of authorial sympathy for the heroine and a valorization of her nonverbal modes of expression. Other textual clues heighten this sense of complicity between the heroine and the female author. By repeatedly framing the hero's speculations about Zaïde with verbs of uncertainty, such as "fancy" (*s'imaginer*), "seem" (*sembler*) or "believe" (*croire*), the author casts doubt on his reasoning, thereby sapping his voice of its authority. An opposite mechanism is at work in *Histoire d'une Grecque moderne*, in which a male author lends such authority to his male narrator's negative preconceptions about the "oriental character" that he effectively undermines the reader's trust in the heroine's words.

Lafayette's hero perceives the heroine's attempts at communication as incomprehensible enigmas, so he invents a story for her that artificially and erroneously motivates all her actions. With the frustration of a myopic voyeur, he watches her look out to sea, presumes that she seeks the trace of a lost lover, and despairs of rivaling that man's hold on her affections. When she appeals to him with her "passionate" gaze, he deflects the meaning of her look onto an unseen third party: "it is not me she sees nor of whom she thinks. When she looks at me, I make her think of the one thing I would fain to have her forget."[21] When she erases a painted figure of his imagined rival, the hero allows for the possibility of her love, but returns to self-pity soon after, since "the small hope this belief gave him could not destroy so many causes of fear."[22] After only a few days in her presence the hero effectively explains away any hope for her love, concluding: "I am in love with Zaïde and Zaïde loves another; and this of all my misfortunes seems the most terrible to me."[23] The specter of an unknown rival fires his passion and stimulates his efforts to win her heart. In the absence of proof he constructs a fiction of Zaïde's private life based on what René Girard has termed "triangular desire," that paradoxical need and fear that we harbor for rivalry and uncertainty in our passions.[24]

Zaïde's dilemma prefigures the painful situation of Prévost's heroine in *Histoire d'une Grecque moderne:* neither woman admits loving anyone, yet her partner is in each case convinced that she loves and is loved by other men. Prodded by their excessive jealousy, the heroes of these works demonstrate an almost pathological fascination (or rather aversion) for the sight of a woman absorbed in her own thoughts. Both Consalve and Prévost's narrator spy on their beloveds, surreptitiously intruding upon the heroine every time she appears to be concentrating or preoccupied. Neither Zaïde nor Théophé has anywhere to hide; foreigners in the heroes' territory, they live in borrowed space—making the hero's penetration easier. With their every moment of absorption broken by peering eyes and attentive ears, the heroines' place in these novelistic universes is reduced, circumscribed by the heroes' jealous, panoptic strategies.

The power of female absorption to inspire male desire and anxiety is graphically portrayed in a nineteenth-century illustration of *Zaïde* (Figure 2). This image presumedly depicts the scene in Tortosa, when Consalve overhears Zaïde confessing her love for him to her confidante, but misidentifies the speakers and so misses the message of her revealing words (130). In the illustration, two women in elegant oriental dress—complete with turbans, jewels, and layered, flowing robes—intimately converse in a garden obscured by night. The private nature of the conversation is emphasized by their physical proximity; it appears one is whispering a secret into the other's ear and gesticulating to mark the importance of her words. Unbeknownst to them, however, a young man in Spanish garb crouches below the promenade, intently trying to seize all their words, taking obvious pleasure in intruding on the sanctity of this moment.

Lest the hero's obsession with jealousy and fear of betrayal appear unfounded, Lafayette presents his past misfortunes with women at the court of Léon in the first inset tale, "Histoire de Consalve." In recounting his past life as a courtier, Consalve describes himself as a victim of society: betrayed by male friends, deceived by his lover and manipulated by the hidden forces of political intrigue. His autobiographical *récit* begins with a debate on the *question d'amour.* The *question d'amour,* a convention of romance (prominently featured in Honoré d'Urfé's *Astrée* and Madeleine de Scudéry's *Clélie*) and a favorite conversation piece in the fashionable salons of the 1660s, typically involves several characters in an open discussion of the psychological sources of love, the merits of friendship as a preliminary to passion, the reasons for disappointment in love and other "precious" concerns.[25] In this case the Spanish nobles Consalve, Don

Figure 2. Frontispiece of Lafayette, *Zaïde, Histoire espagnole*. In *Oeuvres de Madame de Lafayette* (Paris: Garnier frères, "Bibliothèque amusante," 1864). Courtesy of the Princeton University Libraries.

Ramire and Don Garcie discuss what they need to fall in love with a woman. The prudent Consalve demands to know a woman before loving her, whereas the rakish Ramire celebrates "triangular desire," claiming his heart cannot be moved except in response to a rival. As for Prince Garcie, he explains his longing for an unknown woman, unfamiliar with his royal identity (54–56).

This conversation forms a *mise en abyme* of the process of textual motivation in *Zaïde,* reflecting and foreshadowing the possibilities of love in this world. Ramire will in fact become infatuated with his rival Consalve's mistress, and Garcie will fall in love with a sheltered, unknown ingénue. Consalve's later experience, however, absolutely contradicts the maxims he once defended. While he does become acquainted with, then enamored of the lovely Nugna Bella, her eventual duplicity forces him to review his position and take back his hopes of ever really knowing a woman. In view of his past failure with a woman he thought he knew and his present frustration with a total stranger, the narrator concludes his *récit* with the pessimistic maxim: "there is no knowing a woman, they are ever strangers to themselves, and it is only opportunity that decides the sentiments of their hearts."[26]

Lafayette's emphasis on the universal antagonism between the sexes emerges in Consalve's attitude toward Zaïde's Moorish identity as well. Although the heroine's magnificent costume and unintelligible tongue suggest that she is an Arab—and thus an enemy of the Spanish kingdom of Léon—Consalve's anxiety stems less from cultural prejudice or Spanish chauvinism than from his negative conception of "female nature." Even when he realizes that the heroine is Greek, he appears far more threatened by what he sees as her feminine inscrutability than by the character flaws traditionally attributed to her compatriots. The notion that Greeks were a dishonest, conniving people was widely propagated in Lafayette's day, however. Pierre Bayle presents a typical image of Greek unreliability in his *Dictionnaire historique* by citing Cicero's judgment of the Greeks as cunning liars and false witnesses.[27] Prévost will exploit these stereotypes in order to emphasize the moral degeneracy of the Greek woman in his *Histoire d'une Grecque moderne;* for Lafayette's hero the heroine's sex provides cause enough for suspicion.

Driven by his pursuit of Zaïde, that foreign object of desire, Consalve's fictional odyssey becomes a labor of *déchiffrement* or decoding. How can he know what she is thinking, feeling? After following her around for days, peering at her through bushes and gazing at her from afar, the agony of uncertainty becomes too much, and the hero sets out to find an interpreter who speaks her tongue. He begins his Greek lessons by learning to say "I love you." At last, happiness appears close at hand. But when he returns, she is gone.

Alphonse now offers to tell his tale of lost love in order to cheer up his disconsolate friend and thus begins another inset tale, "Histoire d'Alphonse et de Bélasire." Compared to the enigmatic Zaïde, Alphonse's one-time lover Bélasire is absolutely transparent; she readily answers all of his indiscreet questions about her past suitors and feelings, but he remains unsatisfied, plagued by jealousy and doubts. No matter what she might say or write, no matter that her former suitor was then dead, Alphonse suspects a rival in the shadows, explaining: "as I was jealous of a dead man without knowing why, so likewise I was jealous of my friend and believed him my rival."[28] Finally Bélasire gives up on him and on love, concluding: "you have confirmed me in the opinion I had that no one can be happy in love."[29] Bélasire and Zaïde represent extremes in a scale of communication: one tells all, the other cannot tell a thing, yet their lovers both react with suspicion. By projecting their fears of failure onto imaginary rivals, the heroes of *Zaïde* become immune to women's natural, frank expressions of love. It seems that these men will not believe what they hear without the mediating voice of an authoritative third party.[30]

The reunion of Consalve and Zaïde underlines Lafayette's belief that cultural conflicts are secondary to the difficult business of love. After losing his unknown lady-love and returning to the court of Léon, Consalve throws himself into his military duties and regains the king's esteem with heroic feats against their enemies, the Moors. During one of these battles against a Moorish-dominated city the hero deigns to save a distinguished-looking Arab from certain death at the hands of a disorderly group of soldiers. That noble Moor turns out to be the great warrior Prince Zuléma and in following him into the château that he had been defending, Consalve discovers Zuléma's daughter, Zaïde (142–44). Despite the fact that they are now obviously enemies of war, Consalve renews his amorous pursuit and is surprised to discover that she has mastered his native tongue just as he has mastered hers.

A common language, however, is not enough to assure communication. The heroine continues to mystify her frustrated suitor by limiting her speech, anxious not to reveal too much of herself. Her paradoxical manner of self-expression (or rather, self-suppression) seems to work directly at cross-purposes to her genuine fondness for Consalve. She replies with discretion and reserve ("sagesse et retenue") to his questions and becomes visibly troubled by his presence to the point that she can find no other recourse but to flee one encounter deep in confusion and shame (219–20). In another act of noncommunication, she decides to write Consalve a letter, but only on the condition that he not see it until she is gone for good: "I will have that delight, without failing my duty. He does not know who I am; he will never see me again."[31]

Zaïde's self-imposed censure, one discovers, is dictated by the Muslim prohibition of female speech and heterosexual contact, as well as her fear of an unsuitable liaison. We learn the rules that constrain Arab women's lives by reading the female-authored inset tales which suspend the central romance plot at this point. Zaïde's confidante Félime details the social impotence and despair of Arab women by recounting the devastation wrought by a villainous Arab prince in "Histoire d'Alamir, Prince de Tharse." Bound by "insupportable constraint," the women are cloistered morning to night except for an occasional trip to the baths, the mosque or the park. And it is there that Alamir strikes, preying on innocent girls and recent widows. Alamir incarnates the immense power wielded by men in this patriarchal society: he seduces his victims with force, coercing one hesitant lover to surrender by reminding her that his intervention is the only thing that can save her from that "eternal captivity" for which women are destined (194).

Félime's account of Alamir's infamous deeds represents a cautionary tale like the old wives' tales of Western tradition; it communicates a warning of women's vulnerability in society. The unfortunate examples of Naria and Elsibery, who lose Alamir's affection as soon as they confess to loving him, should alert all women to the perils of sincerity and teach them to hide their true feelings from men (178–97). In light of this fear-inspiring model, one understands why Zaïde hides behind mystery and silence instead of freely expressing her passion for Consalve; such protective measures form her sole defense against the hero's indiscreet (and dangerous) curiosity. Women's only power lies in their abstinence and capacity to inspire unrequited love.

I previously portrayed Zaïde as a mute heroine, powerless to control the direction of her life. This accusation of helplessness requires modification, for in the context of Lafayette's novel the heroine's silence could be seen as a strategy to keep her destiny "open." Intentional silence can be used to assert one's power over others and to fortify one's impenetrability to attack.[32] The hero's relentless pursuit of Zaïde gradually moves the romance forward to its climax. This culminating point—when Consalve finally penetrates her mystery—signifies the end of the heroine's autonomy. Once he knows her and knows she loves him, he marries her and her story comes to an abrupt halt. Zaïde's strategic, deliberate silence *protects* her; it provides her with a delaying device, a means to temporarily extend the power that comes from abstinence and to suspend the inevitable outcome of her female destiny (marriage). The heroine herself admits enjoying the comfortable mutism afforded by the language barrier, for as long as she does not reveal her sentiments she is free: "I have, at least, this consolation in my misfortune, that the impossibility of speaking to him hinders me from the weakness of declaring to him that I love him."[33]

Reading between the lines of Félime's autobiographical *récit* ("Histoire de Zaïde et de Félime") discloses other clues that help us to understand the heroine's plight. Stories of other women's loves and losses reveal the usual potentialities for female destiny in this world and thus clarify the parameters of Zaïde's dilemma. They constitute a catalogue of female suffering, representing "all the feminine despair caused by the cold hearts and bad faith of men," including the pain of princess and servant, young girl and widow alike.[34] Growing up in an isolated palace on the coast of Cyprus, Zaïde's world is originally defined as a tiny insular community of women including her mother, her aunt and her cousin. When the girls were but babies, their Arab fathers deserted them, refusing to convert to the women's Christianity. The mothers' bitterness is evident in the maxims passed on to young Félime and Zaïde, who speak of inheriting a great distrust of men, particularly Arab men. Zaïde categorically refuses to marry a Muslim, Félime writes, holding that there is "no extremity which she would not endure rather than consent to marry a man so opposite in religion to hers, and whose laws permitted him to take as many wives as he pleased."[35]

Little by little, as the evidence of the inset tales accumulates, the reader unravels Zaïde's "mysterious" *histoire*. Thanks to Félime's narrative, we learn that when Consalve first encountered Zaïde on the beach, she had just lost her mother in the shipwreck; her tears were not shed for a lover but for the only parent she loved and her only defense against her Arab father. Once Prince Zuléma comes on the scene, Zaïde's dilemma becomes clear. The daughter of an Arab is always an Arab, regardless of her mother's identity. She is not free to construct her own future, for her destiny was determined long ago, when her father announced that she would marry a wealthy Moor. Bolstering his claim with the aid of a fortune-teller, Zuléma convinces Zaïde that she was predestined to marry the man represented on a certain portrait. Since the portrait depicts an African prince, Zaïde logically assumes that her love for Consalve is an ill-fated passion, counter to rules of propriety (*la bienséance*), and impossible to reconcile with her father's law.

Her father's discourse effectively circumscribes Zaïde's existence in both personal and political spheres. While her lover bids her to speak, her father's law of filial duty commands her to remain silent. She thus explains the impossibility of their love to Consalve: "all I can do is to pity you and bemoan myself; and you are too reasonable to ask me to not follow my father's will."[36] The revelation of the father's name coincides with the disclosure of the ties that bind the heroine, recalling the Lacanian paradigm of the "nom/non du père." In French, the name (*le nom*) and the no, or prohibition (*le non*) are homophonic, a resemblance used by Lacanian psychoanalysis to underline the father's commanding role in the child's socialization. When the father emerges as an important figure in the child's life (a significant *nom*) the child learns to submit to his law (his *non*) and by extension, to the conventions of society. According to Lacanian theory, the girl child's realization of her father's *nom/non*, that is, the symbolic order of public action, is a particularly problematic moment in her life. Saddled with a disadvantageous biological destiny, she cannot identify with the father's positive "masculine" values of action and self-affirmation. Rather, she must struggle against the negative connotations that Western society associates with female sexual identity—stasis, submission, silence.[37]

The Arab identity of Zaïde's father (his name or *nom*) symbolizes the sociopolitical obstacles (the societal *non*) that separate the lovers as well. Though raised as a Christian by her Greek mother, Zaïde belongs to her father, who is an Arab prince and a Muslim—and an irrevocable enemy of the Christian Spaniards. Underlining the political problem posed by their different nationalities, she tells Consalve: "Do not complain of me . . . but rather that you have been born a Spaniard; were I for you what you desire, and were my father not prepossessed, your country would still be an invincible obstacle against your wishes and Zuléma would never consent to let me be yours."[38] This love affair seems doomed to failure, for such an unauthorized liaison is paramount to a violation of the law of filial duty and an act of political treason.

Lafayette's heroine finds herself in a Catch-22 situation; if she succumbs to the hero's entreaties, she will bring on the wrath of her father; if she obeys her father's law, she will find herself in a loveless marriage. Stripped of the exotic trappings of Muslim despotism, Zaïde's dilemma appears very familiar; it duplicates the plight of many women in Lafayette's own world. Marriage alliances were a major vehicle through which an individual family (particularly among the nobility) might influence the public life of the monarchical state, so the question of parental authority loomed large under the ancien régime.[39] The importance of assuring the purity of bloodlines among aristocratic families made the control of women's sexuality especially important. "The special character of the ruling-class body lay in its unsullied blood," writes Anita Levy, thus the marriage rules and sexual practices of the aristocracy were governed by a concern with ensuring an elite body enclosed and pure.[40] Legal changes during the reigns of Louis XIII and Louis XIV helped reinforce the power of families to police their daughters' purity. By positing that paternal authority proceeded directly from God and that marriage was not a religious contract but a civil one, seventeenth-century marriage laws strengthened the legal position of fathers at the expense of women. Armed with the law, fathers could not only determine their daughters' futures (threatening to disinherit the recalcitrant bride), they could also manipulate the laws to punish clandestine love affairs. In depicting her heroine's impotence to fight her father's will in *Zaïde*, Lafayette indirectly criticizes the unequal balance of sexual power in her own society. The struggle between a young woman and a tyrannical father figure forms a major theme in the female literary tradition. Given their authors' disadvantaged legal and social status, it is not surprising to find the novelistic heroines of seventeenth- and eighteenth-century women's writings battling with phallocentric logic in its many manifestations.[41]

The dénouement of Lafayette's intricately woven sociopolitical family drama, however, is surprisingly abrupt. As soon as Zuléma recognizes that Consalve is actually the "African prince" of the painting and the prophecy, he resolves to award him the hand of his daughter. But first he vows to convert to Christianity himself and to submit to the Spanish king of Léon. Once the heroine's exotic foreignness is revealed to be but a mixture of Greek and Arab blood, ennobled by a Christian upbringing, her presence is no longer a mystery and the processes of closure go into action. Zaïde's marriage is hastily sketched in the final sentence: the nuptials were solemnized "with all the gallantry of the Moors and the politeness of Spain [avec toute la galanterie des Maures et toute la politesse d'Espagne]" (235). Since the terms *galanterie* and *politesse* are used indiscriminately throughout the novel to describe the customs of Christian Spain and Muslim North Africa, such description remains vague to the point of non-sense. As a symbolic meeting of cultures and an act of political and social unity, this ceremony seems curiously undefined.

One might read the end of *Zaïde* as a successful conversion tale, marking the moral righteousness of Christianity over Islam.[42] But when seen against the sexual antagonism that dogged Lafayette's characters throughout this fiction, Consalve's final possession of Zaïde represents a more profound victory—the triumph of male (European) assimilation over female (oriental) difference. From his very first meeting with Zaïde, the hero's conduct follows a strategy of sexual pursuit reminiscent of colonial assimilation: the heroine is foreign, he learns her language; she is silent, he makes her speak. She is destined to marry a foreigner, he proves he *is* that Other, and finally he owns her. While the correlation between the hero's amorous conquest and a colonial victory is but vaguely intimated in this work, in later novels such as Prévost's *Histoire d'une Grecque moderne* and Monbart's *Lettres taïtiennes,* the conflation of female sexuality and annexable territory will become more explicit.

With all the implausible (*invraisemblable*) elements effaced from her destiny at last, Lafayette's heroine is passed from her father's hands into Consalve's and immediately disappears from our view. In the final scene of *Zaïde,* the hero, the Spanish king and the heroine's father embrace, collectively admiring all the circumstances of "so strange an adventure"—that is, the story of Zaïde, which is now ended. The heroine's life hereafter takes on the status of a mission accomplished, a remarkable story that will circulate among the public. The novel ends with a resounding "the end"—a marriage, a religious conversion and a political truce—a reaffirmation of the contemporary reader's social and textual expectations.

By abandoning the heroine's plot to conventional novelistic closure with such promptitude, was Lafayette making a pessimistic commentary on women's literary, and actual, fate? The marriage scene symbolizes the triumph of the dominant order over the disruptive static (*bruits*)—sexual misunderstanding, religious conflict, political antagonism—that threatened to undermine its power. As a social institution, marriage realizes the integration of potentially threatening elements (foreign, noble) into the sociopolitical status quo and creates a pure political body. In joining the Spanish nobleman and Arab princess by the civil decree of matrimony, the perpetuation of the existing order (European, monarchical, Christian) is secured. The superficial description of the wedding thus represents a deliberate effacing of difference in the name of ideological consensus. *Zaïde* tells a reassuring message to its aristocratic readers in war-torn post-Fronde France: in spite of the many conflicts that separated the hero, the heroine and their families, resolution is possible if one is willing to compromise. But while supporting the cause of national unity, Lafayette questions the means taken to achieve it. In depicting the final scene of reconciliation as an exclusively male event, the author suggests that her heroine's autonomy has fallen by the wayside in the process. And now that her new role as dutiful wife has begun, what has she left to do? The silence that enshrouds Zaïde's presence at the novel's end makes an eloquent reminder of women's impotence in a patriarchal system. Henceforth all decisions, all action will be made by others—her voice is no longer necessary.

In the Margins: Imaginative and Political Landscapes of Greece and Turkey, 1670–1740

Both Lafayette and Prévost use the age-old conflicts between Occident and Orient, Christian and Muslim to amplify the tension between an amorous European hero and an elusive Greek heroine. But while Lafayette ultimately reassures her reader of the uniformity of human nature and the superiority of the Christian, European order, Prévost emphasizes the differences that divide the Occident from the Orient and challenges the notion of European supremacy. Compared to Lafayette's romance, Prévost's memoir-novel appears extremely modern. Instead of resolving thematic tensions with conventional strategies of closure, it presents a fragmented picture of reality which leaves the narrative open to different interpretations. Prévost's characterization of a strong-willed oriental heroine also marks a departure from tradition. One might best locate the modernity of his "modern Greek" (*Grecque moderne*) by contrasting the "Greekness" of Prévost's novel to other contemporary Greek fictions.

The image of a gallant, amorous "Greek" society dominates the novels and *nouvelles* of the late seventeenth century. Marie-Catherine de Villedieu situated her *Carmente, histoire grecque* (1667) in a pastoral Arcadia redolent of *L'Astrée* complete with lonely courtiers and reflective sophisticates disguised as Greek nymphs and shepherds. In the fairy tale, a genre popular from the 1680s well into the eighteenth century, one finds another conception of Greece as the land of magic and wondrous events. In her widely read *Veillées de Thessalie* (1735), Marguerite de Lussan depicts rustic

Greek women spinning tales of their girlhoods, evoking brushes with the gods and supernatural visions as frightening yet inevitable occurrences in their land. The premise of this collection is simple: the women each agree to tell a story of marvels they have seen, "one of those prodigies so ordinary in Thessaly and always attributed to magic."[43] The illustration from Lussan's tales emphasizes this notion of Greece as a land made marvelous, sometimes terrifying, by the proximity of the gods and the prevalence of magic and supernatural forces (Figure 3). "Her cries are heard all the way to the heavens," reads the legend under this shocking image, which shows a young woman in antique dress struggling to free herself from a horrible satyr who is abducting her for his ungodly purposes. The satyr's strange sexuality—his plump female breasts, muscular arms and horse body—contrast with the maiden's virginal appearance and make the scene all the more nightmarish.

Greeks were often characterized as "oriental" and depicted as sages or harlots, depending on their sex. Proverbially, a man who was "Greek" in his field was a man of great knowledge, hence the insult "He is no great Greek [Il n'est pas grand grec]" (*Dictionnaire de l'Académie,* ed. 1694). Greek women, on the other hand, most often embody sexual desire as courtesans or slaves—witness the lascivious portraits painted by Catherine Durand in her pseudo-historical chronicle, *Les Belles Grecques, ou l'Histoire des plus fameuses courtisanes de la Grèce* (1712) and the bold seductresses of François Dubois's *Histoire secrète des femmes galantes de l'antiquité* (1726–32). As figures in a stylized pastoral, gallant or marvelous Antiquity, Greek women are invariably represented as beautiful and passionate, desirable yet morally disturbing.

The title *Histoire d'une Grecque moderne* is provocative, for French readers would normally associate Greece with Antiquity and eighteenth-century France with modernity. While the French idealized the rich civilization and courtly society of ancient Greece, they perceived modern Greece as a fallen land of archaic beliefs and popular suffering. The French voyager Tournefort pointed to their pathetic building practices as an example of the cultural decline of the modern Greeks. Descendants of the greatest architects the world has known, Tournefort writes, these people nevertheless steal blocks of precious marble from magnificent ruins and break them up to use in their squalid dwellings.[44] In the views of such voyagers, it was only right and proper that Europeans should "rescue" all they could of classical remains from the modern inhabitants of Greece. As historian David Constantine explains: "The Greeks, in all their helpless

Ses cris se font entendre jusques aux Cieux.

Figure 3. "Her cries are heard all the way to the heavens." Illustration for Lussan, *Les Veillées de Thessalie*. In *Le Cabinet des fées*, vol. 27 (Geneva: Barde, Manget et cie, 1787). Courtesy of the Princeton University Libraries.

apathy and ignorance, and the Turks, taught by a barbarous religion to detest all representation of the human form, were not fit keepers of a great heritage."[45]

In a European context, however, "modern" had a very positive connotation. According to Prévost's *Manuel lexique* (1755), "modern" meant one of two things to eighteenth-century French readers: that which is recent and new (a modern invention, like the microscope) or that which is in opposition to an ancient paradigm (a progressive theology or science, like Newtonian physics).[46] A modern Greek, then, could signify an enlightened eighteenth-century woman or one who defines herself in opposition to an earlier model, a reformed Greek, as it were. This second definition informs Prévost's heroine, who departs from the tradition of the Greek woman cum courtesan to take on a new, unfixed identity. It is the tension between Théophé's unconventional vision of her future as a free and virtuous Christian woman and the French narrator's conventional mode of seeing oriental women (as fascinating and treacherous love-slaves) that animates the central narrative of Prévost's *Histoire d'une Grecque moderne*.

Yet this novel draws on more than literary and cultural stereotypes to create its picture of Franco-Greek relations. Unlike Lafayette, who used the historical conflict between the Moors and the Spaniards as a mere backdrop to her romance plot, Prévost's choice of a Greek heroine and a Turkish setting forms an integral part of his fictional project. While Prévost's narrative belies a debt to Lafayette's psychological orientation, to understand the psyche of his narrator one must understand the cultural situation in which he lives. The narrator and hero of *Histoire d'une Grecque moderne* is an unnamed French ambassador to Constantinople, the novel (his memoirs) recounts his ill-fated attempts to possess a young Greek whom he has liberated from a Turkish harem. Prévost's depiction of the ambassador's relations with his Greek protégée relies on a knowledge of French diplomatic policies in the Levant that is crucial to our reading.

The fictional ambassador's conduct exemplifies the self-serving attitude of French diplomats and merchants in Turkey during the reigns of Louis XIV and Louis XV. His attempts to "tame" his young charge and to reform her as his Christian daughter/lover represent an experiment in personal imperialism that duplicates official initiatives. French diplomacy in the early eighteenth century was designed solely to establish French sovereignty over the commerce and ideology of the foreign country.[47] The mercantilist expansionism of official policies conditioned French cultural attitudes toward that large, vaguely delineated area designated as "the Orient." Whether Turk or Tartar, Muslim or idolater, the Oriental was believed to inhabit a lawless region consumed by the warring forces of violent sexual desire and repressive political authority.[48] Given its natural tendency toward despotism, it seemed the Orient could only benefit from the stabilizing, civilizing influence of French trade and political intervention.

With the weakened position of the Ottoman rulers in the early 1700s (following defeats by Russia, Austria and Venice), the French position in the Levant become increasingly aggressive. Among the Western powers, France was the only formidable power with the same enemies as the Ottomans and thus enjoyed significant trade privileges in recompense for political support.[49] The French had penetrated the Ottoman market by the end of the eighteenth century and regulated trade by introducing tariffs and rules which expanded French control to the detriment of their British rivals. The spiritual influence exercised by the growing number of Catholic missionaries in the Ottoman states further advanced the prestige of the French. As a guaranteed market for French goods, a receptive audience for Christianity, and a supplier of cheap products for French consumption, Turkey rendered France all the services of a colony without the inconveniences of foreign occupation (Vandal, 16).

The French ambassador to Constantinople held the place of a European viceroy, a sovereign-once-removed; he was privileged with vast influences in the political, military and social arenas of Franco-Turkish contact (Vandal, 37–38). As sovereign of his country home, Prévost's ambassador will set up an idiosyncratic program of assimilation for his Greek protégée that combines his official program of commercial exploitation and political domination with an "enlightened" humanitarian goal of moral reform. The narrator's equivocal distinction between occidental *lumières* (wisdom or light) and oriental *ténèbres* (ignorance or darkness) becomes plain in his efforts to control the elusive object of his desire—as when he figuratively remodels his country home along the lines of a harem, or translates his desire to protect the woman into coercive measures of female subservience. The rigid surveillance exerted over the oriental "guests" on the Frenchman's estate reveals a colonist's desire to control and regulate indigenous elements in the service of his state. Through the tale of the ambassador's obsessive passion for the oriental woman and the follies he commits in his efforts to dominate her, Prévost indicts the imperialism and misogyny that informed French attitudes and policy toward the Orient.

Histoire d'une Grecque moderne, Story of a Fatal Encounter

Critics have long read Prévost's novel as a thinly veiled account of a scandalous event of Regency history, that is, the rumored incestuous relations between the French diplomat Charles de Ferriol and his Circassian protégée Mlle Aïssé.[50] Shifting the focus of critical inquiry from the particular to the paradigmatic, I interpret Prévost's account of a Frenchman's passion for an oriental object-of-desire as an example of ancien régime cultural politics. While the hero of this aborted love story relies on traditional prejudices about oriental inscrutability to stress his beloved's treacherous character, his own words and actions cast a satiric light on the European's superiority over the Orient. An analysis of the contradictions between the narrator's telling (his *récit*) of his tale and the evidence of his lived experience with the heroine (their *histoire*), reveals how Prévost insinuates doubt into the very fabric of his novel and eventually undermines the moral authority, narrative sincerity and cultural perspicacity of his fictional author. The text's pretense of truth-seeking unravels completely when one realizes the distorted morality that motivates the protagonist and, by extension, the hollow epistemological foundations that underlie his ancien régime values.

Presented as a "found object," *Histoire d'une Grecque moderne* recounts the recent past of a famous (nameless) man and the "truth" of a private world. The undependable vision of Prévost's narrator strikes the reader immediately upon opening the novel and finding this confession: "I am in love with the beautiful Greek whose story I am going to attempt to tell. Who will consider me totally honest in this account of my joys and sorrows? . . . what sort of reliability should one expect from a pen guided solely by love?"[51] Following this admission of partiality, the narrator calls on his reader to judge his beloved: "I am a suitor who has been rejected, even betrayed, if I must rely on those appearances of which I shall let my readers be the final judge" (59).[52] The conflicting axes of narration and judgment are thus set up from the beginning: the narrator asks us to offer our (impartial) judgment of Théophé, while his own bias deliberately obscures our vision and troubles the truth value of his narration.

The reader must read between the lines of this novel and follow the progress of two interwoven subtexts—the oriental heroine's plot (*histoire*) and the occidental narrator's psyche, seen in his *récit*. The distinction between these two textual levels is blurred, however, by the nature of Prévost's fictional enterprise. As in *Zaïde,* the hero's misprision confuses the reader's perception of the heroine. But the eclectic structure of Lafayette's romance novel allows for a variety of narrators, representing a variety of perspectives. The reader of her work recognizes Consalve's vision as particular to him and erroneous, whereas the memoir form of Prévost's work means that the reader has little access to any but the narrator's voice and his particular version of reality.

The story of *Histoire d'une Grecque moderne* takes place, for the most part, in a Turkish setting; thus the ambassador is the only non-Oriental in the text. But since he controls the narration, he portrays Turks and Greeks as strangers in his world, or rather as symptoms of the strange ways of the East. He introduces himself as an exemplar of cultural understanding, a veritable "Turkish Frenchman" who effortlessly surmounts the religious and linguistic obstacles posed by the Muslim culture of Ottoman Turkey. His mastery of the Orient is underscored when he recounts his being invited into that highly charged symbol of oriental secrecy, impenetrability and eroticism, the harem.

The narrator's ambivalent attitude toward this spectacle of sexual despotism—a conventional target in Western accounts of the Orient—reveals his problematic sexual politics. As we shall see in Chapter 2, French visitors to the Levant typically condemned the harem as a domestic model of oriental despotism; but Prévost's narrator praises its extraordinary tranquillity. Although he refuses to describe the harem's interior, he details the women's controlled actions at length because, as he puts it, "the prevailing sense of order I saw around me impressed me too much not to be able to recall easily all the details of my visit" (63).[53] Emphasizing the unit's tight organization, he depicts the women moving on demand from solitary handiwork to orchestrated dancing as a "gallant assembly" embellished by the women's "grace and agility." The scene conveys a sense of freedom within confinement: the women are free to choose their own pastimes (though the choice is limited to painting, sewing or embroidery); the pasha speaks to them kindly (but none dare defy his orders); and an ever-present group of non-threatening males (eunuchs) stands guard beside the harem doors to serve the women's desires (and the master's will).

The key to this domestic bliss, the pasha tells the ambassador, lies not in some mysterious Turkish essence, for these women are mostly foreigners. Rather it lies in the exercise of continual, subtle coercion which erodes the women's independent spirits and makes them resigned to their fate. As the narrator recalls: "[The pasha] made some sensible comments to me about the power of education and custom which made the most beautiful of women obedient and submissive" (64).[54] As if to prove his point, the pasha calls over his newest acquisition, a beautiful young Greek. Vivacious and intelligent as she is, this girl has already become a model concubine, thanks to the pasha's well-enforced law—"the strength of our example and customs" (64) ["la force de l'exemple et de l'habitude" (8)].* This lesson is not lost on the Frenchman; later he will devise his own method of assuring female subservience along the principles absorbed in this harem—the principles of control through surveillance and education through habit.

Impressed by the young Greek's obedience to her aging master, the ambassador expounds on the differences between oriental and occidental women and laments women's abuse of freedom in Christian countries, where long-suffering husbands treat their wives as queens rather than slaves and ask for nothing in return but kindness, tenderness and virtue. Soon afterwards he receives a note from the young slave, begging him in honor of "those women who love virtue" to release her from the pasha's control (66). He consents, justifying his intervention as a philanthropic gesture: "I swore . . . that I felt nothing for her . . . thinking only of setting her free" (71).[55] Yet in agreeing to purchase her freedom, he disturbs the fabric of her oriental destiny and creates an ambiguous pact with unknown consequences. Arguing for her freedom, he starts plotting to retain, change and control her. While ostensibly dismantling the Eastern system of sexual slavery, the Frenchman creates a new, equally perverted system in its place.

Indeed the harem forms a central metaphor for the Frenchman's fascination with mechanisms of social manipulation and control. With its monotonous discipline, routine and constant surveillance, the harem transforms individual women into what Michel Foucault calls "docile bodies"—emblems of the master's power.[56] As in *Discipline and Punish,* where Foucault argues that institutionalized enclosures typify the ancien régime mentality, the desire to maintain physical control and psychological domination over marginal social groups is evident on the institutional level of

---

*In this and other short quotes in the text, the first page citation refers to the English translation; the second refers to the French original.

such eighteenth-century inventions as boarding schools and hospitals for vagabonds and paupers. The institution functions according to an invisible network of social and psychological coercion in Foucault's paradigm; the mechanism of colonial control operates similarly in Prévost's novel. The intentional use of "seraglio" instead of "harem" in *Histoire d'une Grecque moderne* emphasizes the political valence of this institution.[57] "Seraglio" refers to the sultan's entire palace and, by extension, to the political organization of the oriental despot, while "harem" designates only the women's quarter in the seraglio.[58] By appropriating the pasha's seraglio for his own use—first purchasing one of his slaves and later creating his own version of the seraglio—Prévost's fictional Frenchman gives full rein to his urges for domination over and colonization of the unruly oriental state.

The ambassador's plans, however, are to be thwarted by his protégée's rejection of her oriental identity. Said maintains that "oriental" connotes an absence or lack of self-definition in European eyes.[59] As if aware of this vulnerability, the young Greek's first actions upon leaving the harem are to create a new identity, changing her appearance and her name. She adopts the manner of a free woman, physically demonstrating her new, improved social status in the hope of reaping its benefits: "She knew the difference Turks make in their behavior toward free women since she had heard about it many times since her arrival in Turkey. . . . her first reaction was to assume the air and look she thought appropriate to such a change in her worldly position" (75).[60]

Second, she changes her name—from Zara to Théophé. The exotic resonance of Zara, like other exotic names in early modern fiction— Zoraida, the Arabic woman who is led out of captivity in Cervantes's *Don Quixote* (1620); Lafayette's Zaïde; Zachi, Zéphis, and Zélis, the frustrated harem wives of Montesquieu's *Lettres persanes* (1721); and Zilia, the ingenuous Peruvian of Graffigny's *Lettres d'une Péruvienne* (1747)—announces a woman who is culturally and graphically different from the European norm.[61] By rejecting that name, with its generic connotations of servitude and sensuality, and adopting the original name Théophé, the young woman sheds the links to her oriental past. The neologism Théophé combines the Greek symbol of divinity, *theo*, with *phé*, derived from the Greek *phema* (voice, rumor, reputation), from *phanai*, to speak. Hence Théophé means "God's voice" or "divine reputation," the ultimate signifier for this eighteenth-century woman who so fervently desires a good reputation.

This name change graphically represents the Greek's readiness to assume a "modern" Western identity, to rewrite the archaic oriental tale of women's passion and malleability in favor of an (idealized) occidental script of virtue and chastity. Recounting her life story, Théophé details the sordid facts of her childhood in the hands of a ruthless, exploitative father and describes the numbing routine of her life as a harem concubine before concluding that her liberation from the seraglio marks her moral conversion to the Western values of self-determination and free will. Claiming to embrace the narrator's principles as guarantees of a new kind of happiness, attainable in his world, she exclaims: "I kept repeating to myself, 'There is a country where people find a happiness that depends on something other than chance and money! . . . Women have other talents which count and other goals to obtain!'" (93).[62] Change, as she understands it, means the freedom to control her existence, her future, her very identity.

Were this little tale independent of the novel, one might read it as a smug occidental philosophical lesson demonstrating the superiority of occidental (implicitly Christian) values over the barbaric oriental system, and suggesting that the woman's plot will develop into a message of redemption through assimilation. The narrative strategies of the ambassador's *récit*, however, make such a reading impossible. Basing his interpretations on a (presumedly) shared antagonism toward the Orient, the narrator repeatedly interrupts his story with ironic asides to his ideal reader (*narrataire*), whom he imagines joining him in a pact of like-minded thinkers who agree on the woman's dubious morality. He frames Théophé's philosophical simplicity in cynicism and undermines her sincerity with suspicion, as when he comments on her self-portrait: "If anyone, after reading Théophé's account, has grasped even a small portion of the thoughts that it evoked in me, then that person ought to expect the sort of reactions which are going to follow" (98).[63] In keeping with his imperialistic, misogynist attitude toward his subject, the ambassador conceives of the ideal community between narrator and *narrataire* as a limited and sovereign community—limited to male readers, sovereign over the cultural space of the Orient.[64] The male gender of the *narrataire* becomes evident when the narrator (ironically) declares Théophé "a unique woman whose conduct and principles ought to be suggested for individuals *of her sex and of ours* to emulate" (241, emphasis added).[65] The European identity of the *narrataire* comes out in gestures of unity against the oriental Other, as when the narrator justifies his distrust of Théophé with a popular slur on

Greek honesty: "Today, as in ages past, to trust a Greek is an ironical saying" (99).[66]

The ambassador's avowed affection for Théophé remains obscured by his evident misogyny and Eurocentrism. His *récit* of her *histoire* depersonalizes the woman's past trials as examples of oriental sexual excess and interprets her will to reform as a typical oriental subterfuge. After relating the story of her childhood, for example, he comments that the cruelty and depravity of her father are but common oriental traits: "Every Turkish province is filled with such infamous fathers who bring up their daughters for a life of debauchery" (99).[67] Likewise, in rationalizing his lust for the heroine he discounts her repeated rejections as feigned decency, asking: "Was Turkey not filled with slaves from whom I could expect exactly the same pleasures?" (143).[68] Through such *exempla*, the *narrataire* is made to believe that Théophé's destiny is predetermined by the perverse logic of the oriental system, which posits social despotism and sexual slavery as a way of life.

The power of this logic is mirrored in the two illustrations from the 1784 edition of *Histoire d'une Grecque moderne,* which depict the shocked and distrustful reactions of Théophé's compatriots in front of her refusal of the two roles traditionally ascribed to oriental women, slave and mistress (Figure 4, Figure 5). The drawings represent two milestones in the heroine's life: the first, when the French ambassador buys her freedom from the harem lord; the second, when she rejects the wealthy Turk's proposition. Her mouth is open but she remains mute in both scenes, as she helplessly witnesses the men's anger from the margins of the image. The legends transcribe the Turks' indignation at her outrageous, ungrateful actions, as in the first image, where the harem lord scolds her, "You should be consoled by the sorrow your loss is causing the Pasha," and in the second, where the disappointed Turk mutters, "Would you have believed it? Would you have believed it?" In both cases Théophé watches in impotent distress while her one-time and would-be owners react in rage and disbelief to her implausible (*invraisemblable*), un-oriental desire for freedom from patriarchal control.

The narrator's shifting judgment of Théophé in his *récit* reveals the arbitrary basis of the ideological opposition of Occident versus Orient. Depending on his interpretation of her actions, they are deemed European or oriental: European being the mode of virtue and self-control, oriental signifying dissimulation and treachery. When she turns down a wealthy

Vous devez être consolée, par le chagrin que votre perte cause au Bacha ;

Figure 4. "You should be consoled by the sorrow your loss is causing the Pasha." Illustration for Prévost, *Histoire d'une Grecque moderne* (Amsterdam: Rue et Hôtel Serpente, 1784). Courtesy of the Princeton University Libraries.

L'auriez-vous cru? l'auriez-vous cru?

Figure 5. "Would you have believed it? Would you have believed it?"
Illustration for Prévost, *Histoire d'une Grecque moderne* (Amsterdam:
Rue et Hôtel Serpente, 1784). Courtesy of the Princeton University
Libraries.

Turk's propositions the narrator likens her to a highborn French woman, "a Parisian lady who was as knowledgeable in the ways of the world as she was intelligent and virtuous" (107).[69] When she rejects the ambassador's own sexual advances, he emphasizes her shameful past and oriental failings, calling her "a girl whom I had taken from a Turk's arms" (208) ["une fille que j'avois tirée des bras d'un Turc" (171)], and considers her refusal a coquettish trick. However when, on another occasion, she herself insists that her lowly status makes her unworthy of his attentions, he reproaches her for using an obsolete vocabulary: "Take back those terms which do not apply to you anymore" (142).[70]

It seems that the essential conflict between the narrator's telling (*récit*) and the actual story (*histoire*) grows out of his equivocal distinction between (her) Eastern vices and (his) Western virtues. His retrospective narrative justifies his desire for her in terms of "oriental" permissiveness, all the while protesting his righteousness in terms of "occidental" philanthropy. His initial reform, as he sees it, is to cleanse Théophé of past impurities inflicted on her by her oriental lovers; he then aims to "purify" her with his ownership, his order: "Had the embraces of her two lovers left their mark on her? . . . Was it not true that a stigma like hers could be erased?" (101).[71] Equating her cleanliness with his possession, he conceives a project of moral reform that will eventually emerge as a thinly veiled reworking of the Turk's "barbarian" sexual despotism.

Motivated by this new mission, he now shifts his sight and declares Théophé's good manners proof of her noble birth (instead of evidence of duplicity), asserting that "in Turkey, as elsewhere, being properly reared is the mark of an individual born to a class much above the common folk" (105).[72] Next, he determines to verify her aristocratic lineage by locating her blood father, whom he believes to be a Greek noble. His eagerness to prove Théophé's paternity is typical of his mixed motives of altruism and sexual frustration. As long as her origins remain obscure, the heroine can call him her adoptive father and thereby shame him into suitably paternal behavior—a title and a practice that he despises. But with the help of her father's authority, the ambassador reasons, he will be able to possess her entirely as her husband—and thus practice the Western equivalent of sexual commerce. Offering to marry her on the condition of her father's recognition, he aims to fix the heroine's past and future into a conventional schema of patriarchal control: "the very day I wanted to become her husband I intended to restore her father to her" (239).[73] The ambassador's obsession with establishing the heroine's paternity and maintaining patriarchal control over her is based on a prescriptive view of woman's role and function in a patriarchal family structure. If sexuality is the woman's essential value and fulfilling men's pleasures her essential function, then the only important virtue she must practice is chastity, that is, availability only for the ambassador's satisfaction.

If one compares the heroine's explicit desires with the narrator's assumptions, however, one finds evidence of a major conflict of wills. She longs to flee the ambassador and his condescending benevolence in order to commence a new life somewhere else, in a Christian country. Instead of helping her, he demands that she abandon her dreams and let him decide her life: "Give up your plans to travel; as young and inexperienced as you are in the ways of the world, you cannot expect anything good to come of it."[74] Although Prévost's narrator has no difficulty understanding the heroine's language, he claims to be baffled by her message (of refusal). When given a chance to express her feelings, Théophé despairs of ever making him comprehend, knowing full well that his blindness is selective: "Alas, have I explained myself badly or are you just pretending not to understand me?" (147).[75] Her longed-for Christian country becomes his domain, her freedom his tutelage, her sky his roof.

The fictional affairs of Prévost's hero and heroine are marked by a constant shift in relational titles, emblematic of the uneasy distribution of power between them. While initially they are (supposedly) equal free people, once Théophé enters the ambassador's tutelage, their rapport shifts constantly between roles of master/slave, father/daughter and preceptor/pupil. The hero's single-minded pursuit of the heroine's affection generates this ongoing psychological combat. Each time he tries to wear down Théophé's defenses, she parries his demands with whatever role will best defend her—slave, daughter or pupil. When the narrator tries to force her to sleep with him, she reassumes the language of a slave, implying that his desire translates as her tyranny: "Alas, what could I rightfully refuse you. . . . Do I have any control over something that belongs more to you than to me?" (141).[76] Like the enlightened Westerner that he is, the ambassador bristles at this suggestion of sexual despotism and retracts his demands. As happens repeatedly in this novel, once he (provisionally) gives up his amorous intentions, she resumes the idiom of a grateful daughter: "'Once again I find my father!' she said to me. 'Once again I find my destiny, my happiness, everything that I have hoped to receive by giving myself over to the fruits of his generous friendship'" (212).[77] With the implied impossibility of incestuous relations, the heroine's daughter role redefines her (indirect) control and advantage over the hero. Her role as pupil similarly makes her impenetrable to his desire. By taking on the ingenuous language of a schoolgirl to rebuff her teacher, she reveals the discrepancy between his theory and his praxis: "do not be offended by the effect that your own lessons have produced upon my heart" (148).[78]

According to Jean Sgard, this indirect power play constitutes a step forward in the heroine's evolution toward autonomy. Claiming that the heroine "makes a defensive arm out of each of the qualities that her lover lends her" and "fortifies herself with his concessions," Sgard concludes that Théophé "conquers her freedom as he loses control over it."[79] This is an exaggeratedly optimistic appraisal of Théophé's role in the novel. Far from proving her "triumph" over the ambassador, the heroine's strategies evidence only a certain pragmatism as regards the Frenchman's sexual politics. As she becomes more aware of his hidden agenda, she learns to develop indirect means of power into effective tools of defense. But she never escapes his tutelage. Victim of an increasingly tyrannical master, Théophé never "conquers her freedom."

While the ambassador originally liberates the heroine from the harem with the promise of passage to a Christian country, he later decides to reform her in his own image. The locus for this social experiment is to be his isolated country house. Arguing that vice contaminates Muslim and Christian countries alike, he proposes that they create an asylum of virtue in his own home: "My house will be a sanctuary; my example will result in all my servants honoring you" (149).[80] Théophé is to become the Frenchman's "work" ("mon ouvrage"), a well-wrought object of Western morality that he—the modern-day Pygmalion—will carve out of the raw materials of the East. In moving her to this lonely place, he initially promises Théophé all the tutors and materials necessary for a European education and pledges to obey her every wish: "I shall see you no more often than you yourself will permit. You will see only those persons whom you wish to receive" (150).[81] Yet he plants a spy in her midst and keeps the woman under increasingly strict surveillance.

The country house serves as an example, a *tableau vivant* of virtue and learning; but for whose benefit? Although Théophé is supposedly mistress of the house, the narrator describes it as "my house," her slaves as "my servants," even her garden as "my garden." Her project of self-improvement becomes "my system," a public structure that symbolizes the ambassador's triumph over the Orient: a microstructure of Western moral and political power in the midst of a distant land. Like the Turkish seraglio, the Frenchman's country house functions on the principle of freedom within confinement. Within the space allotted to her, Théophé is free to choose her pastimes (but the choice is limited to reading the works of French theologians, walking in the garden, or receiving officially sanctioned visitors). When the ambassador's business calls him away, she is mistress of the estate (but his slaves keep a close watch).

Even her efforts at moral reform are mitigated by the cynicism of her occidental overseer. Théophé eagerly absorbs the austere lessons of Christian morality in the *Logique de Port-Royal* and the scholarly *Essais* of the Port-Royal theologian Nicole, yet the Frenchman evinces skepticism about her possibilities for change. Théophé's virtuous conduct is unbelievable (*invraisemblable*), he protests, because of the difference it would imply from her countrymen: "could anyone easily believe that, in the heart of Turkey, right out of a seraglio, a person of your age could not only grasp the idea but even possess the most discriminating perception of virtuous living?" (149).[82] As Norman Daniel points out, the Europeans' superior knowledge or *expertise* was the deepest root of their assumed superiority over Muslim countries, and the instruction they offered, whether by advice, example, or command, was at the heart of their imperial ideal.[83] Like an arrogant colonial administrator, the ambassador directs the "enlightenment" of his indigenous charge without altering his attitude toward her inherently inferior, subaltern lot in life.

It is in their correspondence that the impasse between the ambassador's will to control and Théophé's desire for autonomy comes to light most dramatically. In an exchange that has been characterized as a competition, with the dominant ordering-of-the-world going to the victor, the characters challenge each other's views of themselves and of reality. The ambassador, frustrated by the woman's aloof manner, composes a touching script of seduction that includes "all those fervent and endearing remarks that a heart overflowing with honor and love could possibly use to win her affection" (206).[84] But Théophé appears unmoved; quite aware of his unspoken reproaches regarding her past, nationality and culture, she responds with a letter designed to discourage his affections. She describes herself as "an unlucky girl . . . who had learned the words *honor* and *virtue* from [the ambassador] . . . [and who] did not consider herself fit to inspire any emotion other than pity" (207).[85] In a gesture exemplifying the Frenchman's desire to manipulate the woman's identity, the ambassador erases Théophé's words and sketches a new description that highlights what he sees as her natural perfections. "Here is the person whom I love," he exclaims in front of this new version, "and her features are so firmly imprinted in my heart that it is incapable of being mistaken" (207).[86]

Near the end of the novel, the ambassador and Théophé leave Turkey for France. Their parting gestures reveal a cultural role reversal that exposes the fallacy of the dialectic positing European rationality and humanity against oriental irrationality and despotism. The French ambassador acts like a stereotypical mean-spirited oriental tyrant during the "Fête du Roi" conflict, threatening to blow up his house and guests if the Grand Vizir refuses permission for his fireworks show (250). For her part, Théophé uses her last days in Turkey to leave a legacy of liberality and Christian charity. Declaring the harem system the scourge of oriental women, she cashes in all the jewels and precious gifts that the ambassador and her Turkish suitor had given her and obtains her own buying power in the harems of Constantinople (253–54). Effectively converting her past exchange value as a desirable female into the concrete capital of a businessman, she purchases an entire group of foreign harem slaves and sends them home to freedom. This final act forms a fitting coda to her anti-oriental plot, a living testament to her desire for freedom from sexual exploitation.

The ultimate conflict between the ambassador's moralistic theories and his despotic practice comes to light once Théophé is established in his Parisian household, in the heart of the "Christian country" she had so long desired. Now a sickly old man who has lost his burning passion for the woman, the ambassador nevertheless holds her captive in his home. Twice she asks for release from his house to join a convent—"the only solace I have left and the only one I want," she explains (287).[87] But the Frenchman resolutely refuses her freedom, even to the confinement of a religious order and he sets down new laws for this new prison, challenging her to defy his ever-mounting suspicions: "'You will never leave me,' I said to Théophé, 'and you will act in such a way that you will be above suspicion'" (287–88).[88]

The very limited concept of "liberation" in the narrator's lexicon is thus disclosed: he "liberated" the Greek from her Turkish master for his own use only. Once he is finally forced to admit his failure to win her heart and to mold her into his ideal submissive lover, his persecution grows increasingly flagrant. It is not so much her safety that inspires his concern as his fear of impotence. His greatest worry is not that Théophé should dishonor herself, but that other Frenchmen should know of his failure to possess her: "I surrendered myself totally to a sense of regret that I had . . . brought her to France only to watch some lucky roué obtain those advantages I would sooner or later have obtained myself" (284).[89] The oriental woman represents a materially valuable object, one he cannot stand to lose.

Fear of showing moral or intellectual naïveté is a constant source of paranoia for the oriental and occidental men in this universe. Turks fear being duped by Frenchmen, Frenchmen fear being cheated by Turks, and all men fear the ridicule of women.[90] The cultural and political antagonism generated by the meeting of Occident and Orient is epitomized by the sexual friction felt by the jealous ambassador in front of his indifferent Greek lover. Like Montesquieu's Persian harem lord, Prévost's French ambassador fears proof of female infidelity more than anything, for that would expose the limits of his power. Female power is equivalent to male effeminacy. The same sexual politics that drives these men to confine, control and dominate their lovers reveals their profound apprehension of impotence.

The end of *Histoire d'une Grecque moderne* evokes a spiritual dead end for the heroine in the heart of her promised land and a hell of doubt for the ambassador, whose fears live on in the text. Théophé serves the ambassador until she dies a mysterious death. Yet even in recounting her untimely end, the narrator refuses to admit his unkindness and instead calls for his *narrataire* to begin the inquiry that will solve the "enigma" of her indifference: "I decided to put down on paper all that had happened between this charming foreigner and myself and thus to put the public in a position to judge if I had mistakenly entrusted in her my esteem and my love" (288).[91]

The narrator thus creates an impossible pact with his *narrataire* (and by extension with us, his readers), giving only one side of the picture and demanding an informed judgment of the woman's character. The pseudo-memoir form of *Histoire d'une Grecque moderne* facilitates this narrative bad faith: in the monophonic, monolingual universe of Prévost's work, the speaker is at once narrator, author *and* sole interpreter of reality. How can a reader distinguish the truth value of his *récit* without an outside referent to the *histoire?* In other words, how can we unpack the different levels of Prévost's text to find the real story within?

For eighteenth-century readers, of course, there was a very real historical referent, invoked in the title and clearly implicated in the text: Mlle Aïssé, the one-time harem slave, protégée of the French ambassador to Turkey, and *belle Grecque* of Regency society.[92] Like Prévost's Théophé,

Mlle Aïssé's legacy remains obscure. Accounts of her life portray her either as a martyred saint or a repentant sinner, an exemplar of European virtue or an eternally humiliated concubine. Aïssé and Théophé have much in common as regards their lived experience and the popular images of them that were propagated in the French public. Although both women are bought out of slavery, given Western educations, and placed in upper-class French society, both their histories are shrouded in mysteries of oriental eroticism. Like Aïssé, Théophé's moral goodness—the message of her plot/life—is an arbitrary signifier, granted or denied to her memory entirely by her reader/judge.

Indeed many critics have interpreted Théophé as a Jekyll/Hyde figure. Claire-Eliane Engel, for example, states: "One never knows if Théophé is a talented liar who audaciously pursues a secret intrigue, or if she is a victim of calumny."[93] Such a reading fits the premise of Prévost's narrator to a tee: it accepts his reduction of the female character to a blank slate upon which male insecurities and fears are projected. Théophé's so-called enigma resides in an essentialist conception of oriental femininity as an entity that remains mysterious, opaque and incomprehensible without the enlightened intervention of a Western (male) observer.

One of the most striking features of Prévost's fiction is his lucid portrayal of the masculine blindness that perceives "female nature" in this way. Yet the reader is left wondering, at the end of his novel, if the author did not succumb to the same weakness that he portrays in his narrator. His unequivocal exposé of the French ambassador's tyrannical, arrogant attitude toward the Turks and Greeks under his diplomatic domain coexists with a sensationalized portrait of the Greek woman's troubling, dangerous sexuality. This same configuration—of astuteness on issues of cultural difference and obtusity on issues of gender difference—emerges in the work of Montesquieu as well. As we shall see, the male authors' seeming obliviousness toward the issues of sexual politics marks a great contrast to the female authors' evident concern for accurate representation and exposure of the conflicts, injustices and possible reforms relating to women's place in society. While male authors portray women as creatures defined primarily by their sexual functions, female authors stress their heroines' social identity, thus leaving open the possibilities for other roles besides those of lover, concubine, slave or wife.

The story of Prévost's modern Greek offers a poignant testimony to the moral conflict that haunted early Enlightenment thought. Théophé's miserable existence under a Frenchman's tutelage challenges his optimistic claims of enlightened philosophy and demystifies the moral superiority of his Christian nation. In spite of her efforts at moral reform, she remains an outsider to French society. Perhaps it is the moral hypocrisy of the French that is to blame for her failure to assimilate. In spite of the ambassador's efforts at domination and control, he remains incapable of possessing Théophé or of determining the truth of her life story. Perhaps it is his Eurocentric blindness that is to blame for his failure. These failures point to an essential problem in ancien régime culture, that is, the eroding foundations of its authority—as seen in the rise of secular skepticism, the declining power of the Catholic church, and the increasing trade in parody and political criticism of the monarchical state in the years 1720–80.

Both the *histoire* and the *récit* of Prévost's novel reveal an obsession with fraudulent authority and misplaced sovereignty. The tragic story (*histoire*) of the heroine's ongoing struggle to live a Christian life while in a state of sexual siege reveals the ambassador's corruption of parental authority. The inconclusive narration (*récit*) of the hero's experience reveals his unfounded sovereignty over the cultural space of the Orient and the textual pretense of documentary truth.

In our analysis of *Zaïde,* we considered a heroine whose difference gives rise to a plot of pursuit and courtship, ending with a tableau of reconciliation between two enemy forces—Christian and Muslim, Spaniards and Moors. In *Histoire d'une Grecque moderne,* the heroine ends up unable to join the desired other culture, not for lack of effort or intrigue but because of the basic problem of Western culture, that is, the secret unfoundedness of its authority. Written for an audience anxious about its own place in the increasingly heterogeneous economy of Louis XIV's reign, Lafayette's novel conveys a protective, reassuring vision of a monarchical order that can absorb all manner of potential threats in its flanks and continue functioning unperturbed. Written some seventy years later, during the tumultuous, decadent years of Louis XV's reign and the new enlightened tolerance for moral disbelief and political dissent, Prévost's fiction manifests a profoundly negative message on the legitimacy of French moral superiority and the morality of official government initiatives in oriental lands.

Lionel Gossman tells us that the ambassador's dilemma in *Histoire d'une Grecque moderne* draws on a characteristic anxiety in eighteenth-century philosophy—the unease provoked by the gradual epistemological shift from faith to skepticism, from the absolute truth of the classical age to the universal relativism of the Enlightenment:

> No worldly father, it turns out, has the absoluteness and the self-sufficiency that are associated with ultimate sovereignty. . . . Freed from what it took to be the oppressive and megalomaniac obsession with grandeur of the previous age, enlightened, disillusioned, and cynical, the new society of the eighteenth century nevertheless felt keenly the slipping away of respect for the old rules, the old boundaries, the old distinctions that had sustained both the social order in general and the specific identity and place of each individual in it. . . . Against the efforts of the heroes [Des Grieux and the ambassador/narrator] to limit and control freedom and even to suppress it, the heroines [Manon Lescaut and Théophé] stand for the absolute irreducibleness of the sign and the freedom of a world without mastery or even obligation.[94]

Théophé's indecipherability exemplifies the skepticism of an age when such truths as monarchical absolutism and Catholic dogma no longer retained their symbolic power over the French psyche.

The failure of Prévost's fictional ambassador to capture the oriental woman's love and to reconstruct her character in his narration constitutes a critique of French cultural politics as well. In spite of (or perhaps because of) his occidental confidence in dealing with Théophé, she remains unmoved by his love. In spite of his wide repertoire of myths and legends about oriental peoples, he never succeeds in defining her. Like a frustrated Orientalist, he finds that the assets he had expected in the oriental woman, that is, her malleability, penetrability, and acquiescence to the master's rule, were but chimera of his Western imagination. Unable to decide the truth of the Orient, he is left with no means to control his delirium but this unfinished, fragmentary narrative. Prévost warns against the dangers of Eurocentrism with his clearly paranoid narrator, and he demystifies the dialectic of occidental/oriental conflict with his narrator's excessive, despotic conduct. But once we discard these conceptual and political strategies for dealing with the Orient, once we abandon our hopes of cultural domination over the Other, what do we have left?

Notes

1. David Constantine, *Early Greek Travellers and the Hellenic Ideal* (Cambridge: Cambridge University Press, 1984), 6–8.
2. "[C]ette contrée qui fut autrefois l'asile des sciences et des arts, qui étoit ornée de tant de villes florissantes, n'offre plus aux yeux du voyageur que des masures, des monceaux de ruines, et de pauvres habitans plongés dans l'esclavage, la misère, l'ignorance et la superstition" (Guyot, Chamfort et al., eds., *Le Grand*

vocabulaire françois [Paris: Hôtel de Thou, 1762], 12:414). All translations, unless otherwise noted, are my own. While I have used standard English in my translations, I have decided not to standardize the French language as it appears in early texts. Throughout I will thus retain the spelling, syntax, grammar and accents as they appear in the volumes I use, many of them first editions.

3. Joseph Pitton de Tournefort, *Relation d'un voyage du Levant fait par ordre du roy* (Paris: Imprimerie royale, 1717), 1:156–282.

4. Galland praises d'Herbelot's work: "L'Histoire n'y est ni seiche ni ennuyeuse, par un simple récit de gains de Batailles, de prises de Villes, et de Conquêtes de Provinces. . . . l'étude des trois Langues Orientales, Arabique, Persienne et Turque, est devenue présentement si aisée, que pour les penétrer à fond, et même en peu de temps, il n'y a presque qu'à le vouloir [*sic*]" (Antoine Galland, "Discours pour servir de Préface à la 'Bibliothèque orientale,'" in d'Herbelot, *Bibliothèque orientale ou Dictionnaire universel, contenant généralement tout ce qui regarde la connoissance des Peuples de l'Orient* [Paris: Par la compagnie des Libraires, 1697], unnumbered).

5. Edward W. Said, *Orientalism* (New York: Vintage Books, 1978), 65.

6. "[P]as seulement les Arabes et les Persans; mais encore les Turcs et les Tartares, et presque tous les peuples de l'Asie jusques à la Chine, Mahometans et Païens ou Idolatres" (Antoine Galland, "Avertissement," *Les Paroles remarquables, les bons mots et les maximes des Orientaux* [Paris: Simon Bernard, 1694], unnumbered).

7. Mesnardière, *La Poétique*, 137.

8. "Je fais connoistre les moeurs et les ceremonies des peuples, au moins celles qui peuvent donner quelque contentement aux lecteurs, m'esloignant tousjours des choses qui doivent choquer leur esprit, et qui leur peuvent desplaire" (M. Boisrobert, "Avis au lecteur," *Histoire indienne d'Anaxandre et d'Orasie* [Paris: Frères Pomeray, 1629], unnumbered).

9. "[Q]u'il juge par le témoignage mesme des Orientaux . . . s'ils ont raison de croire qu'ils ne sont pas moins partagés d'esprit et de bon sens que les autres Nations qui nous sont plus connuës à cause de leur voisinage" (Galland, "Avertissement," *Paroles remarquables*).

10. Under the guidance of Jean-Baptiste Colbert, Louis XIV's minister of state and secretary of the navy, France joined the race for international trade and empire-building which was then ruled by the maritime powers of Holland and England. Creating a far-reaching colonial policy inspired by Richelieu's earlier efforts, Colbert extended New France from Canada to the Mississippi, added tropical possessions in Guiana, and established the king's authority on the African coast from the Bay of Arguin to the shores of Sierra Leone. Colbert created a state monopoly in these territories with the establishment of the great royal companies, notably the Compagnies des Indes occidentales et orientales (1664), the Compagnie du Levant (1670), and the Compagnie de l'Acadie (1683). For more on commercial and colonial expansion under Louis XIV, consult Léon Deschamps, *Histoire de la question coloniale en France* (Paris: Librairie Plon, 1891), 139–232.

11. See Edward Turk, *Baroque Fiction-Making: A Study of Gomberville's "Polexandre"* (Chapel Hill: North Carolina Studies in the Romance Languages and

Literatures, 1978), for more on the self-perpetuating mechanism of seventeenth-century literary and moral standards.

12. John Lyons, "The Dead Center: Desire and Mediation in Lafayette's 'Zayde'," *L'Esprit Créateur* 23, no. 2 (Summer 1983): 68.

13. According to novelist Madeleine de Scudéry, history served fiction writers by veiling their mix of invention and truth with the respectable appearance of fact and thus retaining the reader's interest in what might otherwise be considered extravagant or implausible. See the preface to her *Ibrahim, ou l'Illustre Bassa* (Paris: Antoine de Sommaville, 1644).

14. This appropriation of history in the novel was a major bone of contention between "Ancients" and "Moderns." For an example of the Ancients' position against the mixing of fact and fiction see Pierre Bayle's article "Nidhard" in his *Dictionnaire historique et critique,* 3rd ed. (Rotterdam: Michel Bohm, 1720), 3:2091. For a "Modern" argument in defense of the novelist's freedom, consult the Abbé de Charnes's *Conversations sur la critique de "La Princesse de Clèves"* (Paris: Barbin, 1679), 105, 147.

15. "Marroc, Alger, Thunis, et Fez, ne sont pas voisins d'Angola, ni de Congo . . . de plus, les Maures dont il est question ayant quitté l'Afrique, il y avoit près de huit cens ans, n'avoient plus le mesme taint de leurs Ancestres: qui n'estans qu'un peu bruns, avoient laissé une Posterité encore plus blanche [sic]" (Georges de Scudéry, "Au Lecteur," *Almahide ou l'esclave reine* [Paris: Augustin Courbé, 1660], 1:unnumbered). For more on Lafayette's debt to the Hispano-Moorish tradition in French fiction, see Jean Cazenave, "Le Roman hispano-mauresque en France," *Revue de la littérature comparée* (October-December 1925): 594–640; and Thérèse Lassalle-Maraval and Christiane Faliu, " 'Zaïde': du poncif mauresque à 'l'incommunicabilité,' " *Littérature (Annales de l'Université de Toulouse-Le Mirail)* 21 (1974): 149–64.

16. "[E]lle prononça quelques paroles; il en sentit de la joie et du trouble. Il s'approcha pour entendre ce qu'elle disait; elle parla encore, et il fut surpris de voir qu'elle parlait une langue qui lui était inconnue" (Marie-Madeleine Pioche de la Vergne, comtesse de Lafayette, *Zaïde, Histoire espagnole* in *Romans et nouvelles,* ed. Emile Magne [Paris: Editions Garnier, 1970], 45). All references to Lafayette's work refer to this edition unless otherwise indicated. The novel was first published as *Zayde, Histoire espagnole* under the name Monsieur de Segrais (Paris: Claude Barbin) vol. 1, 1670, vol. 2, 1671.

17. "[V]ous l'êtes [malheureux] sans doute de vous être attaché á une personne que vraisemblablement vous ne pouvez épouser" (96).

18. "[S]itôt qu'elle sera guérie, je ne regarderai ses charmes que comme une chose dont elle ne se servira que pour faire plus de trahisons et plus de misérables. Qu'elle en fera, grands dieux! et qu'elle en a peut-être déjà fait!" (44).

19. Michel Serres, *The Parasite,* trans. Lawrence R. Schehr (Baltimore, Md.: Johns Hopkins University Press, 1982), 121, 126.

20. "S'il n'eût point été prévenu de cette pensée, il ne se fût pas cru si infortuné et les actions de Zaïde ne lui devaient pas persuader qu'elle n'eût pour lui que de l'indifférence" (93).

21. "[C]e n'est pas moi qu'elle voit ni à qui elle pense. Quand elle me regarde, je la fais souvenir de la seule chose que je voudrais lui faire oublier" (50–51).

22. "[L]e peu d'espérance que lui donnait cette pensée ne pouvait détruire tant de sujets de crainte" (96).

23. "[J]'aime Zaïde et Zaïde en aime un autre; et c'est de tous les malheurs celui qui m'a paru le plus redoutable" (50).

24. According to Girard, "triangular desire" functions when a model, rival or mediator for the Self enhances desire for the Other by inspiring or threatening imitation. See René Girard, *Mensonge romantique et vérité romanesque* (Paris: Grasset, 1961).

25. For more on the popularity of the *question d'amour* and related topics in seventeenth-century salon society, consult Nicola Ivanoff, *La Marquise de Sablé et son salon* (Paris: Les Presses modernes, 1927), 138.

26. "[O]n ne connaît point les femmes, elles ne se connaissent pas elles-mêmes, et ce sont les occasions qui décident des sentiments de leur coeur" (84).

27. Bayle, *Dictionnaire historique*, 1:753.

28. "[J]e trouvai que, comme j'avais été jaloux d'un homme mort, sans savoir si je le devais être, j'étais jaloux de mon ami, et que je le croyais mon rival" (117).

29. "[V]ous m'avez confirmée dans l'opinion que j'avais qu'on ne peut être heureux en aimant quelqu'un" (123).

30. Lyons, "The Dead Center," 60 ff. Joan DeJean has also discussed the implications of this paradigm of male authority in the novel's larger political context; see DeJean, "No Man's Land: The Novel's First Geography," *Yale French Studies* 73 (1987): 175–89.

31. "J'aurai cette douceur, sans manquer à mon devoir. Il ne sait qui je suis; il ne me verra jamais" (212).

32. Susan Sontag argues: "A person who becomes silent becomes opaque for the other. . . . deliberate silence . . . is also, as behavior, a means of power, a species of sadism, a virtually inviolable position of strength" (Sontag, *Styles of Radical Will* [New York: Farrar, Straus and Giroux, 1966], 16–17).

33. "J'ai au moins la consolation, dans mon malheur, que l'impossibilité de lui parler m'empêche d'avoir la faiblesse de lui dire que je l'aime" (211).

34. Claudine Herrmann, *Les Voleuses de langue* (Paris: Editions des Femmes, 1976), 39.

35. "[I]l n'y avait point d'extrémité où elle ne se portât plutôt que de se résoudre à épouser un homme d'une religion si opposée à la sienne et dont la loi permettait de prendre autant de femmes qu'on en trouvait d'agréables" (173).

36. "[T]out ce que je puis est de vous plaindre et de m'affliger; et vous êtes trop raisonnable pour me demander de ne pas suivre les volontés de mon père" (224).

37. Ann Rosalind Jones, "Writing the Body: Towards an Understanding of *L'Ecriture féminine*," *Feminist Studies* 7, no. 2 (1981): 259. For more on the implications of the Lacanian paradigm in relation to women's writing, consult Xavière Gauthier, "Is There Such a Thing as Women's Writing?" in *New French Feminisms*, ed. Elaine Marks and Isabelle de Courtivron (New York: Schocken Books, 1981),

161–64; and Carolyn Burke, "Psychoanalysis and Feminism in France: Rethinking the Maternal" in *The Future of Difference,* ed. Hester Eisenstein and Alice Jardine (New Brunswick, N.J.: Rutgers University Press, 1985), 107–14.

38. "Ne vous plaignez point de moi . . . plaignez-vous d'être né Espagnol; quand je serais pour vous, comme vous le pouvez désirer, et quand mon père ne serait point prévenu, votre patrie serait toujours un obstacle invincible à ce que vous souhaitez et Zuléma ne consentirait jamais que je fusse à vous" (225).

39. On marriage law in seventeenth-century France, see Sarah Hanley, "Family and State in Early Modern France: The Marriage Pact" in *Connecting Spheres: Women in the Western World, 1500 to the Present,* ed. Marilyn J. Boxer and Jean H. Quataert (New York: Oxford University Press, 1987), 53–63.

40. Anita Levy, "Blood, Kinship, and Gender," *Genders* 5 (Summer 1989): 72.

41. Examples of this topos include Mme de Villedieu's *Mémoires de la vie de Henriette-Sylvie de Molière* (1671–74) in which the heroine must fight off the sexual advances of her adoptive father and Mme de Tencin's *Mémoires du comte de Comminge* (1735), which depicts a pair of star-crossed lovers deploring the unjust prejudices of their fathers.

42. The final conversion of Moslems to Christianity was a well-known convention of "oriental" fictions. According to Claire-Eliane Engel, "Dans tous les anciens romans à cadre oriental, les personnages musulmans sympathiques étaient toujours baptisés en grande pompe à la fin" (Engel, *Le Véritable Abbé Prévost* [Monaco: Editions du Rocher, 1957] 199).

43. "[U]n de ces prodiges si ordinaires en Thessalie, et toujours attribués à la magie" (Marguerite de Lussan, *Les Veillées de Thessalie* in *Le Cabinet des fées* [Geneva: Barde, Manget et cie, 1787], 26:243).

44. Tournefort, *Relation d'un voyage du Levant,* 1:314.

45. Constantine, *Early Greek Travellers,* 8.

46. Antoine François, abbé Prévost, *Manuel lexique, ou Dictionnaire portatif des mots françois dont la signification n'est pas familière à tout le monde* (Paris: Didot, 1755), 2:95.

47. Albert Vandal, *Une Ambassade française en Orient sous Louis XV: La Mission du Marquis de Villeneuve 1728–1741* (Paris: Librairie Plon, 1887), ix–x.

48. For more on European images of the erotic violence and political repression of the Orient, consult Ali Behdad, "The Eroticized Orient: Images of the Harem in Montesquieu and His Precursors," *Stanford French Review* 13, nos. 2–3 (Fall-Winter 1989): 109–26; Alain Grosrichard, *Structure du sérail* (Paris: Editions du Seuil, 1979); and "Contexts: Oriental Travels, Exotic Spies and Enlightenment Philosophy" in Chapter 2 of the present study.

49. Fatma Müge Göçek, *East Encounters West: France and the Ottoman Empire in the Eighteenth Century* (New York: Oxford University Press, 1987), 97–98.

50. Mlle Aïssé was bought at the age of four (in 1698) in Constantinople's slave market by the comte de Ferriol, who had already gained infamy for his irresponsible exploits as Louis XIV's ambassador to Turkey (1692–1711). Aïssé enjoyed renown during the Regency as the "belle Grecque" of the Court and an habituée of the most stylish Parisian salons. Although she devoted herself to the church in later years, her reputation remains tarnished by her oriental origins and her one-

time affection for the scurrilous French ambassador. For the history of Prévost's acquaintance with Mlle Aïssé—the person and the legend—see Yves Breuil, "Une Lettre inédite relative à 'L'Histoire d'une Grecque moderne' de l'Abbé Prévost," *Revue des sciences humaines* 33, no. 131 (July-September 1968): 391–400; and Emile Bouvier, "La Genèse de 'L'Histoire d'une Grecque moderne'," *Revue d'histoire littéraire de la France* 48 (1948): 113–30.

51. Antoine François, abbé Prévost, *The Story of a Fair Greek of Yesteryear,* trans. James F. Jones, Jr. (Potomac, Md.: Scripta Humanistica, 1984), 59. All English quotations from Prévost refer to this translation unless otherwise noted. "Je suis l'Amant de la belle Grecque dont j'entreprens l'Histoire. Qui me croira sincère dans le récit de mes plaisirs ou de mes peines? . . . quelle fidélité attendra-t-on d'une Plume conduite par l'amour?" (Prévost, *Histoire d'une Grecque moderne,* ed. Robert Mauzi [Paris: Union Générale d'Editions, "Bibliothèque 10/18," 1965], 3). All French quotations from Prévost's work refer to this edition unless otherwise noted.

52. "Je suis un Amant rebuté, trahi même, si je dois m'en fier à des apparences dont j'abandonnerai le jugement à mes Lecteurs" (3–4).

53. "[J]e fus trop frappé de l'ordre que j'y vis régner pour n'en pas rappeler aisément toutes les circonstances" (7).

54. "[I]l me tint quelques discours sensés sur la force de l'éducation et de l'habitude, qui rend les plus belles femmes soumises et tranquilles" (8).

55. "[J]e lui jurai si sincèrement que j'étois sans passion pour elle . . . ne pensant qu'à la rendre libre" (16).

56. Michel Foucault, *Discipline and Punish: The Birth of the Prison,* trans. Alan Sheridan (New York: Vintage Books, 1979), 136–209.

57. The "Avertissement" to the 1740 edition of *Histoire d'une Grecque moderne* announces the choice of "seraglio" over "harem": "[L]'on a mis *Sérail* au lieu de *Harem* quoi qu'on ignore point que Harem est le nom des sérails particuliers" (quoted by Breuil, "Une Lettre inédite," 394).

58. Behdad, "The Eroticized Orient," 114, 123.

59. Said, *Orientalism,* 208.

60. "Elle sçavoit, pour l'avoir entendu mille fois depuis qu'elle étoit en Turquie, quelle différence les Turcs mettent dans leurs manières à l'égard des femmes libres. . . . son premier mouvement fut de prendre l'air et la contenance qu'elle crut convenable au changement de son sort" (19).

61. *Z* is the ultimate signifier of foreignness according to Roland Barthes, who interprets the unusual sound and sight of the letter *Z* as disruptions of the French code in *S/Z* (Paris: Editions du Seuil, 1970), 113. For further background and bibliography of exotic Z-names in early modern fiction, see Marie-Louise Dufrenoy, *L'Orient romanesque en France 1704–1789* (Montreal: Editions Beauchemin, 1946), 344–67.

62. "Il y a donc un Pays, disois-je, où l'on trouve un autre bonheur que celui de la fortune et des richesses! . . . Il y a pour les femmes un autre mérite à faire valoir, et d'autre biens à obtenir" (40).

63. "Si l'on a fait, en lisant ce récit, une partie des réflexions qu'il me fit naître, on doit s'attendre à celles qui vont le suivre" (46).

64. My conception of the "community" of narrator and *narrataire* as an entity characterized by its sovereignty over others and its limited membership is inspired by Benedict Anderson's description of the "imagined communities" in nationalistic and colonialist propaganda. See Anderson, *Imagined Communities: Reflections on the Origin and Spread of Nationalism* (London: Verso Editions, 1983), 11–16.

65. "[U]ne femme unique, dont la conduite et les principes devoient être proposés à l'imitation *de son sexe et du notre*" (208, emphasis added).

66. "Aujourd'hui comme du tems des Anciens, la bonne foi Grecque est un proverbe ironique" (47).

67. "Toutes les Provinces de la Turquie sont remplies de ces pères infames, qui forment leurs filles à la débauche" (47).

68. "La Turquie n'étoit-elle pas remplie d'Esclaves dont je pouvois attendre les mêmes plaisirs?" (97).

69. "Une Dame de Paris, avec autant d'usage du monde que d'esprit et de vertu" (55).

70. "Retranchez, lui dis-je, des termes qui ne conviennent plus à votre situation" (96).

71. "[L]es caresses de ses deux Amans lui avoient-ils imprimé quelque tache. . . . Une flétrissure de cette espèce ne pouvoit-elle pas être réparée?" (49).

72. "[L]a bonne éducation, en Turquie comme ailleurs, est la marque d'une naissance au-dessus du commun" (54).

73. "[L]e même jour que je voulois devenir son Mari, je comptois lui rendre un Père" (205).

74. My translation (Jones version incorrect). "Abandonnez vos projets de voyage; jeune et sans expérience du monde, vous n'en devez rien attendre d'heureux" (105).

75. "Hélas! m'étois-je mal expliquée ou feignez-vous de ne pas m'entendre?" (103).

76. "Hélas! qu'ai-je droit de vous refuser. . . . Ai-je en mon pouvoir quelque chose qui ne soit pas à vous plus qu'à moi-même?" (95).

77. "Je retrouve donc mon Père, me dit-elle! Je retrouve ma fortune, mon bonheur, et tout ce que j'ai espéré en me livrant à sa généreuse amitié" (176).

78. "[N]e vous offensez pas de l'effet que vos propres leçons ont produit sur mon coeur" (103).

79. "[D]e toutes les qualités que son amant lui prête, elle se fait une défense; elle s'enrichit de ce qu'il lui concède; elle conquiert sa liberté au fur et à mesure qu'il la perd" (Jean Sgard, *Prévost romancier* [Paris: Librairie José Corti, 1968], 428–29).

80. "Ma maison sera un Sanctuaire; mon exemple portera tous mes Domestiques à vous respecter" (105).

81. "Je ne vous y verrai pas plus souvent que vous ne me le permettrez. Vous n'y verrez vous-même que ceux qu'il vous plaira d'y recevoir" (106).

82. "[P]eut-on croire aisément que dans le sein de la Turquie, au sortir d'un Sérail, une personne de votre âge ait saisi tout d'un coup non-seulement l'idée, mais le goût même de la plus haute sagesse?" (104).

83. Norman Daniel, *Islam, Europe and Empire* (Edinburgh: Edinburgh University Press, 1966), 70.

84. "[T]out ce qu'un coeur pénétré d'estime et d'amour peut employer de plus vif et de plus touchant pour persuader sa tendresse" (170).

85. "Une Misérable . . . qui avoit appris de moi le nom d'honneur et de vertu, et qui . . . ne se sentoit propre à inspirer que de la pitié" (170).

86. "Voila ce que j'aime . . . et les traits en sont si bien gravés dans mon coeur, qu'il n'est pas capable de s'y méprendre" (171).

87. "[L]e seul partage qui me reste, et le seul aussi que je désire" (270).

88. "Vous ne me quitterez point, dis-je à Théophé, et vous tiendrez une conduite qui puisse braver tous les soupçons" (271).

89. "[J]e m'abandonnai au regret . . . de ne l'avoir peut-être amenée en France que pour voir recueillir à quelque Avanturier les fruits que j'aurois tôt ou tard obtenus" (259).

90. After his failure with Théophé, the wealthy Turk angrily accuses the ambassador of sabotaging his efforts with Western methods: "Il est facile à un François . . . de faire une dupe d'un Turc" (183). After his failure with Théophé, the ambassador blames the woman's duplicitous ways: "Je rougissois même d'avoir été la dupe de ces belles maximes qui m'avoient été répétées tant de fois avec tant d'affectation" (225).

91. "[J]'ai formé le dessein de recueillir par écrit tout ce que j'ai eu de commun avec cette aimable Etrangère, et de mettre le Public en état de juger si j'avois mal placé mon estime et ma tendresse" (272).

92. Contemporary readers apparently considered Prévost's title an obvious reference to Mlle Aïssé. Mme de Staal (de Launay) wrote to M. d'Héricourt: "J'ai commencé la Grecque à cause de ce que vous m'en dites: on croit en effet que Mlle Aïssé en a donné l'idée" (quoted by Charles-Augustin Sainte-Beuve, *Portraits littéraires* [Paris: Garnier, 1864], 171). For more on this relation between fact and fiction, consult Breuil, "Une Lettre inédite"; and Bouvier, "La Genèse de 'L'Histoire d'une Grecque moderne.'"

93. "On ne sait à aucun moment si Théophé est une menteuse raffinée qui mène avec audace une intrigue secrète, ou une victime calomniée" (Engel, *Le Véritable Abbé Prévost*, 199).

94. Lionel Gossman, "Male and Female in Two Short Novels By Prévost," *Modern Language Review* 77, no. 1 (January 1982): 34–35.

2. The Exotic Other Becomes Cultural Critic: Montesquieu's *Lettres persanes* and Mme de Graffigny's *Lettres d'une Péruvienne*

> The limits of my language mean the limits of my world.
> Wittgenstein, *Tractatus Logico-Philosophicus*

As fictions of foreign experience, Montesquieu's *Lettres persanes* (1721) and Mme de Graffigny's *Lettres d'une Péruvienne* (1747) present a striking contrast to the novels discussed in Chapter 1. The female figures in Montesquieu's and Graffigny's novels are not only victims and heroines in exoticized love stories, they are also actors and authors of highly visible philosophical and political subtexts. In my readings of *Zaïde* and *Histoire d'une Grecque moderne,* I plotted the exotic heroines' narratological functions and highlighted their symbolic reflections of cultural stereotypes. This chapter considers the Persian and Peruvian women in similar terms and traces their roles in the authors' projects of cultural criticism.

The essence of exotic otherness is portrayed differently in these two chapters. *Zaïde* and *Histoire d'une Grecque moderne* are frustrated love stories, tales of sexual and cultural misprision. They represent Victor Segalen's notion of an "exoticism of the sexes" in that they dramatize the essential difference—of body and mind—that hinders all efforts at heterosexual union. Segalen explains this concept as: "The exoticism of the sexes. And from it all the Difference, all the incompatibility, all the Distance suddenly looms up, shows itself, howls, cries, sobs with love or frustration."[1] These fictions recount the efforts of a male European to decipher what he considers an opaque, practically incomprehensible Other. They tell of romantic friction and cultural conflicts which are resolved, or at least stabilized, within the inflexible parameters of a patriarchal world.

In the *Lettres persanes* and the *Lettres d'une Péruvienne,* the perspective shifts to that of an Other who tries to decipher the rules of a foreign world (Europe). The psychology of the exotic Other is much more developed in these fictions, since it is (s)he who narrates the novels' central plots. The first-person narration and use of foreign terms allow readers to develop a sense of overcoming the linguistic barriers between France, Persia and Peru, and thus to ascertain fundamental similarities between Occident and Orient or the Old and New Worlds.

Montesquieu's *Lettres persanes* is often cited as a classic text of French anthropology. Many anthropologists consider the Persians' reportage a prime example of the Enlightenment ideals of tolerance and relativistic philosophical inquiry and canonize this work as a harbinger of the then nascent science of man.[2] According to Claude Lévi-Strauss, the father of structural anthropology, the anthropologist's work is to suspend the prejudices of his own culture and to look beyond the foreignness of the world's societies to perceive their fundamental structures and underlying universal laws of order.[3] But no matter how impartial such observers may claim to be, anthropologists' choices (subject matter, perspective, emphasis) put their work's documentary value in question. As Montesquieu's protagonists will demonstrate, the anthropologist's limitations are not always caused by his original cultural biases. Like Michel Serres's model of the long-term parasite who gradually becomes absorbed in the host's environment, the scientific observer can err on the side of sympathetic involvement as well as in ethnocentrism. Whatever the causes, these blind spots inevitably show up in the anthropologist's *exclusions,* writes James Clifford, in the ways he silences incongruous voices or deploys a consistent manner of translating the reality of others.[4] The reader must read around the narrative's exclusions and rhetoric in order to distinguish the "systems or economies of truth" that organize the observer's experience. Power and history work through even the best ethnographic texts, Clifford argues, "in ways their authors cannot fully control" (7).

Measured according to Lévi-Strauss's structural model, Montesquieu's Persian spies/anthropologists perform their interpretive duties well: they record the peculiarities of French culture, suggest the archetypal similarities between the Orient and the Occident, and chart the causal relations between laws, morality and political organization. But like the abstract discourse of structural anthropology, the Persians' observations gloss over certain key, potentially problematic aspects of Persian and French culture. Montesquieu's conception of functional laws linking a society's notion of justice to its political order implies that crucial social principles exist a priori, as long as the dominant political structure remains in place. This emphasis on structure over content (or values), left unexamined, is ethically questionable. As the *Lettres persanes* shows, such functionalist logic can be used to explain (and implicitly create an apology for) any sociopolitical order, even the most morally repugnant. The Persians' "scientific" stance crumbles by the end of the novel when their repressive oriental values surface; clearly, the methodological relativism of these "anthropologists" does not imply a moral relativism.

The disinterested personae of the Persian spies/anthropologists point to another aspect of what Clifford calls the "truth system" underlying their selective reportage. Apart from some isolated instances at the beginning and end of the novel, the Persian characters rarely admit their personal feelings or engage in interactions with specific, identifiable individuals. Rather the author uses these characters to construct large-scale comparisons of French and Persian cultural phenomena and to speculate on universal laws of human nature through allusion to generic social types. This rhetorical strategy—which informs both structural anthropology and its intellectual ancestor, European travel writing—perpetuates the ontological advantage of the dominant European (male) observer over a passive, silent (feminized) Other.

In his creation of the authentic-sounding "native scripts" of the harem wives, however, Montesquieu—like his successor Graffigny—will try to challenge this unfair distribution of power and voice. While the Persian men become completely Europeanized and report on their native customs in increasingly abstract, detached philosophical terms, the women's letters, concrete and emotional, indicate how false this Eurocentric notion of "objectivity" is. Graffigny's entire fiction is designed as a corrective to unfair judgments found in voyage literature and in Montesquieu's novel. Her heroine's "Peruvian" virtues challenge the negative portrayal of the Peruvians in contemporary travel writings, just as her heroine's exposé of the sexual injustices underlying ancien régime society contests the notion represented through the Persians' observations that social disorders are caused by a universal, flawed "female nature."

In the introduction, I outlined the narrative devices and ideological assumptions characteristic of travel literature. European travelers' accounts tend to "fix" the foreign Other in a temporal order distinct from the observer's, a timeless, eternal present. Descriptions of foreign peoples as an iconic "they" imply that "their" actions are motivated not by historically specific local events but are typical examples of common custom or rites. Stressing the interpretive powers of the European visitor over the experiential reality of the Other, such descriptions overlook social tensions, presenting instead a coherent, unified image of foreign culture. In the *Lettres persanes,* the conflict between the abstract vision of the scientific observer and the idiosyncratic actions of the exotic Other takes on a gendered dimension. The Persian men's letters compare Persia and France from the lofty advantage of the anthropologist, whereas the Persian women's letters depict specific accounts of suffering in a historically exact time and location, Usbek's harem. The women's forthright condemnation of the harem forcefully debunks Usbek's argument that the harem is natural and necessary to the Persian system and reveals the moral fraudulence of his enlightened, tolerant attitude.

Held up to Lévi-Strauss's model of the detached, impersonal observer, Graffigny's Peruvian spy/anthropologist leaves much to be desired. Instead of distilling her impressions into an abstract, structural comparison of French and Peruvian cultures, Zilia dwells on her feelings, experiences and reactions to the strange new world in which she finds herself. The *Lettres d'une Péruvienne* reads less like anthropological analysis than like anthropological fieldwork gathered firsthand. The highly emotional persona and intimate narrative of Graffigny's Peruvian protagonist necessarily limit her reportage, yet this persona creates an alternative to Montesquieu's model of cultural analysis, suggesting other outcomes for the cross-cultural encounter. The Peruvian's discomfort and alienation in Parisian society enhance her awareness of the inner conflicts that divide this world, particularly the gendered antagonisms arising from women's disadvantages in education and marriage and their financial insecurity. Where philosophical training and personal well-being allow the learned Persians to cultivate a conciliatory, relativistic attitude toward cultural difference, because the preliterate, victimized Peruvian enjoys no such privileges, ethical issues dominate her narrative. The *Lettres d'une Péruvienne* illustrates Graffigny's reworking of Montesquieu's version of cross-cultural comparison. My reading demonstrates that the male author's "impartial" stance on crucial social and political issues goes hand in hand with his superficial, sensationalized treatment of female sexuality.

Contexts: Oriental Travels, Exotic Spies and Enlightenment Philosophy

When Montesquieu published the *Lettres persanes* in 1721, the Orient had long since captured the French literary imagination. Scores of Turkish,

Arabian, Chinese and Indian fictions were based on a vaguely erotic foreign elsewhere. Persia provides the background for many early novels: from lengthy epic romances to pseudo-historical *nouvelles,* fairy tales and "serious" historical writings.[5] The notorious adventures of Mehmed Riza Bey, the Persian ambassador to France, during his Parisian sojourn in 1715 inspired further secret histories (*chroniques scandaleuses*) featuring a violent and irrational oriental character.[6] Standard clichés of the oriental tale, as canonized by Galland's best-selling translation of the *Thousand and One Nights* (1704–17), include tales of genies disguised as wandering beggars, erotic scenes of passion and violence, magical occurrences and sumptuous pageantry. "Oriental" narration was expected to use such archaic and exotic tropes as oral story-telling formulas, lists of unusual flowers, spices and birds, and euphemistic nomenclature—metaphorical or descriptive proper names (Branch of Coral, Sugar Cane, Moon Face).

Montesquieu appropriated few of these "oriental" clichés in his fictional portrayal of Persian culture in the *Lettres persanes.* He is far more indebted to European-oriental travel writers such as Jean Baptiste Tavernier and Sir John Chardin.[7] The characterization of Montesquieu's Persian protagonist reveals the author's borrowings from the spy novel genre popularized by Giovanni Marana's *Turkish Spy.* Cleverly conflating the Eurocentric assumptions of contemporary voyage literature with the ironic perspective of the foreign spy, Montesquieu plots a unique lesson in cultural relativism. Like Tavernier and Chardin, Montesquieu details Persian culture as bizarre and despotic; like Marana's spy novel, the *Lettres persanes* uses Persian spies to expose bizarre and despotic practices of French culture for a (fictional) Oriental reader. Before investigating the philosophical message or narrative mechanics of the *Lettres persanes,* then, we must look to the sources of Montesquieu's exoticism.

While the French enjoyed a privileged position in the Ottoman-controlled regions of the Levant, their efforts toward trade and diplomacy with Turkey's enemy, Persia, were much more problematic. Political and cultural antagonisms often divided otherwise willing trade partners.[8] Texts of late seventeenth-century travelers document French arrogance toward and misunderstanding of their oriental hosts. In Tavernier's account of his voyage to Turkey, Persia and India (1678), for instance, the French author/ traveler describes his journeys as a mercantilist and imperialist venture designed to expand Louis XIV's influence in the Middle East. He compares the ethnographic value of his journals to the monetary value of his foreign purchases; he flaunts his insensitivity toward oriental dignitaries as part of his political service to the French empire. The dedicatory "Epistle to the King" begins:

> I hope, Sire, that these exact and sincere relations . . . will not be less useful to my nation than the rich merchandise that I have brought back from my journeys. . . . In all the countries that I have crossed, my greatest desire has always been to make known the heroic qualities of your majesty and the marvels of his reign. . . . I have often risked my fortune and my life in praising your majesty over all the princes of Europe and the kings of the Orient, even in their presence. I got out of all these perils successfully by impressing respect for your name in the heart of those barbarians.[9]

The term "barbarian" (originally connoting distance from the known, civilized world, from the Greek *barbaros* or babbler, one who could not speak the Greek tongue) here signifies Tavernier's condescending attitude as a French visitor to the Orient. Presenting his text and actions as a gesture of public service to the French nation perpetuates the Eurocentric concept of foreign cultures as alien spaces to be traversed, documented and made knowable to the French reader (who might otherwise be duped by the treacherous oriental Other).

Chardin evinces a more conciliatory, open-minded attitude in his preface to *Voyages en Perse, et autres lieux de l'Orient* (1686). He explains his investigatory approach as combining linguistic mastery, historical analysis and what one might consider an early version of anthropological fieldwork:

> The great desire that I had to know Persia, and to give exact and sincere relations of it, made me employ all that time [from 1671 to 1677] . . . in carefully examining all that could merit the curiosity of our Europe, in comparison to a huge and vast country that we could call *an other world*, because of the distance between places and because of the diversity of customs and manners [between Europe and Persia].[10]

No matter how sympathetic his portrayal of the Persians, however, Chardin's effort to catalogue and distill the strange practices of this "other world" for the European reader ultimately has the same effect as the "informational" discourse of later travel writings: it reinforces the reader's sense of being privy to an extraordinary spectacle, frozen in time and safely distanced from the dynamism of European life.

The timeless, static quality of Persian life is immediately evident when Chardin announces that "in this part of the world, the exterior forms of things, the manners, the habits, even the ways of speaking, were about the same two thousand years ago as they are today."[11] Yet these modern Persians differ from their illustrious ancestors in many ways. Echoing his cóntemporaries' appraisal of the Greeks' sad decline from their once-glorious civilization, Chardin depicts seventeenth-century Persia as a fallen land, the birthplace of the world's oldest and greatest monarchy, presently languishing under the despotic government of the Safavi dynasty. Thanks to the cruel and capricious leadership of Abbas the Great and his successors, Chardin argues, the Persians have lost their original character. No longer the brave, bellicose peoples who fought under the legendary kings Cyrus and Darius, modern-day Persians resignedly accept injustice; they have become lazy, concerned only with sensual and worldly pleasures.

Safavi absolutism degrades all aspects of Persian society, according to Chardin. While the Persians are still "the most civilized peoples of the Orient" because of their gallantry, politeness and eloquence, their civility is not generated by generosity but by self-interest, base fear or hope. "Just as their persons and fortunes are enslaved by a despotic and arbitrary force, their minds and wills are subjugated as well," Chardin declares.[12] The general atmosphere of inefficiency and corruption that governs Persian politics inevitably contaminates the individual's ethics, making the Persians into wily hypocrites whom the French fear and distrust with reason. Chardin targets their dishonest trade practices in particular: "They borrow and never return, and if they can cheat they rarely miss the opportunity to do so . . . [having] no good faith in commerce, where they deceive so craftily that one is always duped."[13]

By emphasizing the repressive, retrograde relations between the Persian rulers and their subjects, Chardin—like Tavernier before him—constructed a politically useful image of the Orient for European consumption. As Talal Asad has argued, the early Orientalists' descriptions of an "unprogressive" and "fanatical" Islamic state offered an ideal pretext for European efforts at commercial expansion and political domination in the Levant.[14] A symbol of political inefficiency and social corruption, the Orient had much to gain from the benevolent intervention of European traders, diplomats and missionaries. The enslavement of Persian women provided further ammunition for European charges of immorality and tyranny in the Islamic state. Conflating the private and public spheres of oriental society, Western commentators translated the domestic tyranny of the harem lord into a potent symbol of the political despotism of the Muslim shah.

Yet the curious mixture of sexual titillation and moral outrage which marks Chardin's harem description makes his ultimate political message unclear. Stressing the difficult access to this place for Western observers, Chardin notes: "It is thus very difficult to know anything certain of what goes on in the harem, or women's apartment, that [place] one can call *an unknown world*," before he assures the reader that his account contains hitherto unpublished facts about harem life.[15] The author thus exploits his reader's prurient interest in the unseen, clandestine side of oriental personal life to add drama to his text. But the main problem with Chardin's harem chapter emerges in the discrepancy between his self-avowed stance of impartial cultural tolerance and his sensationalized image of female sexuality.

Chardin's pseudo-scientific method relies on two explanatory devices that Montesquieu will later use: a structural analysis linking social phenomena to political forms, and the "milieu theory" positing that social life is governed by climate and physical environment. Detailing the Safavi kings' cruel treatment of their concubines and eunuchs, the traveler suggests that the harem is but one more avatar of the Persians' tyrannical absolutism. Yet he makes an apology in general on the grounds that the hot oriental climate requires such structures to prevent the lusty Muslims from killing each other: "as it is generally hot and dry, to such a degree that one experiences the movements of love more profoundly and one feels more responsive, passions for women are extremely violent there; and consequently, jealousy is also stronger there than in most neighboring countries."[16] On one hand, Chardin criticizes the harem as unnatural and despotic; on the other he argues that it is necessary, given the extreme heat that tortures the Persians.

Chardin is similarly ambiguous in portraying the Persian women's sexuality. In their belief that women are good for nothing but pleasure and procreation, Chardin charges, the Safavi kings mark their difference from the noble monarchs of times past. This argument implies that the useless existence of the modern harem dwellers may be a factor in the historic decline of Persian civilization. Yet Chardin approves the strict surveillance and forced immobility of these same women since they are supposed to possess dangerous sexual drives. In a verdict entirely based on hearsay, Chardin concludes that Persian women pose a threat to society with their voracious sexual appetites that undermine the foundations of patriarchal authority, lusting after men and women too: "Oriental women have always passed for 'Tribades' [lesbians]. I have heard it said so often, by so many people, that they are lesbian and that they have ways of satisfying each others' desires, that I take it to be quite certain."[17] Chardin disparages the harem as a wasteful, demoralizing institution without questioning the reality of women's sexual menace to society. His horrified fascination with the possibilities of debauchery and sapphism in the harem supports the continued surveillance and social segregation of Persian women.

The tensions in Chardin's harem chapter emerge from the author's ambivalence toward female sexuality. His lucidity about the political and social injustices of the Persian state coexist with his confused, third-hand account of the sexual politics within the harem. Like the French ambassador of Prévost's *Histoire d'une Grecque moderne* and the Persian correspondents of Montesquieu's *Lettres persanes,* Chardin's fascination with exotic femininity as an enigmatic threat belies his otherwise acute analysis of oriental politics, history and sociology. Clearly, the exotic woman constitutes a land apart, an incomprehensible yet tantalizing no-man's land of sexual apprehension.

The illustration "Persian Costumes" from Chardin's *Travels in Persia* (ed. 1720, Figure 6) reinforces this aura of mystery and impenetrability associated with oriental femininity. Read from left to right, this image shows a continuum of human types going from the familiar to the unknown. The first figure represents a youth dressed in an ambiguous mix of Persian and European styles. His small plumed hat and clean-shaven face indicate European origins, but his short robe and Persian-style leg wraps suggest an oriental identity. (Chardin describes the custom of wrapping linen strips around the legs—as this fellow has done—as a practice typical of Persian servants and country people.) Next to him stand three Persian gentlemen, immediately identifiable by their well-groomed mustaches, the rich fabrics of their tight-fitting *Cabais* (waistcoats) and *Cadabis* (bell-shaped outer robes), their preference for ankle-length trousers rather than European hose, and their elaborate, heavy-looking turbans. Unlike the first four figures, the last, a Persian woman, faces away from the group. Sitting astride a handsome horse, she leans forward slightly as if urging her steed to leave the company of men. Completely veiled in plain fabric, this woman's identity remains a mystery: even her eyes are concealed behind the closely woven black cloth of her face veil. She clutches the cloth at her chin, careful to keep it from slipping open and exposing her to the forbidden male gaze. In opposition to the proud, exhibitionistic poses of the Persian males, the female figure's attitude of nervous mobility exemplifies her unsuitability for the public sphere. She inhabits the marginal space at the edge of the image, her movement away from the group implying that hers is but a fleeting, enigmatic presence.

Persian Costumes

Figure 6. "Persian Costumes," from Chardin, *Travels in Persia*. Trans. Edm. Lloyd (London: J. Smith, 1720; reprint, New York: AMS Press, 1972). Courtesy of AMS Press, Inc.

Turning from the ethnographic sources of Montesquieu's exoticism to his literary models, let us first consider the philosopher Pierre Bayle's efforts to correct the biases of travel reportage in his *Pensées sur la comète* (1695–97). The Eurocentric vision of French travel relations, Bayle charges, forms a telling, negative reflection on the cultural arrogance and political hegemony of Louis XIV's reign. Criticizing the European monopoly on voyage literature, Bayle calls for foreign visitors to France to redress the balance by writing their own cross-cultural critiques:

> If those who come to Paris with ambassadors dared to publish, when they return to their homes, relations [on the French] as daring as those the French publish on foreign lands, I do not doubt that they would have many things to tell. But one fears our nation so greatly that one does not dare print anything which might prove displeasing to it.[18]

Montesquieu may have had Bayle's remarks in mind when composing the *Lettres persanes*. His strategy directly opposes the conventional trajectory of Western-critic-visits-the-East: Montesquieu brings representatives of the Orient into eighteenth-century Paris, reversing the categories of known and unknown and creating a brilliant means to criticize French politics, morality and religion.

Montesquieu did not invent this new manner of writing the foreign, however. The popularity of his *Lettres persanes* rather signals the presence of a flourishing subgenre in oriental fiction: the epistolary novel of the foreign observer or "spy novel." Critics have long debated the origins of this genre, arguing over Montesquieu's debt to Dufresny's *Amusemens sérieux et comiques* (1699); J. F. Bernard's *Réflexions morales, satiriques et comiques, sur les moeurs de notre siècle* (1714); and Addison's *Spectator* articles (1711).[19] In these fictions the foreign visitor is a transparent construction of the author's imagination, a ploy to satirize European manners and to shield the author from charges of subversive content. The quaint language and convoluted logic of the exotic critic make him ridiculous for readers and innocuous for censors.

Giovanni Marana's *L'Espion du Grand Seigneur et ses relations secrètes* (1684), also known as *Letters Writ by a Turkish Spy*, seems the most direct precedent of the *Lettres persanes,* given its political subject matter, its harem intrigue, and the serious, philosophical persona of its protagonist, Mehemet the spy.[20] Like Marana, Montesquieu conceives of his oriental visitor as a learned thinker whose judgment visibly improves as he adapts to French customs and learns the subtleties of Western philosophy.

Marana emphasizes Mehemet's superior intelligence, calling him a "skillful politician" and "wise philosopher." The portrait of "Mehemet, the Turkish spy" illustrates the symbolic attributes of this oriental philosopher/spy (Figure 7). Seated at his desk, pen in hand, Mehemet is surrounded by the tools of his trade in knowledge: a drawing compass, a well-stocked bookcase, opened letters, a globe, bags of coins, loose manuscripts, and an hourglass. The picture of the wanderer hanging under the window alludes to his vocation as a traveling sage who forgoes the pleasures of a settled life in his pursuit of knowledge. Above it all shines the bright light of an oil lamp, symbolizing the ever-burning flame of wisdom.

Voicing a refrain central to the eighteenth-century spy novel tradition, Marana asks his reader, "What matter if it be fiction or truth? Is not reason the same in all times and all countries?"[21] This notion of objective foreign vision, free of blinding prejudice and numbing superstition—the foreigner as reason incarnate—plays a major role in philosophical fiction of the eighteenth century. These philosophers/spies are not mere adventurers in search of exotic novelties; they are what one might call the "reason police," battling crimes of despotism and religious fanaticism. Their mission: to denounce and destroy unreasonable thinking wherever they may find it. Because Montesquieu and Graffigny emphasize this vision of the reasonable foreign critic, one would do well to examine the diverse connotations associated with reason in eighteenth-century thought.

Late seventeenth-century writers projected "reason" as an elitist aesthetic category and as a sociological standard. While theorists of French classicism argued for "naturalness" of expression, they derived their standards of the "natural" exclusively from the world they lived in, that is, the narrow, aristocratic universe of the French salon, court and capital. The influential orator and literary theorist Boileau, for example, used nature as a synonym for reason, but by reason he meant a highly refined state of French *civilisation* (respect for dominant religion, laws and morality) and *civilité* (politeness); as his *Art poétique* declares: "the stage demands exact reason / strict propriety must be guarded there."[22] Endowing the rarefied worlds of Versailles and Parisian high society with the status of "authentic" models, such writers transformed their aesthetic ideals into sociological norms. Ernst Cassirer aptly characterizes classicism as the mentality in which "unnoticed, decorum had superseded nature, and convention truth."[23]

The article "Savages" in Furetière's *Dictionnaire universel* (1691) reflects this confusion of aesthetic and social values under the rubric of reason. Deploying the traditional rhetorical strategy of inversion, Furetière

MEHEMET ESPION TURC
Æt. Suæ LXXII.

Figure 7. "Mehemet, the Turkish Spy," from Marana, *L'Espion dans les cours des princes chrétiens*. Frontispiece, vol. 1 (Cologne: Erasme Kinkius, 1700). Courtesy of the Rare Book Collection, Princeton University Library.

first describes the savage as one who lacks key European values and customs, having no settlements, no religion, no laws, no civil order (*police*), no clothes, and no scruples regarding cannibalism. He then shifts the register from ethnography to morality and claims that the Europeans' social conformity and respect for "reason" proves their superiority to savages, who exhibit such anti-social vices as incivility and skepticism: "[Savage] is said figuratively in moral philosophy, of those who have a capricious spirit or surly habits, who cannot easily be mellowed, *civilized or won over by reason.*"[24]

In the fin-de-siècle epoch spanning the years 1680–1715, the period Paul Hazard has equated with the "crisis of the European conscience," a dramatic ideological shift reverses the connotations of reason. The term loses its association to *honnêteté* (aristocratic propriety and politeness), instead coming to imply a certain irreverence and philosophical curiosity. The *honnête homme* of seventeenth-century tradition practiced noble *civilité* and succeeded in the world by obeying the rigorous rules of *la bonne compagnie*. The early eighteenth century sees the *honnête homme* displaced by the *écrivain-philosophe*, an inquisitive seeker of universal truth and reason, as the new cultural hero.[25] Historian Joan Scott indicates that such contests about meaning "involve the introduction of new oppositions, the reversal of hierarchies, the attempt to expose repressed terms."[26] These changing meanings of reason reverse classicism's conservative deference to the master narratives of Catholicism and monarchy, preferring a more liberal, enlightened stance of spiritual skepticism, and social and religious tolerance.

The *Encyclopédie* (1751–66) exemplifies this connotation of reason as a doctrinal tenet and moral imperative urging new forays into the study of human experience. The religious metaphors of the article "Philosopher" evoke the cachet enjoyed by the *philosophes* in the enlightened circles of Parisian free thinkers: "Reason is for the philosopher what grace is for the Christian. Grace motivates the Christian to act, reason motivates the philosopher."[27] According to the *Encyclopédie,* the philosopher's almost superhuman intellect enables him to examine any science or art and immediately discern its principles or point out its flaws: "There is only the philosopher who . . . is capable of proving that things are as they must be or of rectifying them when they are susceptible to change, by indicating the reason for the changes he wants to make."[28] The philosopher thus defined is the ultimate public servant; his unending search for reason lays the intellectual groundwork for the political reforms that the ideal lawmaker of the pre-Revolutionary age will later pursue.

But much as the *philosophes* and political reformers of the eighteenth century liked to consider themselves laborers in the service of human progress, their definition of progress as change in the direction of greater reason or rationality belies the values hiding beneath the façade of altruism. This criterion of progress as the movement away from irrational or supernatural explanations may be a serviceable measure in the development of physics or astronomy, but it is hopelessly vague when it comes to judging institutions. How can one judge the rationality of a political system without an ideal model in mind? As Marvin Harris argues, "progress" was employed by the *philosophes* to convey their partisan satisfaction with trends they endorsed.[29] The emergence of representative parliaments was thus widely regarded as a progressive change, while the expansion of slave-systems in the New World was not.

This conflict between the *philosophes'* supposedly objective (or rational) method of inquiry and their belief in culturally bound truths about what human society should be features prominently in the *Lettres persanes*. The concept of reason as an impetus to philosophical inquiry appears in the novel's opening letter, where Usbek explains his voyage to France as a mission to discover the secrets of occidental knowledge: "Rica and myself are perhaps the first Persians who have left their native country urged by the thirst for knowledge; who have abandoned the amenities of a tranquil life for the laborious search after wisdom." [30] In his eagerness for the riches of the intellect, Usbek's journey signals his refusal to accept his own culture's wisdom or *lumière* as sole authority: "Although born in a prosperous realm, we did not believe that its boundaries should limit our knowledge, and that the lore of the East should alone enlighten us" (1:9).[31] The Persians' thirst for knowledge epitomizes progressive Enlightenment *philosophie;* the desire to accumulate knowledge about the other culture is inspired not by self-serving commercial or military aims, but by knowledge itself, in an attempt to cross over provincial, national boundaries and access universal truths. The ironic tone and oppositional narratives within Montesquieu's novel, however, cast doubt on this image of the disinterested, public-spirited philosopher.

Lettres persanes: Woman as a Philosophical Entity and *Agent provocateur*

As with other spy novels, the *Lettres persanes* creates a complicitous relationship between the ideal reader (*narrataire*) and the narrator (a.k.a.

the "translator" or "editor") who publicly circulates the foreigner's private correspondence without his permission. Montesquieu stresses the clandestine nature of his work by claiming to have copied and translated the letters of two trusting Persian house guests for a French audience. This deceitful pretext prepares the ironic double perspective of the *Lettres persanes*, that is, the amusing incongruity between the Persians' public discourse, with its high-sounding philosophical discussions and learned political analyses, and their private letters that disclose feelings of jealousy, sexual insecurities and self-loathing. According to the "editor," this represents not a breach of trust or subterfuge but rather a cultural righting of accounts. It is only fair that we Europeans discover the truth about the Orient, since its inscrutable spies so easily see through us: "How much easier it is for an Asiatic to become acquainted with the manners and customs of the French in one year, than it would be for a Frenchman to become acquainted with the manners and customs of the Asiatics in four, the former being as communicative as the latter are reserved" (1:7).[32]

It is the polyvocal epistolary form of the *Lettres persanes*, more specifically the contribution of female voices to the male-dominated narrative, that allows the reader to gain an upper hand on Montesquieu's oriental hero. The letters of Usbek's wives, read against his own missives touching the domestic sphere, disclose the irony of his abstract, intellectual stance of enlightened tolerance in contrast to the experiential reality of his private despotism. By illustrating the interweaving of male and female voices in Montesquieu's novel, this reading highlights the faulty relativism of the Persian as it is exposed by his wives' provocative words and actions.

The older of the two Persians, Usbek, begins the *Lettres persanes* by sending and receiving the first twenty-three letters during his voyage from Isfahan to Paris. These letters are unusual in that they highlight his personal sensitivities: his domestic concerns with the harem, his political reasons for leaving the shah's court, and his anxieties about traveling. Describing his first days in Paris, Usbek bemoans his nostalgia for Persia, claiming to be "depressed both in body and mind," and becoming "daily more melancholy" (1:65). All things considered, however, Montesquieu's Persians are practically on a par—socially and culturally—with the French. Strong diplomatic and commercial links between France and the Levant in the early eighteenth century, including the many visits of the oriental ambassadors to Versailles, reinforce the reader's legitimation of Persia as a refined culture whose representatives were well educated in philosophy and learned in the science of the Ancients. Chardin remarked that "the polite men amongst them are upon a level with the politest men of Europe."[33] Unlike

Graffigny's preliterate Peruvian, Montesquieu's Persians speak French fluently upon arrival and keep their aristocratic status in French society. The Persians' known cultural heritage and worldly *civilité* well prepare them for integration into upper-class French society and within weeks they seem at ease in the refined circles of Parisian salons.

Montesquieu endows his Persian travelers with two distinct modes of representing their encounters with French society. Usbek's narrative voice is that of a speculative philosopher; he considers his experiences as so much data to be classified and analyzed in view of the larger truths—universal laws of human nature, structural relations between politics and morality—that may be discerned therein. Usbek's narrative *récit* creates meaning out of the events of his daily life (or *histoire*) by drawing on the authority of secular and spiritual documents as well, such as travel documents, philosophical treatises and religious texts. After taking in the habits of the French in various locales around the capital, Usbek concludes that French society is organized as a hierarchy of professions or stations (*états*), each group deriving its superiority from its contempt for those immediately below (letter 44). This sociological observation leads him to speculate on the absurdity of human vanity in general, and he cites analogous examples of a vainglorious African and a self-important Mongolian from voyage literature to prove the universal validity of his discovery.

In contrast to Usbek's philosophical generalizations, his young companion Rica speaks with the appeal of a traveling story-teller: he presents his Parisian sojourn in a series of amusing exempla or paradigmatic situations with well-known French social types. There is also a difference in temperament distinguishing Rica's letters. As befits his youthful high spirits, Rica demonstrates moral flexibility and humor in his attempts to make sense out of the French. Usbek, on the contrary, exhibits a more rigid, judgmental attitude toward what he sees as the irrationality and moral duplicity of these people. Rica's portrait of the Parisians in letter 58 exemplifies his humorous story-telling technique. After living in the capital for two years and being taken in more than once by the artful façades of its inhabitants, Rica depicts the city dwellers as practitioners of marvelous paradoxes. Instead of condemning their dishonesty, the Persian professes an ironic admiration for such scoundrels as the coquette (an "adroit woman" whose virginity "withers and blooms again every day"); the fortune-teller (that "skillful wizard" who "can tell you all your life, with the simple proviso of a quarter of an hour's conversation with your servants"); and the professors who "teach what they do not know" and thereby show their great talents (for "much less wit is required to exhibit one's knowledge, than to teach what one knows nothing of") (1:131–32). Like Usbek, Rica often ends his letters with what Chardin considered a typically Persian device—the pithy maxim or moral—in this case: "Everyone who goes from this city, leaves it a warier man than when he entered: by dint of throwing away his means on others, he learns how to keep it to himself" (1:132).[34]

Both Usbek and Rica portray the manners and customs of the French with the detached eye and penchant for taxonomical classification that we witnessed in Chardin's *Voyages*. None of their French acquaintances has a proper name: their identities remain secondary to the sociological evidence they offer as "typical Frenchmen." The Persians' narratives largely deny the historical specificity of the Frenchmen's conduct as well: the many activities and events reported in the *Lettres persanes* come across more as examples of customary practices or rituals than as unique occurrences. But while Chardin's account features numerous material details on the physical differences between life in Persia and life in Europe, including lists of Persian interior decorations, foodstuffs, geographical details, flora, and fauna, the only analogous descriptions in the *Lettres persanes* emerge in Rica's early letters and are not conveyed in the straightforward "informational" style of the seasoned voyager but in the amusing, ironic style of the ignorant new arrival. This brings us to an important distinction between the narrative strategies of voyage literature and the spy novel. In his effort to accurately render Persian geography, politics and mores for the European reader, Chardin tries to efface his prejudices and expectations from the text. Since Montesquieu designed his fiction less as a fair representation of France than as a humorous and philosophical reflection on the French, he incorporates the personal idiosyncracies of his foreign observers into the text as part of his ideological message.

Rica's youthful ignorance thus lays the groundwork for Montesquieu's satirical technique of "defamiliarizing" the known (or criticizing French society through the eyes of one who "doesn't know any better.") Rica's first impressions of Paris as a "city built in the air" or of a comedy as a "dramatic game" seem tame enough, but when he extends this process of metaphorical substitution to such sacrosanct French institutions as King Louis XIV ("a great magician" whose "dominion extends to the minds of his subjects") or the Pope ("an old idol, kept venerable by custom"), the reader realizes the subversive potential of this narrative device. Rica demystifies the rules and rites of the Catholic church by calling rosaries "little balls of wood" and heretics "those who first propound some new doctrine" (1:71). In equating Christian baptism with Muslim daily ablutions, Usbek further deflates the church's authority as unique arbiter of faith. By replacing significant terms with amusingly "defamiliar" material descriptions, Montesquieu uses his Persians to discuss (and to point out the ridiculousness of) subjects generally considered taboo.[35]

The Persians' exposure to French society and *philosophie* gradually affects the style and content of their observations. Toward the end of the book, Usbek's letters resemble philosophical treatises more than personal correspondence. Given his inclination for abstract speculation, it follows that Usbek would adopt the theoretical models found in French *philosophie* to frame his conclusions on French and Persian society. It is surprising, however, to find liberal political ideas issuing from the pen of an oriental patriarch and harem lord. His long series of letters on global depopulation (letters 114 to 122) contrast the presently stagnant Persian state with the burgeoning years of the Roman republic, laying most of the blame on the Persian government's irresponsible attitude toward its citizens. Instead of allowing its people to do as the Romans did and earn money for their labor, become citizens and pursue their own goals, Usbek claims, the Persian state represses its own population growth and financial prosperity by locking its members into dead-end positions as slaves, eunuchs and harem concubines. In what sounds like a defense of the Lockean doctrine of "natural rights," Usbek argues that the state and the citizen have a contractual agreement whereby citizens' productivity depends on being given incentives that encourage the collective well-being of the state.

Many of Usbek's most enlightened ideas, however, are grounded in an essentially conservative world view. Critics have long cited the Persian's tolerance of religious difference as evidence of his progressive thinking. But the rationale behind Usbek's call for religious tolerance does not lie in an appreciation of diverse expressions of human spirituality, but on the practical grounds of national well-being. Minority religions represent a potential source of national prosperity, the Persian asserts: their ostracism from society drives them to accumulate wealth and "embrace the most toilsome of occupations" (2:27). Moreover, all religions are useful in maintaining the status quo, since "there is no creed which does not ordain obedience and preach submission" (2:28). As we shall see, Usbek's so-called liberalism only applies to certain issues of public policy; the private domain remains governed by quite a different set of values.

Rica's enlightenment leaps into evidence in his letters on women's roles in French and Persian society. Nine months after arriving in Paris he ventures a timid criticism of the seraglio, writing that the harem life is "more conducive to health than to happiness, it is so dull and uniform" (1:78).[36] Fifteen months later he openly denounces the Persian custom of forced female subservience and explains his new perspective as a Western revelation: "This I will say: I knew nothing of women until I came here; I have learnt more about them in one month in Paris, than I could have done in thirty years [in] a seraglio" (1:141).[37] Comparing the openness and delightful conversation of French women to the silent repression of their Persian sisters, he condemns the harem as an *unnatural* order: "With us, character is uniform, because it is constrained; we do not see people as they are, but as they are obliged to be; in that slavery of heart and mind, it is only fear that utters a dull routine of words, very different from the language of nature which expresses itself so variously" (1:141).[38]

Once he realizes the extent of women's participation in French society, however, Rica mitigates his early enthusiasm for women's "natural" behavior. His portrayal of the "republic of women" that holds sway over the French monarchy betokens the Persian's antagonism toward women who dare to speak out and assert themselves in the male-dominated universe of politics: "These women are all in each other's secrets and form a sort of republic, the members of which are always busy aiding and serving each other" (2:82).[39] This letter is notable for its depiction of the masculine fear of women's "natural" propensity for secrecy, intrigue and sexual duplicity.

For all his proto-feminist rhetoric, the Persian regards female nature as a threatening entity. The sheer force of their sexuality enables women—in Persia as in France—to reduce government ministers, princes, even kings to passive pawns and to seize the reins of political power for their own, illegitimate ends: "They complain in Persia that the kingdom is governed by two or three women: it is much worse in France, where the women govern generally, and not only usurp all authority wholesale, but retail it among themselves" (2:82).[40] Clearly, women must be reckoned with, managed and controlled, lest they usurp male power over the public sphere.

Usbek's position on the rightful role of women in society is even more problematic. While the early letters of the *Lettres persanes* present him as a concerned husband and advocate of social tolerance, the later ones unveil a discrepancy between his praxis and his philosophy. Usbek's project of cultural comparison leads him to articulate fairly progressive views on human liberty and generally to prefer mild governments over severe ones, but he refuses his own wives the slightest hint of autonomy, invoking the natural order of things. His reasoning adopts the public/private dialectic that informs Prévost's narrator in *Histoire d'une Grecque moderne*. One set of standards rules over public, political policy, another corresponds to private, personal behavior. Hence his argument on the state's obligation to provide citizens with useful occupations (letter 115) does not apply to females: they inhabit the private sphere. Apart from encouraging women's productive potential as mothers, the state has no positive duty toward women, rather it must enforce a negative, police function. Given their natural tendency toward sexual excess, duplicity and irrational behavior, women must be dominated, controlled.

Each political structure devises its own system for keeping women subjugated, Usbek argues, in keeping with its inherent logic and structure. Persian despotism maintains order by forcibly separating the sexes, institutionalizing polygamy and severely punishing unauthorized sexual contacts. French monarchy perpetuates itself by institutionalizing monogamy and, more important, channeling women's energies into the petty intrigues and conspicuous consumption (fashion, luxury, gambling) that rule life at the royal court. In his arguments on justice, morality and politics, Usbek articulates the "woman question" in the cool, abstract language of the disinterested observer. Ethical concerns do not exist.

Seen through the selective vision of this harem lord, the despotic system offers women a better life than the monarchical system. An early letter to his favorite wife Roxane reveals the curious logic behind this claim. Reasoning that the greater the sight of the woman's body, the easier the access to the site of her undoing, Usbek extolls the moral purity of unseen harem dwellers in contrast to their visibly immoral counterparts in France: "How happy you are, [Roxane], to be in the delightful country of Persia, and not in these poisonous regions, where shame and virtue are alike unknown!" (1:61).[41] The Persian women are to be envied, he declares: their seclusion guarantees an unsullied conscience, whereas the French women's freedom of movement hurls them into the quagmire of sexual license and immorality.

Moreover, Usbek conceives of his own harem as an exception to the generally miserable conditions of life under despotism; he represents his own rule as the tender if severe guidance of a loving husband. Counseling his wives to obey his orders and avoid punishment, he says, "For I wish to forget that I am your master, to remember only that I am your husband." Note the significant choice of the pronoun *me* in this declaration of sincerity: "Je voudrois vous faire oublier que je suis votre maître, pour *me* souvenir seulement que je suis votre époux" (1:227). Montesquieu uses the reflexive pronoun required by the French verb "to remember" to stress that it is *Usbek* who insists on this version of reality. Montesquieu's translator, John Davidson, distorts the significance of this passage by replacing Usbek's selective memory with the neutral passive voice ("to be remembered only as your husband" [1:170]). Usbek does not care what his wives think, he wants only to cleanse his conscience of the taint of tyranny. His main regret is that he cannot flatter himself that his government is mild and gentle.

The reader discovers other views on Usbek's rule and the harem institution in the letters of his wives and eunuchs. Authorized by the absence of their master, Usbek's wives take pen in hand to address him and thereby challenge the Persian interdiction on female speech outside the harem. Although they remain captive in a rigorously guarded prison, the women's appropriation of the written word affords them a modicum of autonomy. Self-affirmation—even when limited to the expression of alienation or suffering—is integral to the women's coming-to-writing (*venue à l'écriture*). As time passes and Usbek's once mighty authority over their minds and bodies wanes, the women develop. Where their early correspondence contains primarily lovesick complaints and laments of sexual frustration, a dramatic defiance resounds in the middle of the novel: by the end the women write openly of their disillusionment and disgust with the harem system, demand reparations for their suffering and declare the final break.

Montesquieu endows all the harem wives with one distinct mode of representing their thoughts. Although the letters are attributed to different authors, the women nonetheless resemble one another in their emphatic, emotional style and intimate subject matter. The stereotypical exoticism of the women's names—Zachi, Zéphis, Zélis, Fatmé—further suggests that their identities are interchangeable. Gender dictates fictional voice in the *Lettres persanes*. The male voices, as we have seen, speak with the authority of experts, providers of universally valid sociological *information;* the female voices, on the other hand, articulate passionate accounts of historically and geographically specific *experience*. To the men's large-scale analyses of sociopolitical structures, the women reply with individual reports of localized struggle and conflict within the Persian system.

In spite of the authentic-sounding language and emotions of these "native scripts," Montesquieu's characterization of the Persian women signals his artificial notion of exotic femininity. The composite portrait of the Persian woman that surfaces in the *Lettres persanes* evokes the sensational phantasm of oriental sexuality propagated in voyage literature and "oriental" fiction. Usbek's harem wives are at once passive and insatiable, oppressed and duplicitous, lascivious heterosexuals and sly homosexuals.

Zachi depicts the dilemma of the woman who identifies with her function as a passive sex object—who lives in waiting and depends on others to justify her existence. Seeing herself only as a reflection of male sexual desire, she laments the futility of her existence when deprived of her master's authenticating gaze: "The sighs I heave there is none to hear; my falling tears you are not [here] to pity. . . . Ah! my beloved Usbek, if you only knew your happiness!" (1 : 13).[42] Zéphis's letter contains a double message on the capricious and possibly perverted nature of oriental femininity. Complaining of her eunuch's rigorous constraint, she also lets on the cause of his suspicions: her ambiguous sexual relationship with the female slave Zelida who, she says, serves her "with such affection" and massages her so skillfully ("at whose magical touch new charms appear") (1 : 14).

Fatmé's complaint of sexual frustration adds further evidence to Montesquieu's image of the oriental woman as a creature of voracious appetites: she seems an erotic time bomb just waiting to explode. Yet her comments on the laws devised to keep women's sexuality enslaved to the master's body reveal the woman's critical acumen as well. Temporarily freed from her master's sexual demands, she realizes the emptiness of her role as an "ornament" of the harem and indicts the patriarchal Persian system for forcing women to satisfy men while repressing their own needs: "You men are the cruellest creatures! Delighted when we have desires that we cannot gratify, you treat us as if we had no emotions—though you would be very sorry if that were so" (1 : 19).[43] Depicting the women's concern with sex as the primary vehicle for their interests enables Montesquieu to stress the eroticism of the harem wives even as they critique larger issues of Persian culture.

The physical claustration of Persian women comes under fire in Zachi's letter 47. After an outing in the country where they "hoped to be more free," the women find that even a minor excursion forces them to bear the heavy societal baggage of confinement and fear. They are prohibited even the luxury of saving themselves from peril: when a river crossing suddenly becomes treacherous, the chief eunuch vows to die before he will let the women expose their faces and sully his master's honor. In conclusion Zachi exclaims: "How distressing journeys are for us poor women!

Men are exposed only to those dangers which threaten their lives; but we are in constant terror of losing either life or virtue" (1:103–4).[44] This negative account of travel under impossible conditions is significantly juxtaposed to a letter by Usbek celebrating the renewal of vision and energy that travel affords men. Writing to his friend Rhedi, Usbek exults: "I am interested in everything, astonished at everything: I am like a child, whose organs, still over-sensitive, are vividly impressed by the merest trifles" (1:104).[45] Usbek's joyous realization of his freedom of movement and thought contrasts sharply with the women's bitter awareness of their helplessness and empty lives: this demonstrates the ironic potential of Montesquieu's polyvocal narrative structure.

The letters of Usbek's wives disrupt the narrative flow and help correct our assessment of Usbek's objectivity. Near the mid-point of the novel, Zélis announces a major break with Usbek's law (letter 62). Turning the symbolic order of the harem on end, she claims her freedom from the eunuchs' surveillance and defies Usbek's apparatus of control to tame her independent spirit. Instead of cowering before the specter of institutionalized slavery, Zélis exposes the falsity of Usbek's claim to be an absolute patriarch; she declares that the well-policed seraglio indicates the master's lack of real power, that is, his impotence: "Even in the prison where you keep me I am freer than you. You can only redouble your care in guarding me, that I may rejoice at your uneasiness; and your suspicions, your jealousy, your annoyance, are so many marks of your dependence" (1:140).[46] The dramatic power of this letter is further intensified by the two following it: in letter 63 Rica declares his independence from Persian mores; letter 64, from the chief black eunuch, informs Usbek that his harem is self-destructing.

Writing on the subversive power of the polyvocal epistolary novel, Jean Rousset suggests the ironies created by letter juxtapositions like these: "the simple juxtaposition of two clearly different tones becomes a means of expression, a manner of speaking without having to articulate anything; a white space takes on a meaning; the mute parts of the book themselves enter into the structure of the book."[47] The women's letters, passionate and desperate, concentrate on widening the cracks in the rigid structure of Usbek's seraglio. Given their infrequency in the text (only eleven of the 161 letters are written by women), one might say that the women's voices form the mute parts of Usbek's narrative—the hidden tension of his troubled conscience, symptomatic of a larger problem in his ethics. Montesquieu himself spoke of the letters from the harem wives and eunuchs as a "secret chain" that lends a sense of thematic cohesion to this novel.

The letters from Usbek's eunuchs first alert the reader to the changes occurring in the seraglio, the growing rivalry of the women around their absentee master. As head of the seraglio police, the chief black eunuch describes the atmosphere as one of rampant sedition: "nothing is heard but murmurs, complaints, reproaches; my remonstrances are despised: everything seems permitted in this time of license, and I am nothing but a name in the seraglio" (1:143).[48] In spite of this and other warnings, Usbek's absence eventually provokes a battle, albeit fought in absentia, of mutually opposing sexual codes. While the women call the harem a heinous prison that coerces them into empty lives of forced idleness, Usbek calls it an asylum of innocence, a "sweet retreat, where you find innocence and self-security, where no danger makes you afraid" (1:63).[49] How can members of one (polygamous) family, sharing the same domestic space, see their home in such diametrically opposed terms? The answer lies in the raison d'être ascribed to the harem. Although Usbek's harem was running smoothly at his departure, his absence becomes through time a glaring symbol of the precarious mechanics by which this system operates. The delicate equilibrium balancing pleasure and discipline breaks down when the motivating force behind the harem—the husband's body—is missing. A sexual despotism cannot function without a despot.[50] Without their husband to remind them of their assigned roles in the harem, the women lose sight of the logic behind their confinement and dare to denounce it as ill-founded, even absurd. The place of marital devotion and sexual service, they realize, is but a holding tank, repository of an absent master's playthings.

Usbek, on the other hand, sees his absence from the harem as a temporary hindrance to its smooth operation and demands that the eunuchs guarantee his authority through rigorous policing. Like an amiable visitor (or parasite) who has partaken of a long and satisfying banquet of French *philosophie,* Usbek dismisses the eunuch's warnings and the wives' complaints like so many unsavory leftovers from his past and moves on to more palatable discussions. Usbek's philosophizing late in the *Lettres persanes* recalls Michel Serres's description of the well-fed parasite: "He eats at the house of a great man—the greatest possible. In return, he feeds his greatness. He enjoys belonging. . . . he shares an opinion, an ideology or a rule. Truth surrounds him like a shield. . . . He has finally become specialized; he has a method."[51] When Usbek does admit that the harem has some problems, he couches them in the terms of a philosophically less desirable system. He does not avow any remorse or guilt about his own participation, but rather deflects these issues into sociological arguments about the negative effects of converting potentially fertile citizens into sterile eunuchs and slaves. Avoiding ethical issues by resorting to structural abstractions, Usbek contends that harems constitute an inevitable, natural part of the Persian order. Just as monarchies require an invisible power base to reign over their people, so do despotisms require political and sexual tyranny for their perpetuation (letter 103).

The inconsistency between these progressive ideals and retrogressive practices constitutes one of Montesquieu's most penetrating critiques of the Enlightenment.[52] While Usbek as Persian philosopher sees himself championing religious tolerance and cultural relativism, he clearly prefers the study of abstract ideas over the contemplation of his own distressing domestic situation or his own questionable ethics. A hypocritical *philosophe,* he theorizes the abstract political implications of social constructs when his wives' letters are telling of ever-greater hardships and suffering in his household.

Near the end of the correspondence, faced with proof of his wives' infidelity, the Persian drops his Europeanized persona of disinterested, tolerant observer, quickly returning to his original identity as oriental harem lord. Instead of philosophically analyzing the corruption of the harem as the inevitable result of a system lacking a solid moral foundation, he sees himself as the victim of his wives' vice and sexual excesses. Startlingly severe for an enlightened philosopher, his reaction to the women's treachery is unsurprising for a petty despot: he orders judgment without trial, followed by corporal punishment for all, and death for the deserving.

The last letter of the novel exposes the failure of Usbek's philosophical enterprise. Roxane, Usbek's favorite, prettiest wife, reveals the concrete hypocrisy of his harem in shockingly frank terms: "Yes, I have deceived you; I have led away your eunuchs: I have made sport of your jealousy; and I have known how to turn your frightful seraglio into a place of pleasure and delight" (2:222).[53] In her words Roxane redefines the harem as a woman-oriented place, literally restructuring the sense of enclosure by letting lovers penetrate its drapes and hide within its stone walls. She subverts Usbek's abstract vocabulary as well, rescripting his argument according to her own conception of "natural" law: "I have lived in slavery, and yet always retained my freedom: I have remodeled your laws upon those of nature; and my mind has always maintained its independence"

(2:222–23).[54] Seizing the oppressor's moral and philosophical lexicon, Roxane appropriates his terms to her own uses and reforms the womens' roles to serve the pursuit of happiness and freedom. But just as she assumes this new-found power and speaks this "new language," her story is over. The last letter concludes in an annihilation of self—an abrupt textual closure: "But all is ended now; the poison destroys me, my strength leaves me, my pen drops from my hand; even my hate grows weaker: I die" (2:223).[55] Montesquieu's Persian experiment comes to a conventional conclusion: death, at her own hand, of the misfit woman and the larger social system unperturbed.

Roxane's suicide is often interpreted as a gesture of final freedom, indicating the symbolic death of the master and, by extension, the annihilation of the despotic oriental system. While Usbek's harem is effectively destroyed—his eunuchs poisoned, his wives embittered—at the end of the book, I do not believe this ending suggests a universal condemnation of all sexual tyranny, but rather the logical climax of Usbek's moral and affective bad faith, the ultimate clash between his abstract political philosophizing and the concrete reality of his domestic despotism. The harem's self-destruction makes perfect sense in structural terms as well. As a machine that was missing its one essential cog, a despot-less sexual despotism, this harem had to fall. Others still stand.

In fact the melodramatic dénouement of Montesquieu's novel passes on a profoundly conservative message about women's participation in society. The polyvocal epistolary form of the *Lettres persanes* initially seemed to serve a politics of liberation, allowing the Persian women to denounce their unjust treatment at the hands of their guardians. Yet their challenge to the monolithic authority of their husband ultimately creates nothing more than an *illusion* of female liberation. Though the women speak their minds, they gain no access to power. Moreover, Montesquieu's sensationalized portrayal of the harem women enhances traditional masculinist fears about female nature and reinforces old arguments for the exclusion of women from the public sphere. The women in this novel are untrustworthy, capricious, selfish, sexually demanding, and given to intrigue: such creatures certainly cannot be relied upon to maintain the collective well-being of the state. By stressing the illegitimacy and destructive potential of female action—in the Persian harem and the French court—the author implies that women need to be dominated for the good of society as a whole. The problems in the harem all came about because there was no king, husband or father there to lead them.

The antagonism between Montesquieu's hero and his wives recalls the gendered conflict in Prévost's *Histoire d'une Grecque moderne*. The men in these books are not represented as malicious villains who intentionally hurt the women under their care. Products of social circumstance, they are molded by culture and environment to expect certain things of male-female relationships and are disappointed when their expectations go unfulfilled. Like Montesquieu's harem lord, Prévost's ambassador is an aristocrat. In their relations with women, both characters attempt to safeguard an aristocratic power base through marital fidelity (which ensures the purity of bloodlines) and/or female confinement (which keeps the family unit chaste and closed to outside forces). It is the women's refusal to comply with these rules that brings on their punishment. For the women in these novels are not content to go on living as a commodity exchanged among men: because they want to pursue their own goals and determine their own futures, they are a threat to male dominance and, by extension, to the aristocratic order. The sexual threat of a strong-willed woman is linked to the economic and political threats facing the aristocracy in the early eighteenth century: the economic menace of the socially mobile bourgeoisie and the political menace of a power-hungry absolute monarch.[56] Like a nobleman who fears losing his hereditary privileges to an arrogant king or a lowly merchant, Prévost's Frenchman fears being effeminized by his independent-minded protégée and Montesquieu's Persian fears being symbolically castrated by his disobedient wives. Sexual, economic and political fears are joined in the culturally threatening figure of an inscrutable oriental Other.

Graffigny sets out to desubstantialize such reified notions of gendered and cultural difference in the *Lettres d'une Péruvienne*. Presenting her fiction as the first-person "native script" of an exotic woman, Graffigny abjures the distanced, suspicious perspective of Prévost's novel. Her juxtaposition of informational detail on Peruvian customs and language with an experiential narrative of the heroine's day-to-day actions and feelings lends documentary authority and emotional authenticity to her representation of a Peruvian "spy." By placing her character in the unpleasant situations that young French women experienced—the boring convent and the oppressive parental home—the female author spotlights the *causes* of women's apparent character flaws instead of attributing them to a defective female nature. Her ultimate revisionary act is to keep her heroine alive at the end of the novel and to settle her in an utopian world, turning an aristocratic château into the setting for a life of bourgeois industry and "Peruvian" morality. From the reified image of gendered and cultural conflict in Montesquieu's work, Graffigny thus creates an intimate account of the local forces that affect an outsider's entrance into French society, imagining a positive outcome for French and foreigner alike.

In the Margins: From Persia to Peru— Changing Images of Exoticism, 1721–47

The popularity of the *Lettres persanes* continued throughout the eighteenth century, inspiring scores of sequels and spinoffs. Montesquieu remarks on the prodigious success of his novel and pointedly condemns his imitators in "Quelques réflexions sur les *Lettres persanes*" (1754), but he singles out Graffigny's novel as an exception, rating the *Lettres d'une Péruvienne* alongside Richardson's *Pamela* as the charming successors to the *Lettres persanes*. [57] Graffigny likewise makes an intertextual tribute to Montesquieu in her "Avertissement," stating that she too hopes to educate the French on the ways of another culture and citing the infamous refrain of Montesquieu's prejudiced French socialites, "However can anybody be a Persian?" to underline the ongoing need for such works.

Though she claims Montesquieu's work as her model, Graffigny recasts the exotic spy as an American subject. Why this preference for the New World over the Old? After years of popularity, the oriental locale had lost its sovereign appeal for French readers by the 1740s, as fictional savages, islanders and Indians began to appear in literature from countries hitherto unexplored: the Americas, the Caribbean islands, and later Tahiti. [58] The shift from Orientalism to Americanism corresponds to the many accounts of New World travel that flooded the market in the first half of the eighteenth century. Indeed Graffigny presents her fiction as if it were an authentic ethnographic document, prefaced with a "historical introduction" and supplemented with footnotes defining Peruvian terms and beliefs for the French reader. But in Graffigny's case, the choice of an American protagonist over an Oriental has another, more pointed reason in her project to revise the *Lettres persanes* from a woman's point of view.

In popular stereotypes of the eighteenth century, the Orient was notorious as a place of sexual and political despotism. Oriental women were commodified as sex objects: courtesans, harem wives and slaves. The long-suffering oriental heroines of Montesquieu's *Lettres persanes* and Prévost's *Histoire d'une Grecque moderne* are all portrayed as victims of domineering men; all finish their lives in conventional novelistic endings—marriage, servitude or death. For her novel Graffigny sought a model of exoticism that could question the inevitability of female subservience to men and make plausible a most unusual vision of female destiny. She chose an American, more specifically a Peruvian, because of what Peru meant to her readers.

Let us take a glance at the "Peruvian" literary tradition in Graffigny's day. The illustrations from Gomberville's *Polexandre*, Gueulette's *Peruvian Tales* and Marmontel's *Les Incas* show some typical modes of representing the exotic "Peruvian" in French fiction of the late seventeenth and eighteenth centuries. The scene from Gomberville's epic romance *Polexandre* (ed. 1641) supposedly takes place in the wilds of Mexico when the Peruvian prince is reunited with his beloved (Figure 8). But these New World figures wear the elaborately detailed garb of European courtiers and the scene's locale is the leafy enclosure found in many Baroque illustrations, with no indication of New World flora or fauna. The emphasis is on the Peruvian's similarity to the French; though he may live in an exotic land, this hero's delicate clothing and gallant pose show that he is well acquainted with the classical codes of civility. The illustration from Gueulette's *Peruvian Tales* (ed. 1786), a collection of fairy tales, presents Peru as a marvelous and magical land where the natural often brushes against the supernatural (Figure 9). In this image an eerie glowing hand floats in the air above two toga-wearing, barefoot Incas in a rich setting bedecked with smiling sun heads. This "Peruvian" scene evokes an atmosphere similar to that suggested by the "Greek" figures in Lussan's *Veillées de Thessalie* (Figure 3); both stress the exotic foreigners' mystery and romance, that is, their distance from the Real World.

The early nineteenth-century illustration from Marmontel's *Les Incas, ou la destruction de l'empire du Pérou* (1777) (Figure 10) offers a striking contrast to these highly stylized images of romance and fairy tale. Marmontel's treatment of the Incas' tragic demise epitomizes the anti-colonial fervor and sentimentalism of late eighteenth-century fiction. In this image a Europeanized hero sports a tight-fitting waistcoat and leather shoes, while his lover's attire conjures up an erotic image of "primitive" sensuality with her bare feet, her jewel-encrusted diadem, and her hand-woven robe, which is carelessly draped so as to display her luscious legs, thighs and belly. The legend underlines the exotic woman's function as spectacle for the Western observer: "He opens his eyes and sees Cora: his eyes take in a thousand charms." The female figure's dreamy nonchalance in her lover's

Figure 8. Frontispiece of Gomberville, *Polexandre,* part 3 (Paris: Augustin Courbé, 1641; reprint, Geneva: Slatkine Reprints, 1978). Courtesy of Slatkine Reprints.

Figure 9. Illustration for Gueulette, *Peruvian Tales*. Trans. Samuel Humphreys. In *The Novelist's Magazine,* vol. 21 (London: Harrison and Co., 1786). Courtesy of the Princeton University Libraries.

Figure 10. "He opens his eyes and sees Cora: his eyes take in a thousand charms." Illustration for Marmontel, *Les Incas, ou la destruction de l'empire du Pérou* (Paris: Verdière, 1824). Courtesy of the Princeton University Libraries.

embrace suggests the vulnerability, closeness to nature and gentleness of the Peruvian in contrast to the European's buttoned-up morality and superior military force (symbolized by the sword lying behind the man's hand). Notable as well is the illustrator's attempt at botanical realism, seen in the huge, tropical-looking fronds and berries hanging over the lovers and the cacti at their feet.

Voltaire's play *Alzire ou les Américains* (1735) is cited in the "Avertissement" to the *Lettres d'une Péruvienne* as another "Peruvian" predecessor. These works share a similar historical background, but their portrayal of the Peruvian character could not be more different. Graffigny's heroine expresses her skepticism toward Catholicism and resolutely refuses to convert to the end. *Alzire* concludes with the spectacle of a dying Spanish general admonishing his Inca murderer to learn from his mistake and accept the domination of Christianity and Spanish rule: "Live, superb enemy, be free and remember / What was the duty and the death of a Christian. . . . Educate America, teach her kings / That the Christians were born to give them their laws."[59] Voltaire's hero conquers the spirits of New World savages instead of oriental infidels, but the final moral of this play is the same as in all other conversion tales: given the right motivation, the heathen Other will one day see the light.

Apart from these literary sources, most knowledge about Peru came to the French public in the guise of Jesuit writings, early histories and explorers' accounts. The idealized portrayal of the ancient Incas in Garcilaso de la Vega's *Royal Commentaries* (1609–16; French translation 1633) sets the tone for most historical works.[60] But modern-day travelers brought back vastly different tales of the Peruvian character. The chapters on Peru in Prévost's widely read *Histoire générale des voyages* (1746–80) well illustrate the contentious nature of these early attempts at Peruvian ethnography; as the editor announces: "Our latest voyagers represent the natives of the ancient Peruvian empire so different today than they were at the time of the conquest, that one has difficulty reconciling the modern images with those of the first relations."[61]

Basing his historical overview of Peru on Garcilaso's work, Prévost devotes considerable space to the fabulous origins of the Inca empire, its orderly hierarchical social structure and sun-worshipping religious beliefs. Ancient Peru represents a paradoxical juxtaposition of primitive and civilized: it is a most un-savage model of lawful (*policé*) society. The princes of the Sun are depicted as wise and far-sighted rulers who demand and receive their subjects' submission without conflict, like an exotic version of a European absolute monarch. Proof of the Incas' superior engineering skills is demonstrated in their complex network of roads, bridges and monuments, not to mention their well-known prowess in the mining and treatment of precious metals.

In contrast to Garcilaso's tableau of the Incas' glorious past, the seventeenth- and eighteenth-century voyagers cited in *Histoire générale des voyages* have a hard time explaining the abject misery of the modern Peruvian state. Most agree that the Peruvians they saw are a far cry from their illustrious Inca ancestors, characterizing them as a lazy, secretive and superstitious people. But the observers' rationales vary greatly, ranging from claims of genetic deficiencies to evocations of spiritual plenitude. The "most exact of modern voyagers" (according to Prévost) describe the Indians' moral squalor in the pseudo-scientific jargon of Enlightenment natural science, as a symptom of their degenerate status as a hybrid species (a mixture of various Indian races, Spanish and creole blood). Echoing the famous naturalist Buffon's prognosis of American racial "degeneracy," the Spanish geographer Antonio de Ulloa declares the Peruvians an inferior race: "their imbecility is so excessive, that one can hardly justify placing them above the level of beasts."[62]

Pro-colonial writers compare the benighted existence of the Peruvians with the misery of the Paraguayans before the benevolent intervention of Jesuit missionaries. Their hopes for Peru's future rely upon religious conversion and political assimilation in the Spanish state. As proof of the Indians' potential they cite the greater intelligence and refinement of the Spanish-speaking city dwellers over their illiterate Quechua-speaking country cousins.[63] The illustration from *Histoire générale des voyages* mirrors this attempt to impose European social ranks on the ethnically mixed Peruvian population (Figure 11). In its linear, hierarchical organization of Peruvian types, this image presupposes a New World society not unlike the rigidly class-conscious Old World model. Visually undifferentiated by race, the figures' dress and wearing or non-wearing of shoes, as supplemented by their spatial arrangement and numerical order, clearly privilege wealth and European origins over indigenous blood and such low-class "native" occupations as barber and peasant.[64] Although the pictorial prominence of the Spanish and Indian ladies of distinction suggests that a certain blurring of social boundaries may be afforded the wealthy, Europeanized city dweller, the common Indian of the hills—barefoot and saddled with a baby—remains marginalized in the corner of the group.

Faced with the Peruvians' paradoxical preference for a life of wretched

N. v. d. Meer f. f.

1. Espagnole de Quito.
2. Indienne de distinction.
3. Barbier Indien.

4. Metive de Quito.
5. Paisan Indien.
6. Indienne du Commun.

Figure 11. Illustration for Prévost, *Histoire générale des voyages,* vol. 19 (Amsterdam: E. Van Harrevelt and J. Changuion, 1773). Courtesy of the Rare Book Collection, Princeton University Library.

poverty over acquiescence to colonial rule, other observers describe the Indians as living relics of a lost Golden Age. Hence one writer exclaims: "one could say that the golden age was never more real than for them. Nothing alters the tranquillity of their souls. . . . Though half naked, they seem just as happy as the most sumptuously dressed Spaniard."[65] Eighteenth-century commentators thus replicate the biblical narrative of the fall in an exotic Eden and interpret the Peruvians' fall from grace as the effect of modern-day evils (Spanish avarice and cruelty) on a hitherto unspoiled land. Implicit in all these explanations is the memory of another age, an earlier, purer age when the Peruvian people were most certainly better off.

Lettres d'une Péruvienne: Transgressing the Boundaries of Old and New Worlds

Two central facts of the Peruvian identity—their historical victimization by Spanish conquistadors and their contemporary slander by European travelers—inform Graffigny's choice of the New World locale. Visibly inspired by Garcilaso's history of the Incas, the "historical introduction" to the *Lettres d'une Péruvienne* nevertheless omits certain key aspects of the *Royal Commentaries:* these exclusions point to the peculiar use Graffigny will make of Peruvian history in her novel.[66] The description of the Incas in Graffigny's text stresses the myth of their marvelous origin, their cult of the sun, and their obedience to his "son," the Sun King. Submissive subjects of a just ruler, the Peruvians are seen to work their fields in common, practice an unusually rigorous morality and live in complete contentment. This account ignores some of the most striking details of the Inca Empire— its grandiose expansionist ambitions, rigid sociopolitical hierarchy, and bellicose spirit—to convey the impression of a peace-loving, consensual, primitive society. Consequently this history alludes only briefly to the Incas' rule by a hereditary aristocracy, and neglects to mention the Peruvians' fratricidal battles and violent resistance to conquest. Rather it represents the Peruvians as the innocent, passive victims of heartless colonial aggression: "An entire people, submissive and begging for mercy, was put to the sword. . . . The ignorance of our vices and the naïveté of their morals threw them into the arms of their contemptible enemies. In vain did vast distances separate the cities of the Sun from our world, they became [the Europeans'] prey and most precious domain."[67] Revising the *leyenda negra* to suit Graffigny's purposes, the "historical introduction" translates the

Spaniards' conquest of Peru into the metaphorical rape of a weak and vulnerable, but highly desirable (feminized) land.

Graffigny's indignation with European vilification of the Peruvian national character emerges in the "Avertissement" to the *Lettres d'une Péruvienne*. Instead of offering the Peruvians the respect due them as ancestors of the magnificent Inca culture, she charges, the French look down on them in their misery and blame them for the sheer difference of their language and customs: "Enriched by the precious remains of Peru, we should at least regard the inhabitants of that part of the world as a magnificent people. . . . But always prejudiced in our own favor, we do not grant any merit to other nations except to the extent that their customs imitate ours, or their language resembles our idiom."[68] As one can see from our selection of travel writings, the author does not exaggerate the negative nature of contemporary European stereotypes when she declares: "We scorn the Indians; we hardly admit that these unfortunate people possess the capacity to think."[69]

Just as the Incas' ignorance of Spanish firearms, military tactics and colonial ambitions made them easy victims of the Spaniards' conquest, the modern Peruvians' lack of a written language and written cultural heritage leaves them wide open to the slander of Western observers. Graffigny endeavors to remedy these injustices in her fiction. She redresses the unfair power differential between colonizer and colonized by arming her Peruvian heroine with the cultural know-how to combat European attempts on her person. She rectifies the distorted image of Peruvian character disseminated in travel writing by providing her heroine with the language tools to put her version of reality into writing where it will be safe for posterity. All but the last five of the heroine's letters are addressed to her Peruvian fiancé, Prince Aza, a gesture that reinforces the "Peruvianness" of this text. Finally, in her ultimate act of power redistribution, Graffigny retrieves stolen Inca treasures from the Spaniards and returns them to the heroine, who then liquidates her assets to acquire the single most important possession under the ancien régime system: property.

Like other authors of her time, Graffigny's is a dichotomous vision of Peru, characterized by two opposing images: the poverty of modern Peru versus the splendor of the original Inca Empire. But unlike her more scrupulously historical contemporaries, Graffigny conflates these two ages of Peru.[70] On the one hand she depicts her heroine as a Virgin of the Sun, princess of royal Inca blood and witness to the Spanish conquest of Peru—which transpired in the years 1522–48. On the other hand she brings her heroine into the modern Paris of her day, the 1740s. In a brilliant stroke of literary legerdemain, Graffigny creates a heroine who encompasses both ages of Peru and thus lays the foundation for a most unusual literary destiny. The original dichotomy—ancient splendor versus modern misery—is recast as the symbolic tension between the heroine's admirable natural spirit and her difficult existence in corrupt, unfeeling eighteenth-century French society. By endowing a fictional "spy" with the self-sufficiency and integrity associated with the Incas of the Golden Age, the author establishes her moral superiority and authority as a critic and ultimately motivates her withdrawal from Parisian society at the end of the novel. Graffigny's emphasis on the heroine's Inca goodness thus serves the ends of primitivist polemic and utopian vision in the *Lettres d'une Péruvienne*. The heroine's naïve point of view satirizes French errors in contrast to an ideal primitive past and justifies the author's utopian solution for the future.[71]

Graffigny's choice of a female American over Montesquieu's male Oriental model makes possible a strikingly different account of the encounter between European and non-European. Her protagonist's status as victim polarizes the relationship to two kinds of authority that Montesquieu takes for granted: the authority of French culture and the authority of impartial, informational travel writing. The heroine's uneasy rapport with the French comes out in her fictional plot; the author's dissatisfaction with the master narratives of anthropological reportage comes out in her narrative persona. While Montesquieu's Persians enter Parisian society as peers and internalize its conventions to the point of becoming token Frenchmen, Graffigny's Peruvian comes to France as a prisoner of war and retains an outsider's sensibility during her entire sojourn. Graffigny's resistance to the distanced, "impartial" persona of the travel writer emerges in her preference for reporting the heroine's innermost feelings and contacts with particular individuals over Montesquieu's practice of phrasing the Persians' discoveries in the detached rhetoric of sociological analysis. While Graffigny supplements her tale with informational footnotes explaining Peruvian terms, customs and beliefs, it is the woman's circumstantial narrative of experience that dominates the *Lettres d'une Péruvienne*.

The very premise of Graffigny's fictional plot reveals her heroine's distance from the controlled civility of the Persians. While Montesquieu's heroes set out for Paris with the blessing of their shah and are received by the French as privileged visitors, Graffigny's heroine is wrenched from her native land by marauding Spanish conquistadors, kidnapped by the

French as war booty, and transported to an unknown, alien world. She first meets the French upon waking as a prisoner on their ship and describes them as her "new tyrants" and "officious persecutors." Given her jailers' unbridled curiosity and power over her person, she begins to suspect that their control extends to her mind as well. Perhaps these "savages" can penetrate her brain and read her thoughts, as she remarks: "I make a tiresome task of arranging my thoughts as if they could read them against my will."[72] This fear of transparency effectively stimulates the heroine's desire to learn the French language; it is only by absorbing the foreign culture that the Peruvian can defend herself and repossess her autonomy.

A victim of reverse colonization, the American heroine of the *Lettres d'une Péruvienne* is forcibly moved into the dominant culture and obliged to adapt. The Persians speak fluent French from the start; the Peruvian has but rudimentary language skills. The first letter of the novel underscores her impotence and mutism in relation to the European captors: "held in a narrow captivity, denied all communication with our people, ignorant of the language of these fierce men whose irons I wear, I feel only the effects of my unhappiness, unable to discover the cause. . . . deaf to my language, they are equally unmoved by the cries of my despair."[73]

Frustrated by her inability to communicate orally, the heroine nevertheless manages to express her ideas in knotted threads or *quipus,* the Peruvian textual medium.[74] When we first see Zilia she is knotting *quipus* that textually represent the Spaniards' destruction of the Inca Temple of the Sun and their murder of her religious sisters, the Virgins of the Sun. By describing these atrocities, the hardships of her voyage, and her unfavorable impressions of the French to her lover in *quipus,* the heroine avoids censorship because her captors cannot read the strings. The Peruvian's native text forms a kind of political subterfuge; *quipus* are described as the secret language of an oppressed people: "the same instinct which inspired us to invent [*quipus*] will show us the ways to deceive our tyrants."[75]

Graffigny's emphasis on Zilia's artistry in *quipu*-weaving also signals the feminist implications of this activity. As Nancy K. Miller has argued, in endowing her heroine with the ability to create a persuasive representation of reality by knotting colored threads, Graffigny places her in a female tradition alongside such venerable weavers as Penelope and Arachne.[76] Like Penelope, Zilia weaves and reweaves her *quipus* to keep the memory of her beloved Prince Aza alive, exclaiming: "these knots . . . seem to give more reality to my thoughts; the kind of resemblance I imagine they have with words creates an illusion that assuages my pain: I believe I'm speaking to you, telling you that I love you."[77] Like Arachne, Zilia's weaving represents an implicit threat to those who wish to dominate her, as evidenced by the repeated attempts of the French sailors to take the *quipus* away from her.

But the limited efficiency of this medium outside of Peru is soon revealed when Zilia runs out of strings and the text of the *Lettres d'une Péruvienne* comes to an abrupt (albeit momentary) end. Unable to continue weaving *quipus* for lack of threads and as yet unable to read or write French, the heroine expresses a certain existential angst in letter 17: "Illusions leave me, frightful truths take their place, my wandering thoughts, lost in the immense void of absence, will henceforth be annihilated with the same rapidity as time."[78] Six months later, having learned the French language and mastered pen and paper, she recaptures her voice. Graffigny describes her coming-to-writing as a powerfully positive development that announces her heightened sense of self and foreshadows her ascension to authorhood. As the heroine declares: "I feel new life from this tender occupation. Restored to myself, I believe I am starting to live again."[79] With these words the narrative advances, and the plot of foreign experience unfolds.

Zilia's coming-to-writing announces her acquisition of a voice and the possibility of articulating her ideas in a larger cultural arena. But a language contains more than a system of linguistic signs; it represents an entire body of maxims and prejudices—at once a world view and a system of values. "When we become intelligible," explains Nelly Furman, "we do so by adopting the values upon which communication is predicated."[80] In learning to speak French, then, the heroine must also learn the operative rules of being French.

The equivocal relation between language and social usage is exemplified by her French benefactor, tutor and hopeful suitor, Déterville. Exploiting the Peruvian's ignorance, Déterville teaches her to say, "Yes," "I love you," and "I promise to be yours" as if these declarations of love and surrender were but simple pleasantries. Notice the passivity implied by these words: the Frenchman wants Zilia for his lover, and as long as she does not understand what she says, she keeps that air of docility he finds so attractive. Once she adequately absorbs the foreign culture, however, Graffigny's heroine turns language against her would-be dominator, as in the scene where she redefines "I love you" as "I like you" only (letter 23). This pedagogical backfire recalls the ingenious maneuver of Prévost's heroine in *Histoire d'une Grecque moderne*. Like Théophé, Zilia uses her tutor's precepts to combat his sexual advances and creates a strategy of self-defense out of his manipulative language. These novels differ greatly, however, in the response expected of the narrator's ideal reader (*narrataire*). Prévost's male narrator describes Théophé appropriating his moral rhetoric for her self-defense as proof of her cunning and expects the *narrataire* to share his suspicions of this sly woman. Graffigny's female narrator presents her linguistic artistry as a justified act of self-protection. Her *narrataire* is expected to applaud this maneuver as evidence of the heroine's personal initiative and growing command of French social usage.

Zilia's translation into French marks the shift in Graffigny's fiction from the narrative perspective of a devastated refugee, entirely engrossed in making sense of her alien new environment, to the perspective of an increasingly worldly wise spy on French society. The content of the Peruvian's letters changes accordingly. As she becomes increasingly aware of the complex codes of behavior that dictate polite society, she becomes more critical of their injustices and more aware of her own marginal status in this hierarchically structured world.

As in the *Lettres persanes,* the exotic spy's unfamiliarity with French society gives rise to many amusing "defamiliarized" descriptions in the *Lettres d'une Péruvienne.* Both authors exaggerate the foreigner's surprised reactions to prove an ideological point—the arbitrary nature of prejudice and social custom. Significant differences in tone and content nevertheless distinguish the two novels: while Montesquieu uses the technique of defamiliarization to show the Persians' political perspicacity and sardonic sense of humor, Graffigny uses the same technique to show the Peruvian's extreme ignorance and sexual vulnerability in French society. Usbek and Rica deconstruct such highly charged objects as rosaries and the Pope; Zilia's first discoveries are common material objects, symbols of the most elementary kinds of public exchange: a ship (or "floating house"); a coach ("that machine or cabin"); and horses (*Hamas*—beasts—"of a species unknown to us"). Although the heroine manages to translate some French phenomena into Peruvian terms (philosophers and wise men are *Amautas,* priests are *Cucipatas,* a servant is a *China,* and a leader is a *Cacique*), other marvels escape her for she has no words to describe them.[81] The wonders of French invention, she admits, are simply overwhelming, unfathomable; they disturb her sense of reason and understanding of the world: "These prodigies confound reason and blind judgment; what ought one to think of the inhabitants of this country? Should we fear them or should we love them? I will not take it upon me to come to any conclusion upon this subject."[82] Montesquieu's Persians embrace European learning as a means to supplement their oriental knowledge and advance their pursuit of universal reason; Graffigny's heroine seems daunted by the very existence of a world so unlike her own. She eventually acquires more sophistication, but she never accepts the French mentality as completely as Rica, nor does she adopt its intellectual strategies as readily as Usbek.

Simple, banal household items elicit bewildered reactions from Graffigny's heroine; this enables the author to develop parallels between the Peruvian's growing cultural knowledge and her changing sense of self. Zilia's encounter with a mirror is particularly interesting, for it suggests that in recognizing the differences between Peruvian and French cultures, the heroine comes to see the disparity between reality and representation. Looking at her reflection in the mirror, and thinking—for a moment— that there was another Inca princess in the room, leads Zilia to comment on the tragic difference between her uncomfortable physical presence in France and the infinite possibilities of her representation in space: "What a surprise . . . what an extreme surprise, to find but an impenetrable resistance where I saw a figure moving in a very large space!"[83] Representation, be it pictorial or literary, enables one to imagine other identities, other lives than those allowed by the "real world" of French custom. As she stands next to Déterville, one sees in their reflection an image of their dilemma—a gulf between spatial proximity and cultural understanding. This abrupt confrontation of Self and Other is dramatically rendered in an illustration from the 1797 sequel to the *Lettres d'une Péruvienne* depicting Zilia running to her reflection "with open arms" (Figure 12). The heroine's simple, "Peruvian" attire of sandals, a plain tunic and veil strikes the beholder as extremely unfitting in the ornate setting of a Louis XV salon and next to a man dressed in all the dainty detail of the French aristocracy.[84] The utopian world that Graffigny invents at the novel's end offers an alternative to this conventionally limited, Frenchified representation of reality.

Little by little, Graffigny's heroine loses the timidity of a victim and takes on the verve of an indignant critic. Though she once saw France as an incomprehensible "other world" peopled by "savages" acting in threatening and arbitrary ways, Zilia's daily contact with Déterville and his sister Céline enables her to discern the logic behind their unusual customs. The heroine's growing perception of the general conditions behind particular events reveals Graffigny's narrative strategy of using concrete events in the woman's life as a springboard and source of authority for her cultural critique.

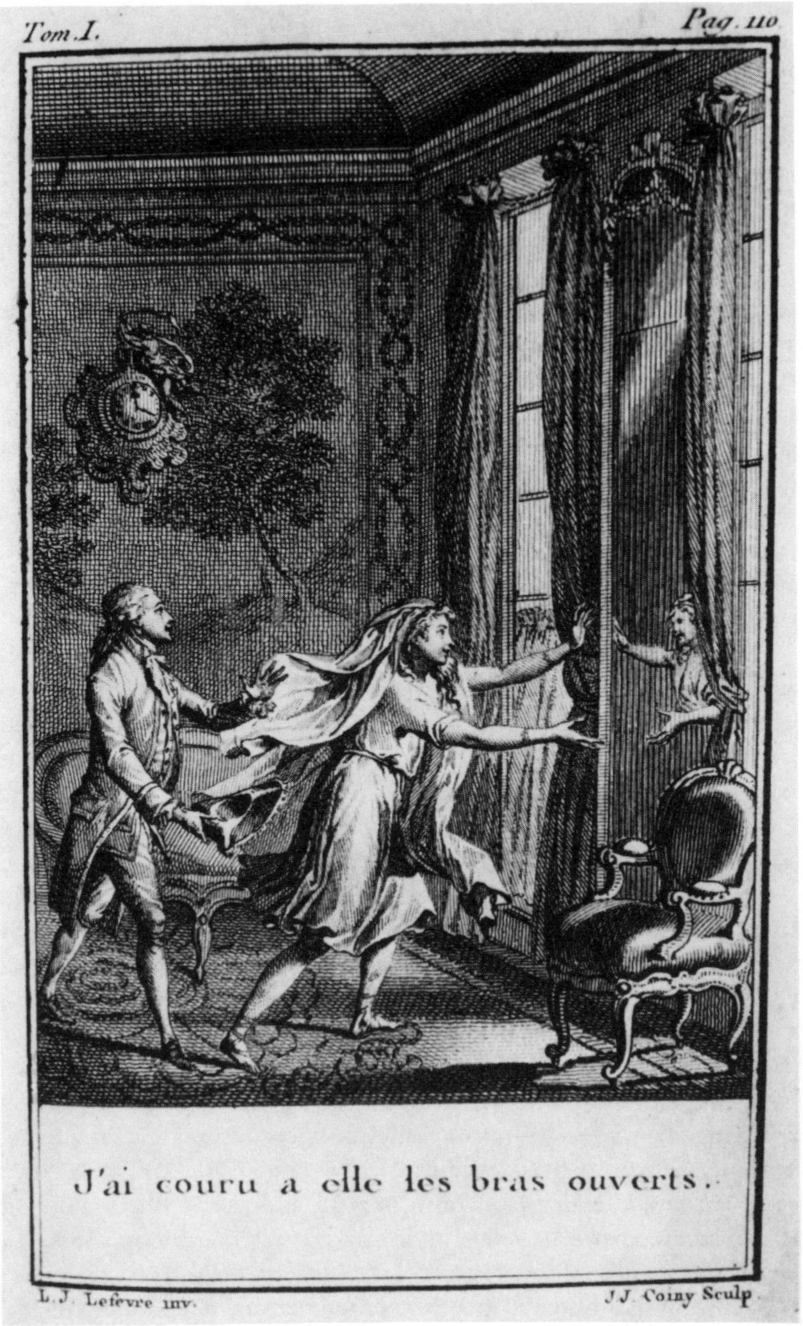
Tom. I.
Pag. 110
J'ai couru a elle les bras ouverts.
L. J. Lefevre inv.
J.J. Coiny Sculp.

Figure 12. "I ran to her with open arms." Illustration for Graffigny [Morel de Vindé], *Lettres d'une Péruvienne par Mme de Grafigny. Nouvelle édition, augmentée d'une suite qui n'a point encore été imprimée*, vol. 1 (Paris: P. Didot l'aîné, 1797). Courtesy of the South Caroliniana Library, University of South Carolina.

During her early days in Déterville's family home, the heroine describes "Madame," Déterville's aristocratic mother, as a stern and reproachful authority figure seeking only to impress her acquaintances in *le monde* (letters 13–15). When Déterville departs on a military mission and leaves his mother in charge of the Peruvian, it is not long before Zilia finds herself locked up in a convent with Céline. She then realizes that the mother's coldness toward her younger children is a product of French family law. Céline's forced confinement and Déterville's forced military service are both justified by the French law of primogeniture, which prescribes passing on the family fortune exclusively to the eldest son in order to keep the family's aristocratic privileges and bloodlines intact. Zilia's sympathy for Déterville and Céline prompts her to condemn this tradition as a "barbaric practice established among the wealthy lords of the land," that is, as a repressive custom by which the rich and powerful maintain their ascendancy over the less fortunate (302).

Zilia's sojourn in the convent gives rise to other unpleasant discoveries about French modes of educating and marrying women. Initially dismayed by Céline's total ignorance of any subjects unrelated to her family or love interests, the heroine later deduces the unsound principles that govern women's education and conduct in France. The French ideal of femininity, she discovers, demands one thing but teaches another; it requires that women act seductive yet remain pure, speak with wit yet forgo book learning, and act piously yet neglect all but the most superficial religious training: "the education that one gives them is so opposed to the goal that it is supposed to achieve, that it strikes me as the masterpiece of French inconsistency."[85]

Observing the women in the convent and *le monde,* the heroine notes that, once married, a woman's social function becomes further reduced to that of a male possession. French husbands reinforce female dependency by urging their wives to pursue only the most insipid and meaningless activities: "With no confidence in her, her husband makes no effort to teach her how to manage her business, her family or her household. She participates in that little universe through representation only. She is an ornament to amuse the curious."[86] Like Montesquieu's Persians, Graffigny's Peruvian decries the French women's superficiality and vapid lifestyle. But while Usbek and Rica dwell on the evils of "female nature," tracing women's faults to their use and abuse of sexual power over men, Zilia seeks out the causes of women's behavior in society not biology, pointing to the institutionalized sexual inequality of the French system as the source of women's errors: "When you discover that power is entirely in the hands of men here, you will not doubt . . . that they are responsible for all the evils of society."[87] Shifting the terms of the argument from sexuality to socialization, Graffigny dispels the myth of female omnipotence in ancien régime French society. Writing from a female perspective, the author replaces Montesquieu's vision of French women as manipulative courtesans and power-hungry adulteresses with a more somber image of isolated and uneducated wives and daughters locked in convents and loveless marriages.

As the Peruvian's sojourn in Paris lengthens, she becomes increasingly self-assured. Thanks to her experience and her readings of French literature and philosophy, Zilia comes to see once feared figures of patriarchal authority—Peruvian and French—in a new light. Eventually she even realizes the impotence of her own ruler: "My mind, my heart, my eyes, everything has seduced me, the Sun himself has deceived me. It shines on the whole world, of which your empire occupies but a portion."[88] Occidental knowledge is painful and reveals the limits of her native system of beliefs. But it also affords her the means to see herself in a different role than as a Virgin of the Sun. By reading the books of the rational, Western philosophical tradition, the heroine gains the power to integrate both systems of value into the quest for knowledge that will be her ultimate (authorial) vocation.

But her attitude toward the authority of French culture is not unproblematic. While she conforms to French codes of language and dress and professes faith in the teachings of French *philosophes,* her religion remains inviolable. Zilia initially honors Catholicism by calling it a variation on "natural law," but a priest's condescending disparagement of her own cult—especially its acceptance of incest—incites her to adopt a more critical stance. Contrasting the priest's self-righteousness and lofty principles with the casual immorality practiced by his parishioners, the Peruvian concludes by firmly resolving never to convert: "I find such a want of connection between [Catholic dogma and practice], that my reason absolutely refuses to accept it."[89]

Graffigny's appropriation of the Peruvian Golden Age myth allowed her to set up a perspective that would make the reader see French norms and customs differently from Montesquieu's "oriental" point of view. By detailing the heroine's sexual vulnerability in the hands of her French captors and her struggles against laws of womanly conduct in the convent, the author heightens the reader's sense of the Peruvian's precarious position in the very world that she criticizes. Montesquieu's aristocratic Persians retain their lofty status in Parisian society; Graffigny's noble Peruvian loses her royal standing in leaving Peru. To the French she is but a destitute victim of colonial aggression, totally dependent upon the charity of others. The heroine's awareness of her marginality leads her to realize the similar plight suffered by all unmarried women in French society: vulnerable in their indigence, they are degraded by work. Bemoaning the inflexible parameters of ancien régime social stratification, Zilia demands: "I have neither gold nor land nor occupation, yet I am necessarily a citizen of this city. O heaven! in what *class* must I rank myself?"[90]

This use of the term "class" in a novel from 1747 is surprising, since such authorities as the historian William Sewell and the *Robert* dictionaries maintain that "class" acquired its modern meaning of rank in a socioeconomic structure with the advent of the Revolution, between 1788 and 1792. Citing Abbé Sieyès's tract, "Qu'est-ce que le Tiers Etat?" (1789), Sewell argues that "class" held no connotations of hierarchy in ancien régime France: "'Class' in Sieyès's time, was an utterly neutral term, with overtones of disinterested scientific precision rather than of nobility and baseness or dominance and subordination, it meant simply 'category.'"[91]

What Sewell fails to recognize, however, is that the very act of ordering people, of creating a sociological taxonomy, implies a symbolic violence that imposes more *value* on some people than on others. The etymology of "class" points to its valorizing function. In Rome the *classici* were the most prosperous citizens and paid the most taxes; the idea of a literary "classic" was imagined by a second-century author who used the *classici*'s pecuniary prominence as a metaphorical label for the best writers. And this "subterranean valorization of economic power masquerading as quality," affirms Richard Terdiman, "has stuck to 'class' ever since."[92] To accept Sewell's claim for the neutral, analytical resonance of "class," then, means erasing history from language. In categorizing things—especially people—one invariably attributes more worth to some individuals than to others, based on criteria that often have nothing to do with ethics but rely on such functional notions as wealth, prestige or productivity. It is just this concept of functional value that Graffigny attacks. Hardly a neutral demographic category, the term "class" wields the force of an emotionally charged label in her lexicon, symptom of an unfair society that fixes individual identity according to the social or economic function one fulfills. Reflecting on her new concern with class identity, the heroine complains: "Although these feelings of shame . . . are foreign to me . . . I cannot help but suffer from the idea that others make of me."[93]

In Peru, Zilia recalls, class tensions did not exist, since the people worked together and the *Capa-Inca* (Inca king) provided for them all. In France the sovereign lives on the toil of his subjects, sharing the wealth with only a few and exploiting the rest (303). Compared to the egalitarian Peruvian ideal, the French monarchy is revealed an untenable order, a society at an impasse between centralized wealth and popular need. Graffigny uses the idealized image of the Inca Golden Age society sketched in her "historical introduction" to support a primitivist critique of French politics here, condemning the corrupt present condition of the French monarchy by evaluating it against a better, earlier model run on the "primitive" principles of communal labor and reciprocal obligation. But in emphasizing the distant, idyllic nature of the Peruvian power structure, the author also admits the vulnerability of that order, which is now irretrievably lost.

Montesquieu and Graffigny both expose the ideological weakness of the French government, but the tone and vision of these critiques differ strikingly. When Usbek contemplates the French political system he evokes an unstable, theoretically unsound institution. The monarchical state, he warns, "is a state in which might is right, and which degenerates always into a despotism or a republic. Authority can never be equally divided between the people and the prince; it is too difficult to maintain an equilibrium" (2:65).[94] Usbek speaks as an impartial observer, an amateur political scientist, considering politics in the abstract terms of institutions, forces of power and ideological warfare. Zilia's analysis, on the other hand, valorizes the experiential impact of politics on the individual citizen. Instead of condemning the instability and injustices of the French economic system in Usbek's terms (as a dysfunctional model), Zilia expresses her argument as a personal dilemma affecting many people, including herself. After disparaging the ruinous custom that demands that one appear wealthy without sullying oneself with labor, Zilia considers the plight of the average citizen, struggling to survive while the rich and titled gentry enjoy lives of ease. Such thoughts soon lead to a dramatic realization of her own, similarly distressing situation: "The knowledge of these sad truths only raised pity in my heart at first, and indignation against their laws. But alas! how many cruel reflections does the contemptuous manner in which I hear them speak of those who are not rich cause me to make on myself!"[95]

The strikingly personal approach of Zilia's philosophizing, seen against Usbek's tendency toward abstraction, suggests an interesting connection between gender and world view. One might well regard Usbek's argumentation as an example of what Catharine MacKinnon terms the "male epistemological stance," that is, "the ostensibly noninvolved stance, the view from a distance and from no particular perspective, apparently transparent to its own reality."[96] By contrast, Zilia might be said to articulate a "female epistemological stance" in that her reasoning draws on an explicitly personal, subjective view of reality; it is involved, empathic and concrete. This divergence between the critical positions of the Persian and Peruvian spies may be linked to the authors' own personae. The baron de Montesquieu was a young, though well-known and respected, member of the Parisian intelligentsia when he wrote the *Lettres persanes*. He wrote with the self-confident authority born of knowing that one's place in *le monde* is assured in advance, thanks to his family's long-standing position in the parliamentary nobility. Mme de Graffigny wrote the *Lettres d'une Péruvienne* as a relative unknown, a newcomer trying to make a name for herself in Parisian society. As a middle-aged widow of modest means, her concerns with financial security and personal autonomy were very real.[97]

Such fascinating incursions into the questions of class and power relations are undermined, however, by the heroine's ultimate re-entry into the aristocracy. Thanks to the *deus ex machina* device of a sudden financial windfall (the recovery of her Inca treasures), Graffigny's Peruvian regains her original privileged rank at the end of the novel and the "noble savage" becomes a socially sanctioned member of the French landed gentry. This abrupt upward mobility makes for an ambiguous message about the value of social rank in the *Lettres d'une Péruvienne,* particularly in light of Graffigny's earlier critique of aristocratic privilege. Indeed the idealized image of property ownership in letter 35 constitutes a glaring contradiction to the glowing picture of Peruvian egalitarianism in the "historical introduction." After being named "sovereign" by a group of admiring peasants, Zilia quickly takes charge of her new estate and visibly enjoys the power of her exalted status, quipping: "I freely gave orders to those servants that I knew were mine; I joked about my authority and my opulence."[98]

It seems Graffigny's liberal anti-privilege stance remains operable only as long as the distant idyll of Peru remained accessible. Once the Peruvian prince Aza has been revealed as a disloyal traitor and the heroine's hopes for returning to Peru are permanently crushed (letter 38), the author abandons the primitivist nostalgia of her cultural critique and adopts a more pragmatic stance toward the heroine's fate. In Graffigny's eyes, the ideal role for a French woman is that of an independently wealthy, unmarried landowner. At the end of the novel, then, the author negotiates the best settlement possible for the heroine in a French context, transforming the Peruvian savage into a country noblewoman. Regardless of the political compromise this scenario suggests, the heroine's well-being and future potential are secured.

But does this arrangement betray a European political compromise? Or does it rather indicate an adroit manipulation of "Peruvian" connotations? Graffigny deploys the notion of cultural difference to two somewhat contradictory ends in the *Lettres d'une Péruvienne,* based on the historical dichotomy set up at the novel's beginning (splendor of Inca Golden Age versus misery of eighteenth-century Peru). The author emphasizes the Other's difference from the French for the purposes of criticizing French customs and institutions. This emerges in her portrayal of the heroine's affiliation with the Incas' idyllic pre-conquest society, as symbolized by her naïveté, moral decency, ignorance of private property and general superiority to European values. Graffigny stresses the Other's similarity to the French, however, for the purposes of assuring a felicitous conclusion to this fiction. This comes out in her depiction of the heroine's un-Peruvian, enlightened appreciation of modern French technology, philosophy and literature, as well as in the final conversion of her Inca treasures into European riches. By endowing the primitive protagonist with golden icons from the Incas' cult to the Sun, and then transforming them into European symbols of wealth (a country manor house and land), the author reassures the reader that her heroine is not so very different from the French. Though she may criticize the inherited prerogatives of the French aristocracy, she too longs for the "noble" privileges of financial security and personal autonomy.[99]

The decoration of Zilia's château underscores the utopian juxtaposition of New and Old Worlds in the *Lettres d'une Péruvienne.* It is equipped with a well-stocked library (symbol of Western culture and French philosophy) alongside an equally well-stocked monument to Inca culture, the secret *cabinet*. Nicknamed the new "Temple of the Sun," the room is brilliantly decorated with icons, mirrors and pictures of Cuzco, complete with a number of royal virgins in the likeness of the princess Zilia. This reconstructed artifact reminds the reader of Zilia's earlier life as a member of Peru's pre-conquest Golden Age society. A brilliant sun attached to the ceiling completes the decor and reinforces the Peruvian's continued devotion to her native cult. The presence of this hidden temple in a French château also adds a note of historical authenticity to Graffigny's narrative, for in the wake of European conquest both the Incas and the Aztecs took their religions underground and built clandestine shrines. Like the colonized Indians, Graffigny's heroine adopts a dual identity: she coexists peacefully with the French in public all the while preserving her Peruvian culture in private.

The rise from marginal to privileged member of society marks the Peruvian's integration into the French social landscape, but on a woman's terms. The estate was purchased, we are told, through a financial "metamorphosis" that converted Peruvian raw materials (the throne of the Inca king) into European symbols of wealth: a home, outbuildings, gardens and land. This commerce between the New World and the Old forms a fittingly subversive metaphor for the process of closure in Graffigny's novel. The Peruvian icon, symbol of a patriarchal cult, is melted down and becomes the foundation for a woman's independent life! What better symbol of the shift from rule by patriarchy to a woman's self-determination in this imaginary universe?

Just as Zilia's *prise de parole* (coming-to-speech) announced her acquisition of a voice and the possibility of articulating a New World perspective in French, her *prise de possession* (coming-to-ownership) inaugurates the heroine's possession of a place and the possibility of realizing her own life-style in France. Mastery of the French language and property ownership secure the foreigner's membership in French society and empower her to control her destiny. After selectively ignoring certain truths about her adoptive society (such as rules that restrict the woman's role to that of obedient wife or passive sex object) and refusing her French suitor's offers of love one last time, the groundwork is set for a unique feminocentric utopia. An innovative system of cultural exchange is set up in this no-man's land as well.[100] Inventing a new kind of salon in Zilia's domain, the author insists that the Peruvian's teachings of natural law will hereafter hold equivalent value as the European's *lumières*. As Zilia explains to Déterville: "You will give me some knowledge of your sciences and your arts; you will enjoy the pleasure of superiority; I will take it [superiority] back by developing in your heart some virtues that you ignore."[101]

The final scene of the *Lettres d'une Péruvienne* shows the heroine—now the author—living and writing in her own home in the country, enjoying her proprietary authority and her new status of voluntary marginality and desired celibacy. Though she may enjoy the privileges of aristocracy, Graffigny's heroine is clearly not about to join the "idle rich." Her plans for the future are brimming with artistic, literary and philosophical pursuits; indeed her emphasis on personal *industrie* reveals a rather bourgeois concern with productivity and individual accountability, with *using* time to worthwhile purpose. Her role as mistress of a country estate and benefactress or "sovereign" to the peasants living nearby presages the association of "primitive" goodness and an idealized, rural morality that we will find in Monbart's *Lettres taïtiennes* as well.

"Re-vision," writes Adrienne Rich, "the act of looking back, of seeing with fresh eyes, of entering an old text from a new critical direction—is for women *more* than a chapter in cultural history: it is an act of *survival*."[102] In her revision of the Persian spy novel Graffigny writes a significantly different destiny for her heroine, symbolic of the woman's survival. Instead of sacrificing her integrity in conversion to a foreign cult or adopting the stance of an eternal victim, Zilia keeps her autonomy: resisting religious conversion, cultural naturalization and seduction.[103] The last time we see the Peruvian she represents that unusual creature—a woman happily alone—demonstrating the existential power of her own voice with the refrain: "I am, I live, I exist [je suis, je vis, j'existe]" (362). This ending effectively sends the reader back to the novel's beginning. We imagine the heroine/author writing and translating the text we just finished reading, and others perhaps; putting her stories into public circulation through her writing.

Surprisingly enough, the ideological content of Zilia's most polemic letters (on the corruption of the French government and the hypocrisy of Catholicism) did not offend contemporary readers; on the contrary, the *Lettres d'une Péruvienne* was reportedly a favorite of Jesuits and Jansenists alike.[104] The novel's dénouement, however, was a major bone of contention for years to come. As an exotic spy Zilia could question political and spiritual authorities with impunity, but as a woman—and a novelistic heroine—she was expected to conform to the standards of female conduct demanded by literary critics and social usage. With her unconventional refusal of marriage, Zilia assumes a place of honor in the female literary tradition, alongside the "scandalous" heroines of Mme de Villedieu's *Mémoires de la vie de Henriette-Sylvie de Molière* (1671) and Mme de Lafayette's *Princesse de Clèves* (1678). Like her literary predecessors, Graffigny too would suffer the consequences of breaking the rules of proper female behavior. Indeed Graffigny's novel was attacked by more than one critic for its unorthodox ending: it struck many as an unfinished work. It was not *vraisemblable* or plausible, they warned, to leave the heroine alone, unmarried, virginal. She ought to be fixed in the novelistic universe, assimilated to the patriarchal French social order.

To judge from responses to the novel, the refusal to inscribe a woman's life into a familiar pattern of love and courtship, or to clearly terminate her story with an accepted gesture of closure—that is, marriage, religious confinement or death—was a major blow to the contemporary reader's horizon of expectations.[105] The sequels to the *Lettres d'une Péruvienne* reveal the unease engendered by this ending: each proposes to rewrite Zilia's story into an "acceptable" novelistic destiny. Ignace Hugary de Lamarche-Courmont makes it his mission to rewrite the Peruvian prince Aza as the heroine's husband and hero in the widely read *Lettres d'Aza, ou d'un Péruvien* (1749).[106] At the end of this novel the two Peruvians are reunited, married, and the French king orders a ship to take them back to their native land. With the heroine married and safely en route back to her own world, the French order is restored, and the reader's expectations are satisfied.

The "editors" of the 1797 volume *Lettres d'une Péruvienne par Madame de Grafigny. Augmentées d'une suite qui n'a point encore été imprimée* declare that their version has the immense advantage over its predecessor of being the product of a woman author. But what does a "feminine" revision entail? The new, improved heroine explains that it means obedience to public opinion and conversion to the dominant order: "How grateful I am that I smoothed out the difficulties in listening to Déterville's wise advice! He made me realize that the true philosophy respects opinion, and dreads the display of total independence."[107] Thus Zilia marries Déterville, her country house becomes his domain, and the Frenchman's authority becomes law where the Peruvian once reigned alone. As Zilia playfully remarks to her husband: "Zilia is not at her home today, you will find her at her husband's home."[108]

In an explicit revisionary gesture to Graffigny's original, the author of this sequel literally effaces the Peruvian's foreignness. By painting over the Inca artifacts on the walls of her private "Temple of the Sun," the revised heroine graphically proves her allegiance to her French master and his order. The illustration of this scene depicts the American's completed assimilation into French society (Figure 13). Sitting at an elegant secretary, wearing a stylish, delicate French gown, the heroine muses about her destiny in front of two significant murals representing Déterville's salutary intervention in her life. The mural on the left represents a maritime battle, on the right a sickbed: two moments when the Frenchman's agency saved her life. In the corner between these enormous paintings stands a small collection of bric-à-brac: porcelain figures of exotic looking animals and a couple of Peruvian icons. This collection, a paltry reminder of her former

Et si j'interroge mon cœur c'est
toujours vous que j'y vois.

L. J. Lefevre inv.

J. J. Coiny Sculp.

Figure 13. "And if I look into my heart, it is always you that I see."
Illustration for Graffigny [Morel de Vindé], *Lettres d'une Péruvienne
par Mme de Grafigny. Nouvelle édition, augmentée d'une suite qui n'a
point encore été imprimée,* vol. 2 (Paris: P. Didot l'aîné, 1797). Courtesy of the South Caroliniana Library, University of South Carolina.

identity, is both framed and dwarfed by the immense works of Western art—a spatial configuration that dramatically summarizes the reactionary message of Morel de Vindé's work. In contrast to the independent, intellectually curious heroine of Graffigny's fiction, this character represents female dependency and sentimentality, as the legend announces: "And if I look into my heart, it is always you [Déterville] that I see." At the end of the novel the old Zilia is gone, definitively replaced by a new, Frenchified heroine, "the overjoyed wife of Déterville [la trop heureuse épouse de Déterville]" (2:231).

While Graffigny originally cast her heroine as a Peruvian in order to reveal the injustices of European cultural and sexual politics, her imitators reacted to her "unfinished" ending as to a threat and tied up the loose ends in conventional patterns. In the sequels the exotic Other is either married to one of her own kind and expulsed from Europe (*Lettres d'un Péruvien*) or married to a Frenchman and molded into the norm (*Lettres d'une Péruvienne, augmentées d'une suite*). Expulsion and assimilation, these two strategies of closure indicate the dominant European responses to non-European cultures during the eighteenth century: both translate a desire to preserve the European moral and social order against the threat of change or innovation. The "errant" savage of the *Lettres d'une Péruvienne* had to be neutralized and immobilized lest her vision of female independence gain larger cultural currency and undermine ancien régime society.

To summarize, let us return to the question of authorial gender and gendered voice in the novel. My comparison of Montesquieu's and Graffigny's works supports Clifford's quote in the introduction: every "other" is also the construction of a "self." Both novelists articulate the narrative of the exotic-spy-visits-Europe in ways that reflect their personal experience and ideological viewpoint. While the aristocratic Montesquieu designed his fiction to expose the hypocrisy behind French religious practices, politics and Enlightenment *philosophie* from the lofty perspective of a man of privilege, the socially and financially insecure Graffigny wrote her story to show the effects of these ill-guided policies on one particular individual, a woman.

If we compare the treatment of the exotic heroine in these two novels, an even more remarkable correspondence comes to light. Montesquieu's Roxane and Graffigny's Zilia both play strategic roles in the articulation of the novels' philosophical message. Given their criticism of masculine values—be it monogamous or polygamous marriage—one might read these heroines as demystifiers of patriarchal culture. Both women raise their voices in protest and represent Julia Kristeva's notion of woman as "perpetual dissident." "Woman is here to shake up, to disturb, to deflate masculine values, and not to espouse them," Kristeva argues. "Her role is to maintain differences by pointing to them, by giving them life, by putting them into play against one another."[109] But while both heroines embody this contestatory stance, only one survives—the one invented by a woman author. Montesquieu suppresses Roxane, the subversive voice in his text, through murder (translated as "suicide," a perennial favorite for quick resolutions). Graffigny, on the other hand, protects the heroine's freedom of expression just as she protects her cultural identity. Graffigny's revision of her male predecessor's model realizes more than a mere literary reform; it posits a new model of feminocentric discourse, a new manner of writing and thinking about female destiny.

Notes

1. "L'Exotisme des sexes. Et là toute la Différence, toute l'incompatabilité, toute la Distance, surgit, s'avère, se hurle, se pleure, se sanglote avec amour ou dépit" (Victor Segalen, *Essai sur l'exotisme: Une esthétique du divers* [Paris: Fata Morgana, 1978], 41).

2. On the *Lettres persanes* as an "anthropological" text see Clifford, "Introduction: Partial Truths," 2. On the tolerance and relativistic values of the Persian characters, see Tzvetan Todorov, *Nous et les autres: La Réflexion française sur la diversité humaine* (Paris: Editions du Seuil, "La Couleur des idées," 1989), 389–401.

3. Claude Lévi-Strauss, *Le Regard éloigné* (Paris: Plon, 1983), 30.

4. Clifford, "Introduction: Partial Truths," 7.

5. Epic romances: *La Sibile de Perse* (Du Verdier, 1632) and *Artamène, ou le Grand Cyrus* (Madeleine de Scudéry, 1643–53); pseudo-historical *nouvelles: Tachmas, Prince de Perse, Nouvelle historique arrivée sous le Sophi Soliman aujourd'hui regnant* (H.F.M., 1676) and *Zamire, histoire persane* (Mlle ***, 1687); fairy tale: Mme d'Auneuil's *Nouvelles persanes*, included in her *Chevaliers errants et le génie familier* (1709); historical writings: Mme de Gomez's *Anecdotes persanes, dédiées au roy*, (1727).

6. Mehmed Riza Bey helped maintain French prejudices against Muslims during his visit by refusing to ride in King Louis XIV's carriage and showing no interest in sightseeing in Paris. Contemporary French accounts depict this Persian emissary as "cruel, eccentric, fierce, rude, unstable in his resolutions, and never willing to listen either to good reason or to good sense" (Maurice Herbette, *Une Ambassade persane sous Louis XIV* [Paris: Perin et cie, 1907], 6).

7. Critics have proposed many theories about Montesquieu's sources of knowledge about Persia; see, for example, Elie Carcassonne's Introduction to the *Lettres persanes* (Paris: Editions Fernand Roches, 1929), xx–xxiii. Besides reading the

well-known works of Chardin and Tavernier, Montesquieu likely gleaned information from the wide variety of travel narratives available in his time, including François Bernier, *Voyages* (Amsterdam: Marret, 1699); and Paul Rycaut, *The Present State of the Ottoman Empire* (London: J. Starkey and H. Brome, 1668; French translation, 1670).

8. After years of mutual suspicion, Franco-Persian relations took a turn for the better in the early years of the eighteenth century, which saw several exchanges of ambassadors between the two countries. The very advantageous treaty of commerce signed in 1715, however, was to bear little fruit, thanks to the financial woes of the French Compagnie des Indes and the political turmoil in Persia (which was invaded by the Afghans in 1723 and thrown into years of chaos and disorder). For more on Franco-Persian contact, consult Paul Masson, *Histoire du commerce français dans le Levant au XVIIIe siècle* (1896; reprint, New York: Burt Franklin, 1967).

9. "J'espere Sire, que ces Relations exactes et fideles . . . ne seront pas moins utiles à ma Nation que les riches marchandises que j'ai rapportées de mes voyages. . . . En tous les païs que j'ai parcourus, ma plus forte passion a toujours esté de faire connoître les qualitez heroïques de Vostre Majesté et les merveilles de son regne. . . . J'ay hazardé souvent et ma fortune et ma vie, en elevant par mes discours Vostre Majesté au dessus de tous les Princes de l'Europe et de ces Rois d'Orient, même en leur présence. Je suis sorti avec avantage de tous ces périls, en imprimant le respect de vostre Nom dans le coeur de ces Barbares" (Jean Baptiste Tavernier, "Epistre au Roy," *Les Six Voyages de Jean Baptiste Tavernier, Ecuyer Baron d'Aubonne en Turquie, en Perse, et aux Indes* [Paris: n.p., 1678] unnumbered).

10. "La forte envie que j'avois de bien connoître la Perse, et d'en donner des Relations exactes et fideles, me fit emploier tout ce temps . . . à y examiner soigneusement tout ce qui pouvoit meriter la curiosité de nôtre Europe, par rapport à un grand et vaste Païs que nous pouvons appeller *un autre Monde,* soit par la distance des Lieux, soit par la diversité des Moeurs et des Manieres" (Jean Chardin, "Préface," *Voyages de Monsieur le Chevalier Chardin, en Perse, et autres lieux de l'Orient* [Amsterdam: Jean Louis de Lorme, 1711], 1:unnumbered, emphasis added). In reading Chardin's accounts of the "other worlds" he found in the East, one must keep in mind that he was himself an outsider to his French audience: he was a Huguenot and a naturalized Englishman.

11. "[E]n cette Partie du Monde, les Formes exterieures des choses, les Moeurs, les Habitudes, les manieres même de parler, étoient à peu près les mêmes il y a deux mille ans qu'elles y paroissent encore aujourd'hui" (Chardin, "Préface," 1:unnumbered).

12. "Comme les Corps et les Fortunes y sont esclaves sous une puissance tout-à-fait Despotique et Arbitraire, les Esprits et les Courages le sont aussi" (Chardin, 2:39).

13. "Ils empruntent et ne rendent point, et s'ils peuvent tromper, ils en perdent rarement l'occasion . . . [étant] sans bonne foi dans le commerce, où ils trompent si finement, qu'on y est toûjours attrapé" (Chardin, 2:36).

14. Talal Asad, "Two European Images of Non-European Rule," 116–18.

15. "Il est donc très-difficile de savoir rien de certain de ce qui se passe dans

les Haram, ou Apartement des femmes, que l'on peut appeler *un monde inconnu*" (Chardin, 2:276, emphasis added).

16. "[C]omme le climat est généralement chaud et sec, à ce degré auquel on ressent plus les mouvemens de l'amour, et auquel on est plus capable d'y répondre, la passion pour les femmes y est extrêmement violente; et par conséquent, la jalousie y est aussi plus forte que dans la plûpart des Païs voisins" (Chardin, 1:275).

17. "Les femmes Orientales ont toûjours passé pour Tribades. J'ai ouï assurer si souvent, et à tant de gens, qu'elles le sont, et qu'elles ont des voyes de contenter mutuellement leurs passions, que je le tiens pour fort certain" (Chardin, 2:280).

18. "Si ceux qui viennent à Paris avec les ambassadeurs osaient publier, quand ils sont retournés chez eux, des relations aussi libres que celles que les Français publient touchant les pays étrangers, je ne doute pas qu'ils eussent bien des choses à dire. Mais on redoute si fort notre nation, qu'on n'ose rien imprimer qui lui déplaise" (Pierre Bayle, *Pensées sur la comète,* ed. A. Prat [Paris: E. Cornély, 1911–12], 2:28).

19. For a concise summary of this criticism consult Alessandro S. Crisafulli, "L'Observateur oriental avant les 'Lettres persanes'," *Lettres romanes* 8, 2 (1954): 91–113; Enea Balmas's introduction to the *Lettres iroquoises* by J.-H. Maubert de Gouvest (Paris: G. Nizet, 1962), 25–38; or G. L. Van Roosbroeck, *Persian Letters Before Montesquieu* (New York: Lenox Hill, "Burt Franklin," 1972), 19–40. For more on the parallel tradition in English literature, consult Martha Pike Conant, *The Oriental Tale in England in the Eighteenth Century* (New York: Columbia University Press, 1908).

20. Proof of Marana's influence on Montesquieu is offered by Dutch editions of the *Lettres persanes* (Amsterdam, 1730) which carry the significant subtitle: "Dans le goût de *L'Espion dans les cours.*" Moreover, researchers have unearthed a copy of *L'Espion turc* (ed. 1717) marked with the arms of the Montesquieus' Bibliothèque de la Brède.

First published in Italian as *L'Esploratore Turco* in 1684, Marana's novel was quickly translated into French as *L'Espion du Grand Seigneur et ses relations secrètes* (1684, 1689, 1696) and into English as *Letters Writ by a Turkish Spy* (1687–93); it was reprinted in all three languages repeatedly throughout the eighteenth century. For details on the publication history and historical content of *L'Espion turc* see Van Roosbroeck, 42–51, and G. Almansi and D. A. Warren, "Roman épistolaire et analyse historique: 'L'Espion turc' de G. P. Marana," *Dix-septième siècle* 110–11 (1976): 57–73.

For a detailed catalogue of the correspondences between Marana and Montesquieu, see Pietro Toldo, "Dell' Espion di Giovanni Paolo Marana e delle sue attinenze con le 'Lettres persanes' de Montesquieu," *Giornale storico della letteratura italiana* 29 (1897): 46–79.

21. "Que ce soit une fiction ou une vérité, qu'importe? La raison n'est-elle pas de tous les tems et de tous les pays?" (Giovanni Marana, "Préface Particulière," *L'Espion dans les cours des princes chrétiens* [Cologne: Erasme Kinkius, 1700], 1: unnumbered).

22. "[L]a scène demande une exacte raison / l'étroite bienséance y veut être

gardée" (Nicolas Boileau-Despréaux, *L'Art poétique,* ed. Guillaume Picot [Paris: Bordas, 1972], 76).

23. Ernst Cassirer, *The Philosophy of the Enlightenment,* trans. Fritz C. A. Koelln and James P. Pettegrove (Princeton, N.J.: Princeton University Press, 1951), 294.

24. "Se dit aussi figurément en Morale, de ceux qui ont l'esprit ou les moeurs fantasques, bourruës, qui ne se peuvent pas aisément adoucir, *civiliser, gagner par la raison*" (Antoine Furetière, *Dictionnaire universel* [La Haye and Rotterdam: Arnout and Reinier Leers, 1691], 2:658, emphasis added).

25. Paul Hazard, *La Crise de la conscience européenne 1680–1715* (Paris: Fayard, "Les Grandes études littéraires," 1961), 300.

26. Scott, *Gender and the Politics of History,* 7.

27. "La raison est à l'égard du philosophe ce que la grâce est à l'égard du chrétien. La grâce détermine le chrétien à agir; la raison détermine le philosophe" (Denis Diderot, Jean le Rond d'Alembert, Louis de Jaucourt et al., eds., *Encyclopédie ou dictionnaire raisonné des sciences, des arts et des métiers* [Neuchâtel: Samuel Faulche (Fauche) et cie, 1765], 12:509).

28. "Il n'y a que le philosophe qui . . . soit en état de prouver que les choses sont comme elles doivent être, ou de les rectifier, lorsqu'elles en sont susceptibles, en indiquant la raison des changemens qu'il veut y apporter" (*Encyclopédie,* 12:513).

29. Marvin Harris, *The Rise of Anthropological Theory* (New York: Thomas Y. Crowell Co., 1968), 37.

30. Charles Louis de Secondat, baron de la Brède et de Montesquieu, *Persian Letters,* trans. John Davidson (London: Privately Printed, 1892), 1:9. All English quotations of Montesquieu's work refer to this translation unless otherwise noted. "Rica et moi sommes peut-être les premiers parmi les Persans que l'envie de savoir ait fait sortir de leur pays, et qui aient renoncé aux douceurs d'une vie tranquille pour aller chercher laborieusement la sagesse" (Montesquieu, *Lettres persanes* in *Oeuvres complètes,* ed. Roger Caillois [Paris: Gallimard, "Bibliothèque de la Pléiade," 1949], 1:133). All French references to Montesquieu's work refer to this edition unless otherwise noted.

31. "Nous sommes nés dans un royaume florissant; mais nous n'avons pas cru que ses bornes fussent celles de nos connoissances, et que la lumière orientale dût seule nous éclairer" (1:133).

32. "[I]l est plus facile à un Asiatique de s'instruire des moeurs des François dans un an, qu'il ne l'est à un François de s'instruire des moeurs des Asiatiques dans quatre, parce que les uns se livrent autant que les autres se communiquent peu" (1:132).

33. "Les gens polis parmi eux peuvent aller du pair avec les gens les plus polis de l'Europe" (Chardin, *Voyages,* 2:37).

34. "Il n'y a personne qui ne sorte de cette ville plus précautionné qu'il n'y est entré: à force de faire part de son bien aux autres, on apprend à le conserver" (1:216).

35. Montesquieu was later compelled to downplay the imaginative power of these passages in order to defend the *Lettres persanes* against the charges of impiety and subversive intent published in such works as the *Lettres persanes convaincues d'impiété,* by Abbé Gaultier. On Montesquieu's problems with the censors, consult

Charles-Jacques Beyer, "Montesquieu et la censure religieuse de 'L'Espirt des lois'," *Revue des sciences humaines* 70 (April-June 1953): 105–31.

36. "[P]lutôt fait pour la santé que pour les plaisirs: c'est une vie unie, qui ne pique point" (1:180).

37. "Je le puis dire: je ne connois les femmes que depuis que je suis ici; j'en ai plus appris dans un mois que je n'aurois fait en trente ans dans un sérail" (1:223).

38. "Chez nous, les caractères sont tous uniformes, parce qu'ils sont forcés: on ne voit point les gens tels qu'ils sont, mais tels qu'on les oblige d'être. Dans cette servitude du coeur et de l'esprit, on n'entend parler que la crainte, qui n'a qu'un langage, et non pas la nature, qui s'exprime si différemment, et qui paroît sous tant de formes" (1:223).

39. "Ces femmes ont toutes des relations les unes avec les autres et forment une espèce de république dont les membres toujours actifs se secourent et se servent mutuellement" (1:291).

40. "On se plaint, en Perse, de ce que le royaume est gouverné par deux ou trois femmes. C'est bien pis en France, où les femmes en général gouvernent, et non seulement prennent en gros, mais même se partagent en détail toute l'autorité" (1:291).

41. "Que vous êtes heureuse, Roxane, d'être dans le doux pays de Perse, et non pas dans ces climats empoisonnés où l'on ne connoît ni la pudeur ni la vertu!" (1:168).

42. "Je pousse des soupirs qui ne sont point entendus; mes larmes coulent, et tu n'en jouis pas. . . . Ah! mon cher Usbek, si tu savois être heureux!" (1:136).

43. "Vous êtes bien cruels, vous autres hommes! Vous êtes charmés que nous ayons des passions que nous ne puissions pas satisfaire; vous nous traitez comme si nous étions insensibles, et vous seriez bien fâchés que nous le fussions" (1:140).

44. "Que les voyages sont embarrassants pour les femmes! Les hommes ne sont exposés qu'aux dangers qui menacent leur vie, et nous sommes, à tous les instants, dans la crainte de perdre notre vie ou notre vertu" (1:196–97).

45. "Tout m'intéresse, tout m'étonne: je suis comme un enfant, dont les organes encore tendres sont vivement frappés par les moindres objets" (1:197).

46. "Dans la prison même où tu me retiens, je suis plus libre que toi: tu ne saurois redoubler tes attentions pour me faire garder, que je ne jouisse de tes inquiétudes; et tes soupçons, ta jalousie, tes chagrins sont autant de marques de ta dépendance" (1:222).

47. "[L]a simple juxtaposition de deux tons aussi différents devient un moyen d'expression, une manière de dire sans qu'on ait besoin de rien formuler; un blanc prend une signification; les parties muettes du livre entrent, elles aussi, dans la structure du livre" (Jean Rousset, *Forme et signification: Essai sur les structures littéraires de Corneille à Claudel* [Paris: Librairie José Corti, 1962], 84).

48. "[O]n n'entend que plaintes, que murmures, que reproches; mes remonstrances sont méprisées: tout semble permis dans ce temps de licence, et je n'ai plus qu'un vain titre dans le sérail" (1:223–24).

49. "[C]ette douce retraite, où vous trouvez l'innocence, où vous êtes sûre de vous-même, où nul péril ne vous fait trembler" (1:169).

50. Critics have interpreted the breakdown of Usbek's harem according to a

variety of interpretive rationales—erotic, political, religious and feminist. For a sampling of this literature consult: Alan J. Singerman, "Réflexions sur une métaphore: le sérail dans les 'Lettres persanes'," *Studies on Voltaire and the Eighteenth Century* 185 (1980): 181–98 (analysis of Persian harem as allegory for Court at Versailles); Josué V. Harari, "The Eunuch's Tale: Montesquieu's Imaginary of Despotism," in *Scenarios of the Imaginary: Theorizing the French Enlightenment* (Ithaca, N.Y.: Cornell University Press, 1987), 67–101 (discussion of the "politics of the body" in the seraglio); and Katharine M. Rogers, "Subversion of Patriarchy in 'Les Lettres persanes'," *Philological Quarterly* 65, no. 1 (Winter 1986): 61–78 (analysis of the harem as a locus of sexual oppression).

51. Serres, *The Parasite*, 194–95.

52. This split between praxis and theory is not atypical of eighteenth-century philosophy. The *philosophes* are famous for their defense of human liberty and their calls for social responsibility, yet many of their writings, not to mention their financial affairs, reveal an unblinking acceptance of racism and the slave trade. Consult Richard H. Popkin, "The Philosophical Basis of Eighteenth-Century Racism" in *Studies in Eighteenth-Century Culture*, Vol. 3, *Racism in the Eighteenth Century*, ed. Harold E. Pagliaro (Cleveland, Ohio: Press of Case Western Reserve University, 1973), 245–62.

53. "Oui, je t'ai trompé: j'ai séduit tes eunuques, je me suis jouée de ta jalousie, et j'ai su, de ton affreux sérail, faire un lieu de délices et de plaisirs" (1:372).

54. "J'ai pu vivre dans la servitude, mais j'ai toujours été libre: j'ai réformé tes lois sur celles de la Nature, et mon esprit s'est toujours tenu dans l'indépendance" (1:372).

55. "Mais c'en est fait: le poison me consume; ma force m'abandonne; la plume me tombe des mains; je sens affoiblir jusqu'à ma haine; je me meurs" (1:373).

56. Joan Landes interprets the misogyny of eighteenth-century writings as an outgrowth of the aristocrat's worries about the "emasculating effects" of absolute monarchical power. For more on this conflation of gendered and political rhetoric, see Landes, *Women and the Public Sphere*, 2–27.

57. "[C]'est une des causes du succès de quelques ouvrages charmants qui ont paru depuis les *Lettres persanes*" (1:129); an earlier version of the preface specified that the "ouvrages charmants" refer to *Pamela* and *Lettres d'une Péruvienne* [1:129, n. 2].

58. Dufrenoy, *L'Orient romanesque en France*, 155–95.

59. "Vis, superbe ennemi, sois libre, et te souviens / Quel fut et le devoir et la mort d'un chrétien. . . . Instruisez l'Amérique, apprenez à ses Rois / Que les chrétiens sont nés pour leur donner des loix" (Voltaire [François Marie Arouet], *Alzire ou les Américains, tragédie* [Avignon: Louis Chambeau, 1764], 43).

60. Garcilaso de la Vega's *Royal Commentaries,* or *History of the Incas* was one of the major sources of information on Peru in Europe for much of the seventeenth and eighteenth centuries. The *History* was reprinted many times, including editions in 1704 and 1744.

61. "Nos derniers Voyageurs représentent les Habitans naturels de l'ancien Empire du Pérou, si différens aujourd'hui de ce qu'ils étoient au temps de la Con-

quête, qu'on a peine à concilier les peintures modernes avec celles des premieres Relations" (Prévost, *Histoire générale des voyages*, 20:35). After Prévost's prolific years of novel production (1730–40s), he turned his efforts to travel literature; the *Histoire générale des voyages* had a tremendous impact on a public fascinated by travel literature and provided the facts to back up many a philosophical debate on foreign peoples. Initially published in 1746, the first seven volumes of Prévost's *Histoire générale des voyages* are translations of John Green's *Travels,* while later volumes are the work of Prévost and a "society of geographers." Quotations all refer to the 1773 edition.

62. "[L]eur imbécillité est si excessive, qu'à peine croit-on les pouvoir placer au-dessus des Bêtes" (Prévost, *Histoire générale des voyages,* 20:36). For more on Enlightenment natural science and the controversies over the American peoples, consult Antonello Gerbi's seminal study, *The Dispute of the New World: The History of a Polemic, 1750–1900,* trans. Jeremy Moyle (Pittsburgh, Pa.: University of Pittsburgh Press, 1973).

63. As the editor of *Histoire générale* explains: "on reconnoît que les Péruviens élevés dans les Villes et dans les grands Bourgs, sur-tout ceux qui exercent quelque métier et qui savent la Langue Espagnole, ont plus d'ouverture d'esprit et moins de grossiéreté dans les moeurs, que ceux des Campagnes" (Prévost, *Histoire générale des voyages,* 20:44).

64. As Leon G. Campbell points out, the racial mixture of colonial Peru made Spanish attempts to impose a racial caste system impracticable. By the eighteenth century a new system of status was installed in which language, dress and diet replaced skin color as definitions of a person's "racial" (i.e., social) category. See Campbell, "Racism Without Race: Ethnic Group Relations in Late Colonial Peru" in *Studies in Eighteenth-Century Culture,* Vol. 3, *Racism in the Eighteenth Century,* ed. Harold E. Pagliaro (Cleveland, Ohio: Press of Case Western Reserve University, 1973,) 323–33.

65. "[O]n pourroit dire que le siecle d'or n'a jamais existé plus réellement que pour eux. Rien n'altère la tranquillité de leur âme. . . . Quoiqu'à demi nus, ils paroissent aussi contens, que l'Espagnol le plus somptueux dans son habillement" (Prévost, *Histoire générale des voyages,* 20:36).

66. This historical introduction is often attributed to Graffigny's friend and fellow novelist Antoine Bret; it was added to the novel in the definitive edition of 1752, along with two new letters (letters 29 and 34) and other revisions.

67. "Un peuple entier, soumis et demandant grâce, fut passé au fil de l'épée. . . . L'ignorance de nos vices et la naïveté de leurs moeurs les jetèrent dans les bras de leurs lâches ennemis. En vain des espaces infinis avaient séparé les villes du Soleil de notre monde, elles en devinrent la proie et le domaine le plus précieux" (Françoise-Paule d'Issembourg d'Happoncourt de Graffigny, *Lettres d'une Péruvienne* in *Lettres portugaises, Lettres d'une Péruvienne et autres romans d'amour par lettres,* ed. Bernard Bray and Isabelle Landy-Houillon [Paris: Flammarion, 1983], 252–53). All French references to Graffigny's work refer to this edition unless otherwise noted.

68. "Enrichis par les précieuses dépouilles du Pérou, nous devrions au moins regarder les habitants de cette partie du monde comme un peuple magnifique. . . .

Mais toujours prévenus en notre faveur, nous n'accordons du mérite aux autres nations qu'autant que leurs moeurs imitent les nôtres, que leur langue se rapproche de notre idiome" (249).

69. "Nous méprisons les Indiens; à peine accordons-nous une âme pensante à ces peuples malheureux" (249).

70. The debate over historicism in the novel began in the seventeenth century and was a major point of contention in the quarrels between the "Ancients" and the "Moderns" well into the eighteenth century, although most novelists continued to mix fact and fiction with impunity. When Graffigny's friend Devaux criticized her work's historical anachronism, the author replied with a flippant quip on her readers' ignorance ("De quoi t'avises-tu de te souvenir du tems de la conquete du Mexiq? Je comptois que tout le monde croioit que c'etoit l'année passée") and cited the well-known inaccuracy of another contemporary fiction: "Je m'étois autorisée sur *Les Anecdotes de Philipe Auguste* [de Marguerite de Lussan] qui assurement ne ressemblent point a ce tems-la [sic]" (quoted by English Showalter in Showalter, "Les 'Lettres d'une Péruvienne': Composition, Publication, Suites," *Archives et Bibliothèques de Belgique* 54, nos. 1–4 [1983]: 19).

71. On the temporal differences and thematic similarities of primitivist and utopian discourses, see Todorov, *Nous et les autres,* 297–303.

72. "[J]e me fais une étude gênante d'arranger mes pensées comme s'ils pouvaient les pénétrer malgré moi" (271).

73. "[R]etenue dans une étroite captivité, privée de toute communication avec nos citoyens, ignorant la langue de ces hommes féroces dont je porte les fers, je n'éprouve que les effets du malheur, sans pouvoir en découvrir la cause . . . sourds à mon langage, ils n'entendent pas mieux les cris de mon désespoir" (257).

74. In the historical introduction the Peruvians' *quipus* are described as an all-purpose narrative of colored threads, a sort of macramè with meaning: "Les *quapas* ou les *quipos* leur tenaient lieu de notre art d'écrire. Des cordons de coton ou de boyau, auxquels d'autres cordons de différentes couleurs étaient attachés, leur rappelaient, par des noeuds placés de distance en distance, les choses dont ils voulaient se ressouvenir. Ils leur servaient d'annales, de codes, de rituels, de cérémonies, etc." (255). Graffigny's text thus lends mimetic representational value to a medium that was essentially an arithmetic system of recording. Thanks to its scientific trappings, the *Lettres d'une Péruvienne* long enjoyed popularity as a source book on Peru, inspiring (and deceiving) later writers on Peruvian customs. For more on the functions of the *quipu* in Inca society and the fantastic uses attributed to the *quipus* by Graffigny's successors, see L. Leland Locke, *The Ancient Quipu or Peruvian Knot Record* (New York: The American Museum of Natural History, 1923).

75. "[L]e même sentiment qui nous fit inventer leur usage [des *quipos*] nous suggérera les moyens de tromper nos tyrans" (260).

76. Miller argues that the *quipus* guarantee Zilia's identity as a "feminist" writer in *Subject to Change,* 137–57.

77. "[C]es noeuds . . . semblent donner plus de réalité à mes pensées; la sorte de ressemblance que je m'imagine qu'ils ont avec les paroles, me fait une illusion qui trompe ma douleur: je crois te parler, te dire que je t'aime" (270).

78. "L'illusion me quitte, l'affreuse vérité prend sa place, mes pensées errantes, égarées dans le vide immense de l'absence, s'anéantiront désormais avec la même rapidité que le temps" (299).

79. "Je me sens ranimer par cette tendre occupation. Rendue à moi-même, je crois recommencer à vivre" (299).

80. Nelly Furman, "The Politics of Language: Beyond the Gender Principle?" in *Making a Difference: Feminist Literary Criticism,* ed. Gayle Greene and Coppélia Kahn (New York: Methuen, 1985), 72.

81. "J'ai une infinité d'autre raretés plus extraordinaires encore; mais, n'étant point à notre usage, je ne trouve dans notre langue aucuns termes qui puissent t'en donner l'idée" (294).

82. "Ces prodiges troublent la raison, ils offusquent le jugement; que faut-il penser des habitants de ce pays? Faut-il les craindre, faut-il les aimer? Je me garderai bien de rien déterminer là-dessus" (280).

83. "Quelle surprise . . . quelle surprise extrême, de ne trouver qu'une résistance impénétrable où je voyais une figure humaine se mouvoir dans un espace fort étendu!" (280).

84. This episode, which so charmingly evokes the heroine's cultural naïveté, is actually based on an inaccuracy. According to Garcilaso's account of Peruvian society, the mirror was a well-known object to women of all social standings: "Quant à leurs miroirs, les Dames de sang Royal en avoient d'argent poli, et les femmes du commun n'en avoient que de léton ou du cuivre, parce que l'usage de l'argent leur étoit défendu" (Garcilaso de la Vega, *Histoire des Incas, Rois du Pérou,* trans. Jean Baudoin [Amsterdam: Gerard Kuyper, 1704], 1 : 227).

85. "[L]'éducation qu'on leur donne est si opposée à la fin qu'on se propose, qu'elle me paraît être le chef-d'oeuvre de l'inconséquence française" (341). Graffigny's description of this sad logic echoes many contemporary writers on female education. In her 1728 treatise, *Avis d'une mère à sa fille,* Mme de Lambert expresses a similarly disparaging view: "Rien n'est donc si mal entendu que l'éducation qu'on donne aux jeunes personnes: on les destine à plaire; on ne leur donne des leçons que pour les agréments; on fortifie leur amour-propre. . . . Il y a une injustice, ou plutôt une folie, à croire qu'une pareille éducation ne tourne pas contr'elles" (Anne Thérèse, marquise de Lambert, *Oeuvres* [Amsterdam: Par la compagnie, 1766], 56).

86. "Sans confiance en elle, son mari ne cherche point à la former au soin de ses affaires, de sa famille et de sa maison. Elle ne participe au tout de ce petit univers que par la représentation. C'est une figure d'ornement pour amuser les curieux" (344).

87. "Quand tu sauras qu'ici l'autorité est entièrement du côté des hommes, tu ne douteras pas . . . qu'ils ne soient responsables de tous les désordres de la société" (345).

88. "Mon esprit, mon coeur, mes yeux, tout m'a séduit, le Soleil même m'a trompée. Il éclaire le monde entier, dont ton empire n'occupe qu'une portion" (300).

89. "[J]'y trouve au contraire une inconséquence si remarquable que ma raison refuse absolument de s'y prêter" (306).

90. "Je n'ai ni or, ni terres, ni industrie, je fais nécessairement partie des

citoyens de cette ville. O ciel! dans quelle *classe* dois-je me ranger?" (304, emphasis added).

91. William H. Sewell, Jr., *Work and Revolution in France: The Language of Labor from the Old Regime to 1848* (Cambridge: Cambridge University Press, 1980), 81.

92. Richard Terdiman, "Is There Class in This Class?" in *The New Historicism,* ed. H. Aram Veeser (New York: Routledge, 1989), 226.

93. "Quoique tout sentiment de honte . . . me soit étranger . . . je ne puis me défendre de souffrir de l'idée que les autres ont de moi" (304).

94. "[La monarchie] est un état violent, qui dégénère toujours en despotisme ou en république: la puissance ne peut jamais être également partagée entre le Peuple et le Prince; l'équilibre est trop difficile à garder" (Montesquieu, 1:281).

95. "La connaissance de ces tristes vérités n'excita d'abord dans mon coeur que de la pitié pour les misérables, et de l'indignation contre les lois. Mais hélas! que la manière méprisante dont j'entendis parler de ceux qui ne sont pas riches, me fit faire de cruelles réflexions sur moi-même!" (304).

96. Catharine A. MacKinnon, "Feminism, Marxism, Method, and the State: An Agenda For Theory," *Signs* 7, no. 3 (Spring 1982): 537–38.

97. In many respects Zilia's plot resembles an exotic, idealized version of Françoise de Graffigny's life. Like her heroine, Graffigny knew what it meant to be an outsider in Paris; she had firsthand experience of personal and financial hardship. Married at sixteen, Graffigny lost all of her children very young, and suffered years of violence and brutality under an abusive husband from whom she eventually separated. She occupied a position as lady-in-waiting at the court of Lorraine until it was dissolved in the late 1730s when Lorraine was ceded to the Polish crown. In 1739 (at the age of forty-four) she followed her protectress, the duchesse de Richelieu, to Paris. When the duchesse died the next year, Graffigny found herself without resources. After a series of posts as lady-in-waiting to wealthy aristocratic women and sojourns in Parisian convents, Graffigny eventually took her own home and became a modestly successful *salonnière*. But even after the success of the *Lettres d'une Péruvienne* and her play, *Cénie* (1750), Graffigny was obliged to spend most of her time trying to secure financial security through aristocratic pensions and favors.

98. "J'ordonnais librement à des domestiques que je savais être à moi; je badinais sur mon autorité et mon opulence" (352).

99. Hayden White holds that the concept of "nobility" was one of the most problematic concepts confronting eighteenth-century writers, aristocratic and bourgeois alike: "However much they resented the inherited prerogatives of the nobles, they still in general honored the idea of a social hierarchy. Such a hierarchy might be conceived to be based on talent and wealth, rather than birth, but it still presupposed a humanity divided into 'haves' and 'have-nots'" (White, "The Noble Savage Theme as Fetish" in *First Images of America,* ed. Fredi Chiapelli [Berkeley and Los Angeles: University of California Press, 1976], 2:131).

100. Janet Gurkin Altman argues that the *Lettres d'une Péruvienne* advances the notion of a "Peruvian enlightenment—a language, history, and philosophy worth preserving, studying, and disseminating to western Europe" in Altman,

"Graffigny's Epistemology and the Emergence of Third-World Ideology" in *Writing the Female Voice: Essays on Epistolary Literature,* ed. Elizabeth C. Goldsmith (Boston, Mass.: Northeastern University Press, 1989), 172–202.

101. "Vous me donnerez quelque connaissance de vos sciences et de vos arts; vous goûterez le plaisir de la supériorité; je la reprendrai en développant dans votre coeur des vertus que vous n'y connaissez pas" (362).

102. Adrienne Rich, "When We Dead Awaken: Writing as Re-Vision," in *Lies, Secrets, and Silence: Selected Prose 1966–1978* (New York: W. W. Norton and Co., 1979), 35, emphasis added.

103. Showalter, "Les 'Lettres,'" 25.

104. Showalter, "Les 'Lettres,'" 23. One might add, however, that the novel was placed on the infamous "Index" by the Vatican in 1765.

105. Elizabeth J. MacArthur discusses the moral and social implications of Graffigny's novelistic closure in MacArthur, "Devious Narratives: Refusal of Closure in Two Eighteenth-Century Novels," *Eighteenth-Century Studies* 21, no. 1 (Fall 1987): 1–20.

106. The success of this novel is confirmed by the fact that most later editions of *Lettres d'une Péruvienne* include Graffigny's text alongside Hugary de Lamarche-Courmont's as part 1 and part 2.

107. "Comme je me sus bien gré d'en avoir applani les difficultés en écoutant les sages avis de Déterville! Il m'avoit fait sentir que la vraie philosophie respecte l'opinion, redoute d'afficher une entière indépendance" ([Mme Morel de Vindé, *Lettres d'une Péruvienne par Madame de Grafigny. Nouvelle édition, augmentée d'une suite qui n'a point encore été imprimée* [Paris: P. Didot l'aîné, 1797], 2:220).

108. "Zilia n'est pas chez elle aujourd'hui, vous la trouverez chez son mari" (*Lettres d'une Péruvienne . . . augmentée d'une suite*, 2:226). This conventional ending contrasts sharply with what we know of the author's own intention. Graffigny explicitly portrays her will to keep Zilia unmarried in a letter of September 1750, wherein she declares, "tranquilise-toi, Zilia ne sera pas mariée, je ne suis pas assés bête pour cela [*sic*]" (quoted by Showalter, "Les 'Lettres,'" 23).

109. Cited by Josette Féral, "The Powers of Difference," in *The Future of Difference,* ed. Hester Eisenstein and Alice Jardine (Boston, Mass.: G. K. Hall and Co., 1980), 92–93.

3. Woman as an Island: La Dixmerie's *Sauvage de Taïti aux Français* and Mme de Monbart's *Lettres taïtiennes*

> It is thus . . . the ignorance of the savages which has enlightened the civilized peoples.
>
> Raynal, *Histoire philosophique et politique des établissemens et du commerce des Européens dans les deux Indes*

French writers have long depicted Tahiti as a metaphorical woman, witness Victor Segalen's claim that "the whole island came to me like a woman."[1] Since 1767 marks the arrival of Tahiti's earliest European visitors, Tahiti was truly a "virgin" land for eighteenth-century observers, that is, a land as yet unpossessed by any European power, with all its bountiful natural resources still intact. The physical and spiritual distance of this untouched paradise from the known world inspired much speculation in French travel and anthropological writings. The Tahitians' geographic isolation in the midst of the vast South Pacific gave rise to theories on the exotic (possibly Asian or American) origins of this people and hypotheses claiming Tahiti as a model of man's "natural state." Like a prelapsarian Eden, Tahiti seemed to have escaped man's malediction to work with its blessedly temperate climate and generous, natural supply of food. But the topic of greatest fascination was the Tahitians' bizarre code of morality which, in giving women the same sexual rights and prerogatives as men, enhanced the island's status as an upside-down world (*monde à l'envers*) in French eyes.

Drawing on such images of Tahiti, Nicolas Bricaire de La Dixmerie's *Sauvage de Taïti aux Français* (1770) and Marie-Josephine de Monbart's *Lettres taïtiennes* (1784) present the encounter of Europe and Tahiti in a primitivist rhetoric that conflates problems of cultural and sexual difference. While the plots of Prévost's *Histoire d'une Grecque moderne* and Graffigny's *Lettres d'une Péruvienne* suggest that the meeting of European and non-European cultures could provoke a gendered conflict between an aggressive male (European) suitor and an elusive or combative female Other, this tension is underscored, almost caricatured, in the works of La Dixmerie and Monbart. The Tahitian's encounter with Europe appears inherently, inevitably associated with a drama of sexual possession. Stressing the metaphorical connection between the political body of the Tahitian state and the erotic body of the Tahitian woman, La Dixmerie and Monbart portray the meeting of Europe and Tahiti as a situation fraught with peril for the fragile island culture. This sense of external threat comes across in the authors' evocation of the island as a territory at risk of invasion and in need of (male) protection (as in the *Sauvage de Taïti aux Français*), or as a land already ravaged by foreign influences, a lost paradise of moral innocence (as in the *Lettres taïtiennes*).

Clearly members of the spy novel tradition, the heroes of La Dixmerie's and Monbart's fictions subtly alter the formula of cultural critique designed by their predecessors to reflect a "Tahitian" mentality and message on European colonialism. In both novels representatives of Tahiti come to France and report on the differences between the two cultures. Much of the criticism of French society derives from the contrast between the unhappiness and disadvantaged social status of women in that enlightened land and the complete freedom and happiness afforded women in backwards, unenlightened Tahiti. While French women suffer under the chains of ill-suited monogamous marriages demanded by Christian morality, Tahitian women remain free to pursue the partners of their choice under the natural, polygamous system of Tahitian morality. Instead of using Tahiti as a term of comparison to prove that all cultures have equally valid social structures and systems of belief (the cultural relativist argument), these works project an idealized vision of the island culture to disprove the myth that European, civilized nations are superior to less advanced societies and to argue in favor of protecting the primitive from the civilizing influences of trade and colonial expansion (the primitivist argument).

The encounter with French society incites a crisis in the Tahitian character, a realization of the dangers of political penetration and social corruption on the island. But the plots of the *Sauvage de Taïti aux Français* and the *Lettres taïtiennes* suggest very different outcomes for the future of Franco-Tahitian contact. The narrator of La Dixmerie's novel is a Tahitian king who, all the while protested his lack of cultural sophistication, presents a philosophical attack on the many injustices he observes during his

sojourn in French society. Returning to his homeland at the end, the Tahitian vows to put his knowledge about the French to practical use and
create new laws to protect the Tahitian people from the foreigners' corrupting influences. La Dixmerie thus depicts the Tahitians' distance from
Europe as a philosophical tool and strategic advantage in their battle
against foreign penetration.

Monbart, on the other hand, interprets cultural isolation as a sign of
vulnerability and weakness. The narrators of her sentimental fiction are
two young Tahitian lovers who are separated when the hero decides to
board a French ship on its return to Europe. Like La Dixmerie's narrator,
this young islander reports on the many surprising discrepancies in French
morality. But as time passes, he falls prey to the tantalizing traps of civilized society, loses his Tahitian decency, and becomes the very model of
the French *roué*. Meanwhile, back on Tahiti, the heroine reports the cruelties inflicted on the islanders by sex-crazed French and English sailors in
their midst. Her narrative reaches a climax when she herself is raped by an
English ship's captain and betrayed by her compatriots for the Englishman's gold. In this context the Tahitians' ignorance of European mores
makes them into malleable victims of colonial corruption, presaging the
end of their primitive idyll.

The different visions of Tahiti in La Dixmerie's and Monbart's novels
indicate the influence of two styles prevalent in late eighteenth-century
literature: the public service-minded "philosophical" style and the intimate, tearful "sentimental" style. The philosophical polemics of the *Sauvage de Taïti aux Français* belie La Dixmerie's desire to use literature as a
vehicle for participating in the increasingly polarized intellectual climate
of the 1770s. His image of the ideal Tahitian lawmaker recalls the optimistic reform-oriented discourse of much pre-Revolutionary political propaganda. The emotional language and tragic message of the *Lettres taïtiennes*
reveal Monbart's fascination with the reigning vogue of sensitivity (*la sen-
sibilité*) in literature, and its call for the analysis of human feelings over
intellect. Much like Rousseau's wildly popular *roman sentimental, La Nouvelle Héloïse* (1761), Monbart's *Lettres taïtiennes* underscores the unsophisticated style and unreasonable actions of the Tahitian lovers to prove the
authenticity of their texts.

But in their portrayal of French penetration of the Tahitian woman/
state, these novels also constitute timely commentaries on contemporary
debates on colonialism. The French popular press of the 1770s sensationalized the Tahitian woman as the literal object of male erotic desire, the

sexy and welcoming love kitten of the tropics. While warning against the adverse effects of miscegenation on the French population, pro-colonial writings propagated a similarly idealized vision of the island as a desirable woman, symbol of Tahitian generosity, docility and abundant natural resources. But these topoi were later recast as Europeans became increasingly aware of the problematic consequences of their contact with primitive peoples. By the 1780s the glorified image of the Tahitian woman's unfettered sexuality was tarnished by news of widespread syphilis among the islanders, as well as sobering accounts of sexual prostitution and class division in this supposedly idyllic land. Reading La Dixmerie's and Monbart's fictional accounts of Franco-Tahitian encounters in the light of contemporary voyage literature and anthropological writings shows how the author's differential uses of the Tahitian locale formed part of the larger shift in the French mentality away from the pro-colonial politics of the 1760s and 1770s and toward the anti-colonial activity of the 1780s.

Contexts: Anthropological Theories and Colonial Ambitions in the Austral Lands

The philosopher Pierre Louis de Maupertuis called for expeditions to the "Austral Lands" (the legendary continent of the South Seas) as early as 1752 and proposed that examples of the strange people found there be brought back to Europe to participate in a kind of international think-tank or "Collège des sciences étrangères." Maupertuis's description of the Austral people embodies the popular belief that the most primitive savages were not completely human but rather a hybrid man/beast species, and typifies the "scientific" curiosity of eighteenth-century *philosophes:* "It is in the islands of that sea that voyagers have reported seeing wild men, hairy men with tails; a middle species between monkeys and us. I would rather spend an hour in conversation with them than with the wittiest man in Europe."[2]

Maupertuis's efforts were consolidated in 1756 with the publication of the monumental *Histoire des navigations aux terres australes* by the Dijon parliamentarian Charles de Brosses. De Brosses's work explicitly defends French colonialism in the South Seas, drawing a sharp distinction between the cruel, ruthless Spanish conquest of America and the peaceful, commercial infiltration of the French into Austral lands. According to de Brosses, this colonization will serve both parties: the "Australians" will receive the valuable aid of French technology in return for their obedience to French rule; the French will reap the profits of their fertile country in exchange for civilizing its inhabitants.[3] But the fine print of his plans reveals a more sinister end—repression, if not extermination, of the indigenous culture. In de Brosses's ideal colony, the Europeans would avoid sexual contact with the natives in order to people the island with a pure French race even as they would gradually expand French control over the natives' economy and territory: "[The colony] will gradually expand into the country around its central warehouse: it will push the savages farther away."[4]

Subsequent to a humiliating defeat at the hands of the British in the disastrous Seven Years War and the colonial losses incurred by the Treaty of Paris in 1763, French expeditionary interest in the mysterious *Terra Australis* ran high in the late 1760s. The islands of the South Seas symbolized a second New World, a possibility for colonial territory, commercial prosperity and scientific progress.

When Louis-Antoine de Bougainville, well-known army officer, mathematician and socialite, embarked on the circumnavigation that was to lead him to Tahiti in 1766, he left with the blessings of King Louis XV and his influential foreign minister the duc de Choiseul, who reminded him to insist on French rights against British claims for colonial possessions. The French saw their expansionism as a gentler form of colonialism than the violent conquests of their rivals, the English and the Dutch. In his instructions to Bougainville, Choiseul emphasized that colonies are primarily commercial partners, not extensions of the French state. Nevertheless, the French administrators were to oversee the colony's economy as closely as possible, and to subjugate the natives to "the most austere prohibition" against trade with other nations.[5] As it turned out, Bougainville's symbolic claim of Tahiti for the French crown was to prove entirely useless.[6] But the ten-day stay of the French crew provided rich material for philosophical debates in years to come.

Given that contemporary theorists considered the Tahitian race a branch of the Indian race and that Bougainville's Tahitian protégé Aotourou was called a "Patagonian" by his Parisian acquaintances, we must keep in mind the very flexible boundaries and abstract nature of French concepts of "primitive" ethnicities at this time. Thanks in part to Jean-Jacques Rousseau's *Discours sur l'origine de l'inégalité* (1755), when late eighteenth-century writers wrote of primitive societies they often conceived them as mythic constructs for proving theories on the origins of human society or arguing the advantages of nature versus culture. Rousseau dips into ethnographic texts often in his treatise, but only to use the various savages found on European expeditions to illustrate the stages of human society in its fall from nature. His radical questioning of societal progress raised a number of philosophical controversies. Was the savage's subsistence living preferable to the civilized man's alienation, envy and competitive survival? If so, was the role of woman in primitive societies also preferable to civilized woman's experience?[7] Was the natural order of relations between the sexes based on forceful subjugation or consensual freedom?

Some theorists saw the organization of savage societies as manifestations of an ideal order of natural ethics (*le droit naturel*) embodying all human freedoms, including sexual liberation. It is this pro-nature premise that explains one commentator's claim that "in most savage societies girls enjoy total freedom."[8] But other observers argued just the opposite and portrayed the savage life-style as a miserable, dog-eat-dog struggle for survival. The academician Antoine-Léonard Thomas contended that women are necessarily oppressed in primitive societies: "More than half of the globe is covered with savages; and in all these societies women are very unhappy. Savage man, at once ferocious and indolent . . . despotically commands over beings that reason made his equals, but which weakness makes his slaves."[9]

In his essay, "Sur les femmes," Diderot also denounced the myth of primitive indolence in the name of woman. Far from enjoying a life of ease, Diderot argues, primitive women must work twice as hard as women in civilized societies.[10] These arguments rest upon the "Four Stages of Mankind" theory: a vertical conception of progress that categorizes human societies according to their economic and social organization and means of subsistence. The relations between the sexes supposedly improve when a society moves up the ladder of technological progress, away from hunting and gathering toward agriculture and finally commercial trade. On the scale of potential happiness, the primitive savage holds the bottom rung, surpassed by the pastoral shepherdess, the farmer's wife and, at the apex of civilized emancipation, the bourgeois matron of industrial society. This theory, espoused in various forms by the *philosophes* of the late eighteenth century, equates the development of complex social institutions with civilization and the creation of a capitalist economy with rational progress. "Civilized man was supposed to have literally thought himself out of the state of nature," Marvin Harris explains, "by steadily inventing more and more clever and reasonable institutions, customs and subsistence processes."[11]

Tahiti was a paradoxical exception to such theories. The first and most influential accounts of French explorers to Tahiti argued that Tahitian women were not only free of the subsistence gathering and backbreaking labor characteristic of other primitive peoples, they were also encouraged by the menfolk to be sexually active, even promiscuous. Tahiti represented an anomaly: a primitive subsistence economy that nonetheless ensured the freedom and happiness of all participants. How could this be? As we shall see, much of what was taken for "Tahitian" in the French press was but a myth, an eminently appealing myth at that.

The earliest account of Tahiti to reach the French public was an article published in the *Mercure de France* in 1769, in which Bougainville's botanist Commerson describes the discovery of a land dedicated to the cult of love, "New Cytherea." Commerson glosses over the actual antagonism that the French encountered on the island by depicting their arrival as an occasion for making love not war, and characterizing the Tahitian culture as one founded upon generosity and hospitality toward foreigners: "all strangers are admitted into these happy mysteries [Tahitian lovemaking]; it is even one of the duties of Tahitian hospitality to invite them in."[12] Using rhetoric reminiscent of Rousseauean philosophy, Commerson describes the islanders as children of nature, who have not yet "degenerated into reason."[13] Strangers to the very notions of social hierarchy or political dissension, these people regard their kings as benevolent family patriarchs. Like Rousseau's image of the happy Caribs in the *Discours sur l'inégalité,* the Tahitians are seen to inhabit that delicate equilibrium between asocial nomadism and institutionalized injustice. Technologically unsophisticated, they live in rudimentary structures and have yet to discover the arts of metallurgy or agriculture.

But "this is no horde of vulgar and stupid savages," Commerson asserts. Though they may be ignorant, the Tahitians display uncommon artistry in the construction of their canoes and huts, and show great curiosity in French techniques of boatbuilding, sailmaking and food preparation. Excusing the islanders' thievery as evidence of their communal philosophy and lack of private property, the Frenchman demands: "this property right, is it in nature? No, it is pure convention."[14] In conclusion he judges Tahiti a paragon of civic and moral harmony and underlines the freedom of women in Tahitian society as proof of their humanity and difference from other savages: "We admired the simplicity of their customs, the decency of their conduct, especially toward their women who are in no way subjugated among them as they are among savages."[15] Unlike the man of nature imagined by Rousseau, whose goodness comes from his isolation from society, the virtues that Commerson celebrates in the Tahitian man of nature are social, active, positive; they manifest an aptitude for civilization.[16] Commerson's selective vision of Tahiti reveals the combination of anthropological observation and political instrumentality that typifies the government-supported scientific voyages of the 1770s.

Like Commerson's account of the Tahitian paradise, Bougainville's *Voyage autour du monde* (1771) smoothes over the historical truth—the battles and bloodshed which actually occurred when the French arrived on Tahiti—by describing the island in an idealized, ahistorical context. Bougainville's relation contains a veritable catalogue of utopian images borrowed from the Western tradition. He describes the women who welcome the ship as beguiling nymphs, whose beautiful nudity charmed his sailors just as Venus's apparition charmed the Phrygian shepherd.[17] The island's marvels are described as attributes of New Cytherea, the garden of Eden, a pastoral idyll, and the Elysian Fields. This accumulation of other-world imagery has the effect of situating Tahiti on top of an imaginary pedestal, as a distant yet accessible paradise.

Bougainville contributes to the eroticization of Tahiti by depicting the island as a haven for the sex-starved European sailors. The Tahitian women offer themselves to the Frenchmen ingenuously, he claims, like creatures from an amoral Golden Age. The very atmosphere of the island resonates with sensuality: "The air one breathes, the songs, the dances, which are almost always accompanied by lascivious poses, everything reminds one at all times of the pleasures of love, everything calls for one to take part."[18]

Contemporary book illustrations further propagated this vision of Tahiti as a docile and inviting woman. The illustration from Bérenger's *Collection de tous les voyages faits autour du monde* (1789), titled "Amusements of the Tahitians and the English," shows naked Tahitian women swimming up to an English ship and beckoning to the sailors to come frolic in the waves (Figure 14). Two sailors proffer a string of beads and a mirror as evidence of their willingness to engage in sexual commerce with the islanders, while a third sits perched astride the ship's boom in a striking pose of phallic symbolism. Note the complete lack of "Tahitian" racial specificity and the cartoon-like landscape of the island, which is identified only by a few palm trees. Clearly, this artist was less concerned with

Amusemens des Otahitiens et des Anglais.

Figure 14. "Amusements of the Tahitians and the English," from Bérenger, *Collection de tous les voyages faits autour du monde par les différentes nations de l'Europe*. Frontispiece, vol. 8 (Lausanne: J. P. Heubach et cie, 1789). Courtesy of the James Ford Bell Library, University of Minnesota.

rendering an authentically documented foreign locale than with populariz-
ing an image of Tahiti as a paradise for European mariners.

The illustration from the travel journals of Captain Cook depicts two
Tahitian women coyly posing for the European observer. These women
appear frozen in time, seized in the middle of ritualistic actions: dancing a
ceremonial dance and presenting a formal gift (Figure 15). Their dress is
simple yet erotic. The dancer's feathery bra and swaying pose draws attention to her voluptuous figure, while the present-bearer's robe leaves one
breast bared and the other only negligently covered by a simple cloth.
Although the legend announces her function as a gift-presenter, with no
gift visible in the picture one wonders if she herself is to be given away to
the European visitor.

Just as Tahiti's sexual utopia disproved the need for European-style
morality, the islanders' social harmony put to shame the divisive spirit and
repressive practices of European governments. Shifting from the register
of ethnographic reportage to philosophical speculation, Bougainville announces the utility of the Tahitian model for Europeans seeking clues to
their own humanity in his last journal entry before leaving the island:

> Lawmakers and philosophers, come here and see, completely established [a
> society] your imagination could not even dream of. A numerous people,
> composed of handsome men and pretty women, living together in [nature's]
> bounty and health, with all the signs of the greatest harmony, distinguishing
> between "yours" and "mine" enough to keep good order but not so much as
> to create paupers and rogues.[19]

Tahiti symbolizes the ideal other world of the *philosophes,* an egalitarian,
harmonious, liberal utopia.

After leaving the island on their voyage, Bougainville and his men
grew somewhat disenchanted with "New Cytherea," however, thanks to
the presence of their Tahitian companion Aotourou.[20] Not only did
Aotourou sour the Frenchmen's dreams of paradise through his rudimentary conversation, he also dispelled illusions of noble nature with his im-
petuous conduct. Indeed in the eyes of his cosmopolitan observers, the
Tahitian prince proved to be a rather ignoble savage. His relentless sexual
advances toward Commerson's assistant Jeanne Baré, for example, were
most offensive to the French crew. Jeanne Baré's story is part of the myth
of Tahiti and bears telling here. According to many historians, she was
the first woman to circumnavigate the globe. By wrapping her breasts
and dressing in men's clothes, she managed to get hired for Bougainville's

Figure 15. Illustration for Cook, *A Collection of Voyages Round the World Performed by Royal Authority. Containing a Complete Historical Account of Captain Cook's First, Second, Third, and Last Voyages*, vol. 5 (London: A. Millar, W. Law and R. Cater, 1790). Courtesy of the Princeton University Libraries.

voyage as cabin boy and assistant to Dr. Commerson. Legend has it that suspicions had been raised about her gender early in the trip, but no one had been able to verify her femininity until the ship arrived at Tahiti. The Tahitians, apparently more attuned to sexuality than the repressed Westerners, noticed her authentic gender at once and tried to force her to have sex with their tribesmen in exchange for all the Tahitian women given to the French.[21]

On arriving in France, Bougainville's Tahitian did much to reinforce the myth of the lusty Tahitian. He reportedly refused to get dressed, so loathe was he to cover up his resplendent posterior and hide his noble tattoos.[22] In Paris it is said that he attempted to ravish the first lady he met, and on another occasion indelicately suggested to a certain Mlle Heinsel that she tattoo her bottom also![23] Aotourou was commonly described as a man driven by his avid sexual appetite, a weakness typical of the Tahitian character. After a period of popularity in which he was invited to Versailles and received in all the best salons, contemporary writers admit being disappointed with their long-awaited *bon sauvage,* who on closer look appeared dull and small-minded, lustful and coarse. Instead of the visiting sage envisioned by Maupertuis, who would reveal to European scientists the secrets of his native culture and profit from European training to bring his nation into the modern age, Bougainville's Tahitian turned out to be an average man, passionate, untaught and uncouth.

Bougainville nevertheless defended Aotourou against his European critics. While his hopes for the islander were not a little based on French colonial aspirations in the South Pacific, he also made a point to commend the Tahitian's intellect—"he possesses in intelligence what he lacks in beauty [il possède en intelligence ce qui lui manque du côté de la beauté]"—and to criticize the arrogant ignorance of Parisian high society (*Voyage,* 253). Bougainville's high hopes for Aotourou's visit ultimately fell flat, but in La Dixmerie's novel the tables are turned and the Tahitian visitor criticizes the French for their woeful disregard for other peoples.[24]

Le Sauvage de Taïti aux Français: The Complaint of a Primitive Philosopher

La Dixmerie takes up the Tahitian's defense in *Le Sauvage de Taïti aux Français, avec un envoi au philosophe ami des sauvages,* transforming an uneducated islander into an eloquent partisan of political and social justice.

The first-person harangue form of this text, with its many apostrophes and direct challenges to the reader, shows the author's belief in literature's power to affect public opinion and reflects the intellectual climate in which he was writing. As Georges May has shown, by the 1760s the novel was widely accepted as a genre *engagé,* expressing a commitment to an ideological cause.[25] The term *philosophe* underwent a significant semantic evolution during these years, losing its association with the learned seeker of universal "reason" for a new connotation as the combative "man of letters" (*homme de lettres*) fighting in defense of a partisan "true philosophy" (*la vraie philosophie*). In the *Dictionnaire philosophique* (1764), Voltaire describes the *homme de lettres* as a militant educator-martyr who takes great risks in publishing his ideas, but does so anyway for the good of society.[26] Bolstered by such ideas, literary authors became ever more outspoken on controversial issues: by the 1770s the polemical "citizen-writer" (*homme de lettres-citoyen*) was glorified in the popular press as a "guardian of the public interest" (*vengeur de la cause publique*). As befits their new pedagogical personae, many authors began demanding greater commitment from their readers. "For them, reading should be a serious matter," Roger Chartier explains, "and should imply the active participation of the reader, whose very thoughts and existence should change."[27] In the increasingly polarized atmosphere of La Dixmerie's day, writers used literature to do more than depict the reality of contemporary society, it was to offer a plan of reform, a means of improving on the real. But just as the *philosophes* themselves had gradually left behind their marginal status to assume prestigious positions in the ancien régime's literary establishment, their urgent appeals for political justice and social equality had gradually become conventionalized as a "democratic" form of wit.

The first generation of *philosophes* (Montesquieu, Voltaire, Rousseau, d'Alembert) had espoused revolutionary ideals in their early days, articulating and propagating an ideology that undermined the traditional values Frenchmen had inherited from their Catholic and royalist past. But as their influence grew, their connections with the aristocratic elite improved, and eventually the hungry young men of the 1720s, 1730s and 1740s were enjoying lives of relative ease as academicians, writers for the state-sponsored press (*Le Mercure de France*), and recipients of noble privilege and protection. Similarly, the ideas that had seemed so subversive in the early eighteenth century (skepticism, religious tolerance, criticism of monarchical absolutism), in becoming popularized, had lost their power to disturb. "Voltaire's *Lettres philosophiques* may have exploded like a 'bomb' in 1734," writes Robert Darnton, "but by the time of Voltaire's apotheosis in 1778, France had absorbed the shock."[28] The democratic ideals of the *philosophes* had become common cultural currency by the late eighteenth century, and were integrated into officially sanctioned rituals of legitimation—scholastic competitions and literary contests. Candidates for academic honors in the 1770s and 1780s tried to outdo each other in eloquent declamations on once-potent philosophical abstractions, such as "man's pursuit of happiness," "the value of human dignity," or "independence."[29]

Like many idealistic young men born in the 1730s and 1740s, La Dixmerie left his native province at a young age and came to make his literary fortune in Paris. An aspiring writer, he was likely inspired by the vision of the republic of letters that the great *philosophes* had described: a society of independent but fraternal individuals who rally together in the service of a common cause. What he found, of course, was that the real world of letters functioned like everything else in the ancien régime: individuals got ahead as best they could in a labyrinth of baroque institutions, relying not on talent but on the old devices of privilege and protection.[30] La Dixmerie's early writings show his understanding of these mechanisms; his first literary enterprise was a collection of flattering epistles to King Louis XV, after which he became a regular contributor to the *Mercure*. The Tahitian's harangue on French customs and institutions in the *Sauvage de Taïti aux Français* (and the amusing "envoi" to the "philosopher, friend of the savages" that follows it), reveal the combination of philosophy and pragmatism that characterizes this age. Daring enough to challenge the reader's intellect, La Dixmerie's reformist rhetoric nevertheless falls short of sweeping change to remain within the acceptable bounds of a popular "democratic" ideology.

La Dixmerie's narrator is a nameless Tahitian sovereign writing on the eve of his departure from France. He addresses the French reader as an equal, yet his own simplicity initially puts his narrative authority in question. Given the primitive state of Tahitian culture, with what authority can he hope to teach a lesson to the French? After writing only a few pages he pauses in a crisis of self-doubt: "But I feel my hand wants to stop, my mind is becoming muddled. Who! Me? Dare to write to you?"[31] This narrative self-consciousness recurs as a leitmotif in La Dixmerie's fiction, signaling the candor and honesty of his savage speaker and emphasizing the Tahitian's uneasy relations with the French.

Indeed, looking at the description of Tahiti in the prefatory "Avis de l'éditeur," one may well wonder at this speaker's audacity. La Dixmerie characterizes the island culture as an inverted, backward reflection of European civilization. The Tahitians' cuisine requires no cooking pots; the islanders drink no wine or liquor; their civil organization reveals no discord; since they have no weapons they also have no murders nor wars; and their cultural heritage contains neither written prose nor any historical record. What the Tahitians do possess, however, is the privilege of living in harmony in a benevolent, naturally bountiful land. While their cultural achievements are admittedly limited, their concepts of beauty, truth and justice are purer than the Europeans', for they are based solely on sensorial impressions and common sense instead of being distorted by the falsely authoritative jargon of "experts." Appealing to the French readers' guilty sense of living in a corrupt age, the "editor" exhorts them to demonstrate their integrity by listening to the Tahitian's tale: "There was a time when one would only have been interested in knowing if this island produces much gold; it is possible that today that question has not even been asked. I hope so for the honor of philosophy. We need morals more than wealth."[32] The Tahitian's prestige derives from his pure, uncompromised morality. But the narrator will nonetheless attempt to reinforce his authority repeatedly in La Dixmerie's text.

"I am leaving you, oh affable and arrogant people . . . I only drew your glances; you captured my attention. You ignore my existence, and I know you."[33] Thus begins the Tahitian's narrative in the *Sauvage de Taïti aux Français* and already the structure of La Dixmerie's polemic stands out. The Tahitian speaks the unknown language, the unheard voice from the outside to denounce the unlistening, unfeeling chatter of a complacent society. Instead of getting involved in social, romantic or political intrigues with the French (like the other exotic spies we have studied), La Dixmerie's hero remains on the margins of society from beginning to end as a reasonable, albeit misunderstood, observer. As a narrator, however, the Tahitian involves himself deeply with the French reader. "The Tahitian author seeks to be read," declares the "Avis de l'éditeur"; his urgent appeals to the reader evidence his desire for recognition or at least a reaction, if not admission that he is right (xxiv).

This marks La Dixmerie's major difference from the spy novel tradition: his work demands no literary subterfuge between a duplicitous "translator" and a sly reader, for this text is public, not clandestine. The narrator's ideal *narrataire* is the French population, not a distant friend or lover. The *Lettres persanes* and the *Letters d'une Péruvienne* presented more or less veiled social criticisms through their fictions of an exotic character's education and admission into the Parisian aristocracy. The emphasis in these books was on the character's gradual discovery of the mechanics of French society, with its complex rituals and codes of proper behavior. As an explicit, undisguised attack on French customs, politics and social institutions, the *Sauvage de Taïti aux Français* marks a later development in French literature.[34] Like Montesquieu's Persians and Graffigny's Peruvian, La Dixmerie's Tahitian undergoes humiliating treatment at the hands of the French nobility. But instead of attempting to understand what social principles make the Parisians perceive him so differently (like the Persians) or lamenting his alienation in private (like the Peruvian), he takes his complaints to a public forum and lambastes the French reader with a list of French hypocrisies, injustices and cruelties.

With the bravado of a self-righteous *homme de lettres,* the Tahitian narrator turns his weaknesses and vulnerability vis-à-vis the French into the very foundations of his textual and political authority. His difficulty with the French language and embarrassed mutism in social situations thus becomes a symbol of his work's utility: "It is because I was never able to speak that I am taking it on me to write," he declares, "I could never verbally answer any of your questions."[35] Since the Tahitians possessed no written language, this process of transcribing his thought into writing suggests great effort. But La Dixmerie's narrator describes the translation from orality to writing as a concession for his French reader rather than a sign of Tahitian ignorance. After all, he argues, the Tahitian language is far superior to French: "If only you could understand our [language]! It does not weary those who speak it; it pleases the ear of those who hear it. We all pass for eloquent and we owe it our eloquence."[36]

La Dixmerie's "Tahitian" critique of French culture inverts the value of such traditional oppositional pairs as savage/civilized and natural/artificial from a primitive point of view, and redefines key concepts like "barbarian" and "cannibal" as terms of morality not ethnography. The Tahitian "savage"'s lack of a written legal code, for instance, enforces a civilized, orderly form of conduct; "None of our laws are written and none have ever been broken [Aucune loi parmi nous n'est écrite, et jamais elle ne fut transgressée]" (10). Unimpressed by the highly touted courtesy (*politesse*) of the French, the narrator deflates social etiquette into a question of artful, misleading appearances: "All that exterior [façade] could not impose on me; it could not deceive the eyes of a man who sees through the eyes of nature."[37] And just as he redefines "barbarian" to mean one who metaphorically attacks human dignity by valuing wealth over virtue, he calls "cannibals" those who feed on the suffering and pain of their compatriots—like lawyers and magistrates (36, 93).

La Dixmerie employs a clever literary strategy to lend credibility to the voice of his primitive philosopher. By periodically interrupting the savage's harangue with questions on his authority, the author gives the narrator an opportunity to forestall his critics' opposition and to reinforce the righteousness of his stance. These challenges range from skeptical comments from an unseen third party, such as, "Someone will say perhaps: this is too much erudition for a savage. How did you learn to reason?" to first-person admissions of self-doubt, that is, "But a savage who writes to you, will he be worth reading?" [38] The narrator responds in each case by reaffirming his *difference* from French norms. How did he learn to reason? By avoiding the French reliance on "experts" and seeking out the truth for himself. Will his text be worth reading? Whatever the French may think, the Tahitian knows his work is valid, for it constitutes a totally disinterested, unbiased exposé of the truth. Instead of holding him back, the Tahitian's cultural isolation and lack of education thus serve as his best defense against the weighty force of French culture. His unlearned, natural distrust for anything smacking of hypocrisy forms the most compelling criterion for his authority and his book's utility.

The Tahitian narrator's most sustained critique of French usage pertains to the "woman question," which he examines from all angles: aesthetic, moral and political. Focusing on the female body, he interprets the different styles of clothing found in Tahiti and France as metaphoric gauges of women's freedom and social justice. The Tahitian women's simple, semi-transparent dress symbolizes their sexual liberty and closeness to nature: "Look at our beautiful Tahitian women! Their clothing floats in the wind. An ingenious gauze hides their nudity from sight, but lets one see their charms. Nothing fights against desire; everything excites it." [39] The French women's complicated and constraining apparel, on the contrary, betokens their prudishness and social vulnerability. La Dixmerie satirizes the French women's repressed sexuality by describing their clothing with terms borrowed from the vocabulary of warfare and penology. The women's tight-fitting gowns hold them captive like "painful shackles" ("pénibles entraves"), while their corsets (symbolic "cuirasses" or suits of armor) and other articles of clothing or "entrenchments" ("retranchemens") contribute to make them practically "inaccessible" to the male gaze: "They say you are not impregnable, [yet] you fortify yourselves as if you wanted to be."[40]

Women's physical behavior offers other clues to their social position in Tahiti and France. While the Tahitian's pleasure-oriented morality ignores decorum and allows women to run and jump "like young deer," the Europeans' social codes, which prohibit women from walking or exhibiting their bodies unnecessarily, indicate their women's oppression. In contrast to the joyful play of the Tahitian women, French women only exercise if they have to. Physical exertion depends on class status; immobility is a privilege of the rich. "You would walk well, if you could walk," charges the Tahitian, "but it is not considered good taste to use one's legs. You leave that privilege to the petty bourgeoises, who use it with great restraint."[41]

Given the narrator's "Tahitian" penchant for eroticizing social customs, his discussion of women's physical conduct leads inevitably to a comparison of courtship rituals in France and Tahiti: for why do women need to move, if not to seek out or escape from men? With her remarkable speed and agility, the narrator remarks, the Tahitian woman "would escape from us easily, if she did not want to be caught [elle nous échapperait facilement, si elle n'aimait pas qu'on l'atteignît]" (48). But thanks to their permissive moral code, the island women do allow themselves to be caught and give themselves to men without reserve. Such unions are characterized by consensus and respect, according to the Tahitian (reporting, of course, from a male point of view): "We believe a beautiful woman is the greatest gift that nature gave to man. We receive this gift with gratitude, we use it; but we always recognize its value."[42] What is striking about La Dixmerie's description of the Tahitians' gender roles is his image of woman as an object or gift proffered to man. For all her freedom of dress and movement, liberated though her conduct may seem, she still lives within the boundaries of a patriarchal mentality that posits man as hunter/seducer and woman as the playful, but fundamentally passive, prey or goal. In portraying the Tahitians as passive sex objects instead of Amazons, the French writer protects his male reader from a potential threat to his masculine ego.

The Tahitians' hunt-style courtship appears vastly preferable to the French practice, which is described as a "battle" between the sexes. With mystery, guile and resistance their sole weapons against male domination, the French women try to make their lovers' pursuit last as long as possible.

Once they capitulate, they lose their power. Although a Frenchman may act respectfully toward his lover during his campaign to conquer her heart, once married he disposes of this façade to assume his rightful position as absolute sovereign of the household. As the narrator puts it: French husbands "stop being submissive as soon as they can command [Ils cessent d'être soumis aussitôt qu'ils peuvent commander]" (82).

Shifting his critique to the domain of politics, La Dixmerie's narrator judges the Tahitian and French governmental systems by comparing their inclusion and exclusion of women, peasants and commoners. He describes the Tahitian order as an ideal patriarchal family: "We are all children of the same family; we treat each other as brothers."[43] Their society has no class or labor divisions, because it has no classes and very little labor: "Every inhabitant of our island is a man in our eyes. We would value all occupations equally, if we had occupations."[44] Although the masculinist resonance of La Dixmerie's language, with its references to brotherhood and manly equality, may lead one to wonder about women's participation in this order, the narrator assures us that women are treated as equals under the few laws that they have. Condemning the French women's forceful exclusion from the elite Académie française, he argues: "I doubt that there will ever be an academy on Tahiti, nevertheless I vow that women would not be excluded from it."[45]

In contrast to the simple, consensual Tahitian government, the French monarchy seems excessively complex and unjust. La Dixmerie's Tahitian passes negative judgment on many manifestations of inequality under the ancien régime, including the divisive prestige of wealth, rank, and family origins and the unfair division of labor between the idle gentry and the hard-working commoners. The archaic system of French law (written "in a foreign language, made 2,000 years ago") comes under particular attack as a symbol of French disregard for natural truths and authentic values (60). Exposing the legally sanctioned power imbalance between the sexes, the narrator charges that boys are allowed unlimited sexual freedom under the law, while girls are dishonored and even sentenced to death for satisfying their natural impulses (and hiding the results through infanticide or abortion). He exhorts the French reader to end such injustices: "Spare her the shame, and I assure you the crime will disappear. Simplify your laws."[46]

In his most provocative inversion of primitive and civilized perspectives, La Dixmerie's narrator indicts women's lack of rights under French law. Inspired by the inclusive Tahitian model, he calls on the French to offer women the same privileges as other citizens, and to open the public sphere of professional activity to them: "[Your laws] seem to rob them of their civil status. I do not see . . . any profession available to women. Eh! Why forbid them? There are some occupations that they would perform better than you."[47] Directly attacking the source of male dominance under the ancien régime, La Dixmerie's savage argues that women may not only be as good as men, they may be better. Those who are already accomplished thinkers and writers should be allowed entrance into the Académie française; others could easily be trained to practice medicine—and may well prove more adept at it than men (83–85).

Yet for all his incendiary rhetoric, La Dixmerie's polemic stops short of revolutionary praxis to remain in the safe, albeit ideologically charged realm of fiction. Although the Tahitian speaker denounces class divisions as "barbarian" and reveals the miserable existence of the French peasant, he does not demand a restructuring of ancien régime society. Instead he merely asks the upper classes to recognize the peasants' essential contribution to society and to sympathize with their plight: "That family . . . devoted to the hardest jobs, does not expect any relief from you. They merit your gratitude, and can barely avoid your contempt."[48] The feudal system of nobleman and peasant is not wrong in itself, this passage suggests, a simple "Thank you" will suffice to improve the peasant's life. This timid conclusion to an otherwise fiery critique recalls the limp ending of Diderot's *Supplément au Voyage de Bougainville* (written 1772, pub. 1796), where B. winds up his long complaint about French customs with an admission of impotence: "We will speak out against unreasonable laws until they are reformed . . . meanwhile we will obey them."[49]

It seems even the most innovative *homme de lettres* respected certain limits in social criticism. While their writings might expose sensitive political and social issues of Louis XV's and Louis XVI's reigns, they did not extend to a subversion of the established order in its entirety, but rather targeted discrete items for reform. Similarly, the readers' response to this polemic, *engagé* literature was largely one of benign tolerance. Paradoxical as it may seem, the inflammatory, "philosophical" rhetoric of late eighteenth-century fiction was very popular among aristocratic and wealthy bourgeois readers. This is because the readers, all the while championing the cause of their favorite *philosophes,* were convinced in their heart of hearts that this literature could never actually affect their elite status or inherited privileges, nor provoke any substantive change in the social order. As the comte de Ségur, a witness to this age, testifies:

Although it was our rank, our privileges that they were mining under our feet, we liked that little war; we did not feel its attacks, we only saw the spectacle. It was but a combat of pens and words, [it] did not seem to do any damage to the superiority we enjoyed and which a precedent of several centuries made us feel was unshakable.[50]

When it came to the "woman question," contemporary readers proved even less amenable to change. Just as the daring call for women's suffrage in Condorcet's *Lettres d'un bourgeois de New-Haven* (1788) fell on deaf ears, the appeal for women's full participation in the professions in La Dixmerie's text did not significantly affect the mentality of his day.[51] Such claims appeared too incongruous to the majority of readers, who considered women as sexual and reproductive beings above all, worthy of protection and even deification in the domestic sphere, but wholly unsuited to functions in the public realm. While they enjoyed reading and tossing about such reformist notions in coffeehouses and salons, few readers considered them practicable, given the seemingly inalterable structure of ancien régime society.

At the end of the *Sauvage de Taïti aux Français,* the Tahitian leaves France for his native isle and vows to devote the rest of his life to protecting Tahiti from pernicious European influences. As king and primary lawmaker of the Tahitian people, he sees himself single-handedly saving the country from destruction. This image of the lawmaker's power to reform society echoes the *Encyclopédie* entry for "Législateur" and Rousseau's ideal lawmaker in the *Contrat social;* as he declares: "I said while shedding my chains, let us be free and go govern a people which must remain free. They are not numerous, but they are faithful. My people respect me and I love them. What I demand is always in their best interest, and what they desire is always what I can allow."[52] Tahiti remains the faraway ideal, the *monde à l'envers* or upside-down world that embodies all that is lacking in France—compassion, love, justice, freedom and wise government. While acknowledging that the Tahitian utopia resides on a delicate equilibrium, La Dixmerie affirms that it can be maintained indefinitely under the guidance of a wise ruler.

The amusing "envoi" to Rousseau, the "philosopher friend of the savages," which follows La Dixmerie's novel reinforces this sanguine attitude. After gently ridiculing Rousseau's demand (in the *Discours sur l'inégalité*) that man return to a semi-bestial natural state, living naked and exposed to the elements, the Tahitian invites the philosopher to join him on his island. Although he will not find an unadulterated state of nature there, the savage admits, he will find a society under the care of a benevolent leader, united in its desire for peace and freedom from external influences: "Come and see us when your stay in the forests becomes tiresome. . . . You can live in a cave, but leave us our huts. You can go naked; but allow us to dress lightly. . . . you will be free; but allow our chiefs to protect your freedom."[53]

This optimistic vision of the Tahitians' future political autonomy from Europe bespeaks a pointedly anti-colonial message when one recalls the historical context of La Dixmerie's text, that is, the official expansionist initiatives represented by Bougainville and sponsored by King Louis XV and his minister, the duc de Choiseul. In fact, La Dixmerie's narrator openly denounces French colonial ambitions at one point, exclaiming: "Eh! you dare to call yourselves a humane people, a people made to civilize others? How cruel you are!"[54] After seeing the shortcomings of the ancien régime system revealed against the idyllic picture of Tahitian freedom and unity, the reader leaves La Dixmerie's fiction hoping that Tahiti might somehow avoid French domination.

It seems the Tahitian who actually visited France in 1769–70 incited an analogous effect on the French public. Instead of creating enthusiasm for the official projects of French commerce and settlement in Tahiti, Aotourou's naïveté and crude manners inspired nostalgia for the unspoiled simplicity of his world. The description of Tahiti in Bougainville's *Voyage* also had a tremendous effect on the growing anti-colonial sentiment of 1770–1780. But this message was not exactly what Bougainville, who saw himself as the first French governor of Tahiti, had in mind. Historian Jean-Paul Faivre contends that Bougainville's writings worked directly against his political goals:

> Bougainville brought to a surprised Europe the revelation of Tahiti which, renewing the old myth of the Good Savage, stirred up a philosophical and anti-colonial hornet's nest. Of all his appeals, the appeal to colonization was thus the least regarded.[55]

Monbart draws on this emotional appeal of Tahiti for French readers, but her prognosis for Tahitian society in the *Lettres taïtiennes* is radically different from that of the other Tahitian texts. Unlike the joyous natives of Commerson's and Bougainville's travel accounts and the ideal natural creatures of La Dixmerie's novel, the Tahitians of Monbart's fiction inhabit a fallen land. By the end of the *Lettres taïtiennes*, the Tahitian utopia is no longer intact. Evil outside influences have ruined its natural equilibrium, bringing corruption and death in their wake.

In the Margins: The Demystification of Tahiti, 1770–84

The pessimistic message of Monbart's novel may have been inspired by the discoveries of later eighteenth-century expeditions to the Pacific. In the 1770s and 1780s French and English readers were inundated by a flood of writings on Tahiti and Oceania which revealed several distressing truths about the islands. The claims of Tahitian pacifism and sensitivity put forth by Commerson and La Dixmerie were refuted by evidence of bloody intertribal warfare, infanticide and human sacrifices.[56] The popular male fantasy of Tahitian women as welcoming maidens who gladly offered their bodies to European mariners gave way to a more disheartening image of sexual coercion among the islanders, with lower-class Tahitian girls exchanged for nails.[57]

Tahiti nevertheless retained its exemplary status in the European imagination. In spite of their flaws, the Tahitians were more appealing than the other inhabitants of Oceania, who had acquired a notorious reputation as dangerous and bellicose peoples. Tales of treachery at the hands of the Samoans and carnage among the cannibals of New Zealand put many a reader's hair on end, especially after a crowd of furious Hawaiians murdered England's beloved Captain Cook in 1779. Attacks on European ships and sailors multiplied in the 1780s, leading to the surmise that these acts of aggression expressed the natives' desire to avenge the misdeeds of previous European visitors.[58]

Philosophers had long warned that the delicate equilibriums of primitive societies could be disrupted, even destroyed by contact with Europeans. The venereal disease that was ravaging the youth of Tahiti was a prime subject for such debate. The English blamed the French and the French blamed the English for introducing this dread disease to the isolated islanders, but it was clear to both that the Tahitians' syphilis was of European origin.[59] In his *Journal* (1772–75), Captain Cook expresses shame over the corrupting influence of European penetration into these lands:

> such are the consequence of a commerce with Europeans and what is still more to our shame civilized Christians, we debauch their morals already too prone to vice and we interduce among them wants and perhaps diseases

which they never before knew and which serves only to disturb that happy tranquillity they and their forefathers had injoy'd [*sic*].[60]

Diderot's *Supplément au Voyage de Bougainville* shifts all the blame for the Tahitians' vices to Europe and suggests that their thievery and prostitution were caused by the presence of foreigners in their midst. As Diderot argues in the first version (1771) of the *Supplément:* "Hardly had you shown yourselves among them that they became thieves; hardly had you entered their land that it was tainted with blood."[61] By 1784 Tahiti had become the locus of much political and moral debate, symbol of a delicate natural state in danger.

Lettres taïtiennes: A Woman's View of Tahiti

In the *Lettres taïtiennes* Monbart builds upon many of these concerns, including the feeling of witnessing a pivotal, tragic moment in Tahitian history caused by European intrusion on the island. Her nostalgia for the lost, idyllic world of Tahitian unity comes out in the background description of the island as well as in the narrative of the Tahitian lovers' separation and fall from grace. Gone is the lofty, distanced perspective of La Dixmerie's philosophical observer, speaking in retrospect. These Tahitians live in the present of the sentimental epistolary style popularized by Richardson, Graffigny and Rousseau; they compose their thoughts in the midst of their tumultuous lives. Moreover the "Avertissement" warns us that Monbart's hero "is not a REASONABLE BEING [n'est point un ETRE DE RAISON]": he is a creature of passions and emotions, subject to the same foibles as all men—and then some.[62] Underlining the tragic youth and naïveté of her protagonists, Monbart calls them "two simple young people, who have never had any other master than nature."[63]

But what a remarkable master that is! A *locus amoenus* of unparalleled tenderness, the Tahitian natural environment described in Monbart's "Introduction" incarnates the sensuality for which its people were famous. Nature is personified as a loving and gentle force that protects the Tahitians from harsh external elements: "Trees of all kinds, covered by a multitude of birds, softly bend their entwined branches to embrace [the Tahitians'] cheerful huts, which they hide from view and shelter from the sun's rays."[64] Monbart's use of terms often associated with lovemaking—entwined ("enlacées"), embrace ("embrasser"), hide from view ("dérobent à la vue")—heightens the voluptuous resonance of this description.

The same clemency that characterizes the Tahitian climate governs their social organization as well. With no laws but the code of nature, these people live in perfect harmony, untroubled by prejudices. Like the idealized savage societies described by early explorers to America, Monbart's Tahiti conjures up the image of a beautiful body without divisions, unsplit by trade, partitions or hierarchy.[65] The two scandalous aspects of Tahitian culture, polygamy and human sacrifice, are reinterpreted so as to stress their role in assuring the unity of this order. The Tahitians' polygamous relationships are thus represented as bonds that knit the social fabric together in an extended pattern of conjugal fidelity. Their practice of sacrificing evildoers to the gods is seen as a means of ridding the populace of unworthy elements, a service to the state (1:ix).

Against this idyllic setting, Monbart presents her story of loss. Using the epistolary form, the author depicts the European corruption of Tahiti from two points of view: the hero Zeïr chronicles his moral degradation while visiting Paris, and the heroine Zulica reports the sexual and political destruction of Tahiti by French and English sailors visiting the island.

The hero's story follows two familiar trajectories: in volume 1, he represents the primitive spy who criticizes French customs in comparison with his culture's superior, "natural" practices; in volume 2, he plays the role of the natural man who assimilates into civilized society and suffers its baneful influences. Monbart's project of cultural critique in volume 1 mirrors La Dixmerie's in many respects. But while La Dixmerie took great pains to prove his narrator's authority as an unlearned yet wise observer, Monbart's Tahitian hero claims no such authority. He speaks the plain, unadulterated language of the heart; ignorant and unsophisticated, he blunders first and then philosophizes. Both critics address such weighty issues as morality, justice and religion, but their approaches—like their personae—are very different.

Monbart's critique of the contradictory demands made on women's sexuality in France is a perfect case in point. Upon first arriving in France, the Tahitian Zeïr is taken in by the St. Val family and soon falls under the charms of their young daughter Julie. Their meetings are characterized by the conflict between his lusty advances and her coquettish yet prudish refusals. After many a frustrating scene, their relationship explodes when Zeïr tries to force himself on her and Julie, bursting into tears, resolves to join a convent. The Tahitian then realizes the double standard that governs male-female relationships in France. Since he cannot possibly marry Julie, she cannot love him for fear of dishonor. The confinement of convent life, as she sees it, is the sole solution to keep her wayward passions at bay. Zeïr concludes that she is but one of many victims of a misguided education and an unjust moral code that punishes women for loving, or as he puts it: "the farther one goes from nature, the more one is lost, that is the product of the severe lessons that one gave to Julie and the extravagant novels that one let her read."⁶⁶ La Dixmerie presented his critique of this issue in a direct attack on the French legal system; Monbart arrives at a similar conclusion but in a much more novelistic (*romanesque*) manner.

While the hero's letters criticize French custom according to the "primitive" values exemplified by La Dixmerie's novel and the travel accounts of Bougainville and Commerson, the heroine's story marks a departure from primitivist conventions. By representing her Tahitian heroine as an articulate writer and active participant in the plot, Monbart debunks the European myth of Tahiti's sexual utopia from a woman's point of view. Along with her significant subtitle (*Suite aux Lettres péruviennes*, "Sequel to the Peruvian Letters"), Monbart's rendition of the Tahitian woman's coming-to-writing reveals her debt to the female tradition in French fiction. Underscoring the importance of female authorhood, the novel opens with the heroine exclaiming: "Blessed be the honest Frenchman, my dear Zeïr, who taught me the art of fixing my thoughts and of communicating the movements of my soul to you."⁶⁷ Like other famous letter-writers of the female tradition—Héloïse (lover of Abélard), Mariane (fictional author of the *Lettres portugaises*), and Graffigny's heroine Zilia—Zulica is initially drawn to writing through loneliness, because she is separated from her lover. And like her predecessors, the Tahitian's early letters to her beloved are characterized by an "aesthetic of disorder," marked by insistent questions, exclamations and dreamy digressions on her changing states of mind and growing sexual frustration.⁶⁸

With the passage of time, however, Monbart's heroine comes to perceive her writing in a different light and uses it for other purposes. In letter 14 Zulica responds to Zeïr not only as a heartsick lover but also as a thoughtful moralist, articulately explaining the reasons behind her skepticism on French cultural superiority. The woman's powers of self-expression are emphasized in letter 19, where Zeïr reports his French friend's impressed reaction to Zulica's letters: "[St. Val] was surprised that a Tahitian could express herself so easily in a foreign language . . . he seemed even more amazed by the clarity and soundness of the ideas."⁶⁹ This affirmation of female intelligence reflects the author's concern for women's education. (Like many women novelists, Monbart also wrote pedagogical tracts: *Sophie, ou de l'éducation des filles*, 1777, and *De l'éducation d'une princesse*, 1781.) The heroine's writing has the same symbolic value in the *Lettres taïtiennes* that it had in the *Lettres d'une Péruvienne,* signaling the woman's ascendancy to the status of writer, with the intellect and self-determination necessary to control her destiny.

The heroine's identity as a member of primitive Tahitian culture makes her coming-to-writing particularly significant. By recording the (albeit imaginary) "native script" of a hitherto unrepresented group, Monbart can expose the real story behind traditional European myths of Tahiti and make a lasting testament to the Europeans' devastation of the island culture. This shift from orality to writing marks another link with Monbart's predecessor Graffigny; both authors set their fictions of coming-to-writing in preliterate societies that had been or would soon be destroyed. The creation of a written history seems predicated by the end of the primitive's Golden Age. Just as "Adam did not begin to think historically, in terms of the past, until he had been driven out of Paradise,"[70] the primitive heroines of the *Lettres d'une Péruvienne* and the *Lettres taïtiennes* do not begin recording their memories and experiences until they are either driven from their homes or threatened by imminent invasion. Perhaps history, the desire to fix events in a text, can only come into being when there is a past to lament and idealize.

The *Lettres taïtiennes* is a "heroinical" text, to use Ellen Moers's term, a Tahitian story told from a woman's particular point of view.[71] While echoing many Tahitian topoi found in voyage literature, Monbart nevertheless uses the island locale differently than did her male predecessors. Her changes are particularly geared toward challenging dominant, masculinist assumptions on Tahitian sexuality. Unlike La Dixmerie, who portrays Tahitian polygamy solely from a male perspective—as a system in which women give themselves to men—Monbart stresses the advantages for women of a society that encourages polyandry as well as polygyny. Hence a footnote affirms: "The plurality of men and women is alike permitted on Tahiti," and the heroine's first letter portrays Zeïr's ex-lovers easily finding solace in other men's arms after his departure: "My companions also regret your absence, but they can still find pleasure; they miss you, but they are still happy."[72]

Virtually all the male authors we have examined depict Tahitian women giving themselves joyously and indiscriminately to European mariners. Monbart demystifies this myth of unlimited sexual circulation. Recounting her horrendous experiences with French sailors on the isle, the Tahitian heroine complains of their interference in Tahitian life: "Why did these strangers land on our island? Why did we let them participate in our pleasures? Cruel men! . . . they have sown discord in these peaceful lands."[73] Furthermore, she informs the reader that the Tahitian women's intercourse with foreigners forms part of a ritual ceremony of welcome, it is only a one-time privilege. The Frenchmen's continued demand for sex thus constitutes a flagrant, criminal abuse of Tahitian hospitality: "these proud and jealous strangers, forgetting the sacred rights of humanity, dared to violate the asylum which we had accorded them."[74]

This state of sexual and cultural antagonism takes a turn for the worse when the English arrive on the island. In a gesture reminiscent of the age-old animosity between the British and the French, the French author Monbart depicts the English sailors wreaking permanent, irreversible damage on the island culture. The French sailors may be brutes, but the English are worse because they undermine the very foundations of Tahitian unity. Thanks to her language skills, Zulica spends much time translating for the English ship's captain; soon he demands that she be his lover too. And this is where Monbart makes her greatest departure from conventional (masculinist) conceptions of Tahiti. Projecting a European battle between the sexes onto the Tahitian locale, Monbart rewrites the traditional topos of Tahitian accessibility—which serves male interests— as an attempt against the Tahitian woman's body/land. Zulica is a far cry from the wanton sex object of legend; indeed she struggles forcefully against that stereotype when the Englishman demands her favors: "their chief . . . has tried to force me to give myself to him on the authority of Tahitian custom. My tears, my repugnance . . . my continual and humiliating refusal, nothing can thwart his mad passion."[75] Monbart inverts the Tahitian utopia: the much vaunted sexual freedom of the Tahitian woman becomes an offensive weapon in the hands of an uninvited, European seducer.

The crisis in Zulica's plot pivots on her control over her sexuality and as such reminds one of other eighteenth-century heroines' tales of "virtue in distress" (such as those of Pamela, Clarissa and Marianne). But while the sexual struggles in *Pamela* and *La Vie de Marianne* are grounded in class struggles between a lower-class heroine and a nobleman, the dilemma of the *Lettres taïtiennes* is based on a clash of cultures, or rather of cultural stereotypes. As we have seen, European travelers' accounts touted the open sexuality of Tahiti and portrayed Tahitian women as sensuous creatures who gladly offer their favors to the first comer. Zulica's refusal to have sex with the Englishman does not make sense, according to this received knowledge. By shifting the perspective on Tahiti from that of a male

European observer to that of a native woman (as seen by a French woman), the author makes us see that the traditional myth of the lascivious Tahitian is actually a European male fantasy of control and dominance that doubly oppresses the heroine.

Monbart's focus on the experiential reality of cultural conflict allows her to show the results of European vices that La Dixmerie referred to in theory only. Thus while the narrator of the *Sauvage de Taïti aux Français* speaks hypothetically about wealth and commerce as disruptive social forces, Zulica's experience dramatizes the power of the Europeans' capitalist currency to disrupt the primitive barter economy of the Tahitians. For when the Englishman gives up trying to cajole the heroine into submission, he resorts to commercial tactics and offers gold in exchange for her body: "he bought my freedom with his dangerous treasures and my cowardly compatriots, seduced by false goods, congratulate themselves for their treason."[76] In allowing the European to purchase one of their women, the islanders symbolically surrender to foreign domination. This commercial exchange heralds the establishment of a new morality, symbolized by the European's economics. Zulica represents what Peter Brooks has called "the precious but primitive 'found' resource, belonging to an economy of abundance, enjoyment and waste."[77] Her prostitution to the Englishman signals her new value as a commodity belonging to an economy of scarcity and repression. Sounding an ominous presage for the future of Tahiti, Zulica complains: "I have no more friends, no more relatives, no country, in a word I no longer own myself."[78]

The heroine's rape and enslavement announce an attempt upon the Tahitian social order. By coercing one of their women into prostitution against her will, the islanders pervert the very principles upon which their society rests, that is, mutual trust and reciprocal responsibility. The ease with which the Englishman convinces the (presumedly male) Tahitian leaders to sell out casts a pall on this supposedly ideal system and projects a pessimistic message on women's social participation in general. If a woman cannot retain her autonomy even under this paragon of natural justice, if she cannot enjoy the privileges of equality even under this egalitarian government, what hope can a French woman have for improving her lot under the recognizably unjust, hierarchical ancien régime? The conflicts involved in the European's attempt to "civilize" the Tahitian savage as his lover thus suggest analogous problems in the process of "citizenizing" the female subject in the French (or Tahitian) state. For all the Tahitians' rhetoric of value consensus and respect for women, they treat

Zulica much the same as Europeans treat their women—as an object to be exchanged among men.

This stunning scene concludes with a warning. The heroine informs her lover that the society they once loved is now corrupt beyond repair, he can never go home again: "Don't ever come back to this unfortunate island, all the vices of the Europeans have entered here with them, sincerity and generosity have been banned; debauchery has taken the place of love, and our angry gods have taken away our pleasures."[79] In violating the sexual body of the Tahitian woman, the Englishman also violated the political body of the Tahitian state, marking the end of its utopian distance from the real world. No longer a pristine paradise of social harmony, Tahiti is now divided, polluted; the Europeans' contact has disrupted the delicate equilibrium of the political order and transformed the natives' unique morality into an unabashed justification for prostitution.

This letter marks the turning point in Monbart's fiction and underlines the Tahitians' estrangement from their native land. With the heroine abducted from the island and transported to England, the scene shifts permanently to Europe where Zeïr, the "natural man," has meanwhile become increasingly unnatural ("dénaturé"). Whereas he previously defended Tahitian culture against European attacks, he now endeavors only to conform to French custom. His early letters recounted his frustration with the seemingly contradictory rules of French propriety, religion and gender relations. Once he realizes the superficial nature of French morality, he becomes quite adept at playing the social game. Hence his later letters depict his triumphs in the elite world of Parisian aristocracy, especially among its female members. Volume 1 closes with an image of Zeïr entering a haughty noblewoman's bedroom, where he finally discovers how to use his "Tahitian" qualities (i.e., his lusty sexual appetites) to advantage: "Docile to the movements of my heart, I dared in that instant to be Tahitian, and the duchess did not seem to take offense."[80]

Zeïr's letters in volume 2 trace his increasingly vicious, "Frenchified" conduct. Recounting the great pleasure he takes in deceiving his wealthy mistresses, the hero proudly declares his progress in acculturation: "All my friends say that I have made marvelous progress in that *Wickedness* which is so fashionable in Paris," and asks his correspondent: "Well, St. Val, do you recognize a compatriot, have I finally understood the national character?"[81]

The footnotes that supplemented the text of volume 1 with translations of Tahitian terms and details of Tahitian customs now assume a different role. As if to underscore her work's pedagogical utility to the French reader, Monbart intervenes with ironic asides on the "Frenchness" of the hero's dissolute behavior. In letter 1, for example, where Zeïr recounts deceiving a duchess with his artful lies, the author notes: "It seems to me that the Tahitian is already quite French [Il me semble que le Taïtien est déjà bien François]" (2:3). In the middle of Zeïr's explanation of his new "French" understanding of love (as an acquired taste, more important to pleasure than happiness), the author comments with a cynical maxim on his citified mores: "When love dies, the heart becomes corrupt; that is why there is so little real passion in big cities."[82] The original thematic opposition between the Tahitian and the French gives way to a new model, more relevant to the French reader: country dweller versus city dweller, more specifically, provincial peasant versus Parisian aristocrat. While upholding the primitivist belief that moral goodness increases with distance from the known world, Monbart relocates the novel's cultural conflict to sites within the French nation and thus demonstrates the local significance of her message.

The parallel between provincial, peasant rusticity and Tahitian simplicity was already drawn in volume 1, when the Tahitian hero described his friend St. Val's estate in the Midi as a pastoral idyll à la Tahitienne, complete with a warm, fertile environment and lively, joyous natives whose songs and dances recall the "loveable ingenuity of our good Tahitians [l'aimable ingenuité de nos bons Taïtiens]" (1:103). St. Val's feudal governance likewise recalls the benevolent leadership of the Tahitian patriarch/king; his fief is characterized as a cheerful country in which the master's kindness makes the peasants into "happy children" who willingly cultivate the lands of their "good father" (2:91). Monbart underlines the conflict between the immorality of the Parisian city dweller and the goodness of the provincial peasant by juxtaposing Zeïr's accounts of his scurrilous intrigues among the Parisian aristocracy with St. Val's letters on the simple pleasures of living among the contented peasants of Southern France. Like the voice of Zeïr's conscience, St. Val warns his friend to beware the dangerous charms of Parisian women and the vain promises of his acquaintances at court, and urges him to return to the country before it is too late.

When Zulica finally gains access to writing again, we learn that she has arrived in London and, with much resistance, has successfully refused to assimilate to that barbaric land: "The country of my tyrant, his language, I hold it all in horror [La patrie de mon tiran, sa langue, tout m'est en horreur]" (2:18). Like the committed Francophile that she is, Monbart glosses over the past cruelty of the French toward the Tahitian woman and her compatriots and presents her heroine's journey to France as the key to the lovers' future happiness. What follows is a highly implausible series of events that highlight the heroine's singularly plucky character, intelligence and determination. She escapes from her English master, crosses the Channel, and hides in a convent near Zeïr's lodgings until he passes by, when she drops him a letter expressing her eternal love. After a period of soul-searching, Zeïr's love for her blooms anew. The heroine's forceful intervention in his life saves him from his rapid descent into that den of iniquity that is Parisian high society and, on a textual level, puts into gear the mechanism of closure.

The conflict between European and Tahitian in this novel serves the ideological purpose of proving the superiority of the primitive over the civilized, but it also serves the purely literary ends of romance. The Europeans' unexpected arrival on the island sets in motion a romance plot that posits Tahiti as a happy beginning but unattainable end. As the novel opens, French sailors have convinced the hero to come away with them, thus separating the lovers. In the middle of the story the English ship's captain ravishes the Tahitian heroine and takes her off to England, thus commencing her romance quest. For the rest of the novel, the heroine endures many hardships and fights many obstacles before finally finding her lover in France. At the novel's end, the Tahitian lovers are reunited and the romance cycle has come full circle, or at least almost full circle, for they are reunited in *exile*.

The Tahitians' exile on French territory marks Monbart's appropriation of the exotic native voice as an instrument in a French national script. Their original utopia extinct, the Tahitians find another world of communal harmony and natural bounty among the peasants of the Midi. Their retreat to the French countryside represents the path to social unity and personal redemption; it is there that Zeïr hopes to rediscover the "happy calm" and "pure joy" that he once knew in Tahiti (2:137–38). By describing the French peasants as happy, simple folk who preserve the customs and mores of an earlier, better age, Monbart (herself a member of the aristocracy) smoothes over the political injustice and social abuses associated with the feudal system. Like Rousseau's glorified image of the peasantry in *La Nouvelle Héloïse,* Monbart conveniently avoids the issues of manual labor or poverty to stress the friendly cooperation, sincerity and naïve goodness of the peasantry. This idealization of the rural low class as the so-called savages of Europe communicates a politically conservative message. In stressing the contentment and superior morality of the poor, the author implies that the power structure that maintains the feudal system of land (and people) management is a just and good order—on the condition, of course, that the noble master play the role of an enlightened, benevolent patriarch/protector to his subjects.

In its fictional relocation of a Tahitian idyll to the fields of Languedoc and the concomitant idealization of the peasant as *bon sauvage,* Monbart's novel gives credence to Gilbert Chinard's contention that European travel writings could be used to confirm and justify ancien régime social institutions.[83] But the scathing portrait of French barbarity on Tahiti in the *Lettres taïtiennes* reveals her moral challenge to official projects of colonization in the South Seas. When La Dixmerie used the Tahitian myth as a vehicle for cultural criticism, he attempted to resolve the French threat to the island. But his solution of making a native hero into a wise lawmaker who will return to protect his people from foreign contact begs the question of the inevitability of corruption; he merely puts it off to some unforeseen future. Monbart's novel constructs a more comprehensive metaphor of conquest than do any of her male precursors. Directly addressing the evils of European expansion into primitive countries, she shows the firsthand results of cultural exploitation and demystifies the notion of a Tahitian sexual utopia by portraying Europeans raping the island women. Although Monbart's strong-minded heroine manages to cross oceans and travel hundreds of miles to be reunited with her lover, even she cannot stop the Europeans from destroying the island home to which none of them may return.

Contemporary ideological debates visibly color both La Dixmerie's and Monbart's visions of the Tahitian Other. Yet in spite of the increasingly precise and scientific documentation of Tahitian plants, geography and wildlife which was available in the 1770s and 1780s, the physical detail of their settings is minimal. Both authors make perfunctory praise of the breadfruit tree and wax poetic on nature's bounty, but their descriptions of the Tahitian environment are more suggestive than scientific. The French public had to wait for Bernardin de Saint-Pierre or Chateaubriand before writers became aware of the possibilities of integrating natural detail with fictional narratives.

However, the limited exotic detail of the *Sauvage de Taïti aux Français* and the *Lettres taïtiennes* is relevant here in that it reflects the mode of writing the foreign that held sway in the late eighteenth century. French writers incorporated exotic locales and native Others in their writings mainly to advance their own French national scripts. This function of exoticism is graphically evident in Abbé Raynal's best-selling *Histoire philosophique et politique des établissemens et du commerce des Européens dans les deux Indes* (1770). Raynal's compendium of colonial history covers a wide variety of peoples and places, but the reader finds very little material detail to distinguish one exotic locale from another. The author appears less interested in the natural settings of foreign societies than in the moral attributes they incarnate; he uses his exotic subjects primarily as ammunition to prove his ideological arguments. Raynal illustrates this strategy in an early article on Greenland: "I am delighted to know that there is a people like the Greenlanders, who, with no notion of Divinity, no moral principles, no laws nor government, are gentle, sociable, humane, and live in perfect equality and union."[84] The Greenlanders are worthy of interest because they provide living proof of Raynal's contention that atheism is not incompatible with virtue. But the author's interest in these people is limited, as he remarks: "I am not eager to learn that these Greenlanders wear no shirts, have bad smelling breath and do not wash the plates on which they eat."[85]

The illustrations from Raynal's *Histoire philosophique et politique* demonstrate the polemical nature of late eighteenth-century exoticism. The first image evokes the positive presence of European settlers in America, showing one Quaker (dressed in a long, ample robe, flat-rimmed hat and sturdy shoes) embracing a family of half-naked, barefoot savages while his cohort throws the Indians' bows and arrows onto a pile of discarded weapons (ed. 1776, Figure 16). Behind them one sees a busy port filled with European sailing ships; a good-sized settlement of European-style houses and buildings circles the bay and spreads onto the hill above. A lonely palm tree on the edge of the community marks the sole indication of the American locale. The Indians look out of place in this bustling scene of colonial prosperity: an iconographical hint of their necessary conversion to European mores.

The second picture, "Charity of a Savage Family of Canada Toward the French [Bienfaisance d'une famille sauvage du Canada envers des Français]," represents the disastrous results of French attempts to colonize Canada (ed. 1781, Figure 17). Here, an Indian woman dressed in a buckskin tunic and boots and flanked by a clinging toddler, a dog and a female companion, reaches out her muscular arms in a gesture of friendship to a

Figure 16. Frontispiece of Raynal, *Histoire philosophique et politique des établissemens et du commerce des Européens dans les deux Indes,* vol. 7 (La Haye: Gosse fils, 1776). Courtesy of the Rare Book Collection, Princeton University Library.

Figure 17. "Charity of a Savage Family of Canada Toward the French [Bien-
faisance d'une famille sauvage du Canada envers des Français]." Frontispiece
of Raynal, *Histoire philosophique et politique des établissemens et du commerce des
Européens dans les deux Indes,* vol. 8 (Geneva: Jean-Léonard Pellet, 1781).
Courtesy of the Princeton University Libraries.

visibly distraught group of Frenchmen. The Europeans' desperation is evident in their beseeching gaze, suppliant pose, and prayerful upheld hands. In contrast to the first image, symbols of Indian culture dominate this scene of European–non-European encounter. A large earthware vase and dish sit in the foreground in front of the woven wall of the Indians' dwelling. In the bay behind the Frenchmen a pirogue is moored at a dock with other Indians aboard watching the spectacle. The message is clear: the Indians' humanitarian aid is the Frenchmen's sole hope for survival in this wilderness.

The powerful symbolism of Raynal's illustrations complements the author's ideological purpose: to appropriate the foreign subjects to the best advantage of his arguments for and against European colonialism in America. (Note that the later edition portrays European settlement in the New World in a much more negative light—an indication of the growing anti-colonial sentiment of the 1780s.) Similarly, for La Dixmerie as for Monbart, it was Tahiti's reputation of sexual equality and social justice, along with its precarious situation vis-à-vis European colonial powers, which inspired the authors to base their fictions on the island locale. The vague image of a tropical paradise lends added interest to these novels, but the itineraries traced by their plots follow essentially moral, political voyages.

Notes

1. "Toute l'île venait à moi comme une femme" (Segalen, *Essai sur l'exotisme,* 61).

2. "C'est dans les isles de cette mer que les voyageurs nous assurent avoir vu des hommes sauvages, des hommes velus, portant des queues; une espèce mitoyenne entre les singes et nous. J'aimerois mieux une heure de conversation avec eux qu'avec le plus bel esprit de l'Europe" (Pierre Louis Moreau de Maupertuis, *Lettre sur le progrès des sciences* in *Oeuvres* [1768; reprint, Hildesheim, RFA: Georg Olms Verlagsbuchhandlung, 1965], 2:382–83).

3. Charles de Brosses, *Histoire des navigations aux terres australes* (1756; reprint, New York: DaCapo Press, "Bibliotheca Australiana #1," 1967), 1:17. De Brosses's pro-colonial writings were undoubtedly supported by his influential family connections: his brother-in-law, the marquis de Crèvecoeur, was one of the biggest investors in the state-sponsored Compagnie des Indes.

4. "[La colonie] s'étendra peu-à-peu dans la contrée au tour de son magasin principal: elle écartera plus loin les sauvages" (de Brosses, *Histoire des navigations,* 1:41).

5. Albert Duchêne, *La Politique coloniale de la France* (Paris: Payot, 1928), 101–2.

6. French hopes faded for Tahiti with the death of Aotourou and the arrival of Captain Cook, who inaugurated the British presence in the South Seas. The first group of British missionaries arrived in 1797 and Tahiti remained under the rule of British evangelization—if not political protection—until 1839. The English government twice denied the Tahitians a protectorate (1825, 1839) before the Tahitian king finally accepted the aid of the French king Louis-Philippe. Tahiti officially became a French protectorate in September 1842 and was annexed to the French crown in 1880.

7. For Rousseau, who saw woman as the appendage of man, this question was indifferent. In the *Discours sur l'inégalité* the woman of nature is portrayed solely in relation to natural man: as the necessary vessel for his sexual urges and the vehicle by which the propagation of the species is assured. See Jean-Jacques Rousseau, *Discours sur l'origine de l'inégalité*, ed. Jacques Roger (Paris: Garnier-Flammarion, 1971), 200.

8. "Chez la plupart des peuples sauvages les filles jouissent d'une liberté entière" (M. Gudin de la Brenellerie, *Aux Manes de Louis XV, et des grands hommes qui ont vécu sous son règne* [Lausanne: n.p., 1777], 408). The question of what constitutes *le droit naturel* is complex; for some the concept implies the fundamental values at the base of all human societies, for others it suggests the law of the wild. For a discussion of this important concept in eighteenth-century thought, consult Paul Hazard, *La Pensée européenne au XVIIIe siècle de Montesquieu à Lessing* (Paris: Boivin et cie, 1946), 1:196–216.

9. "Plus de la moitié du globe est couverte de sauvages; et chez tous ces peuples les femmes sont très-malheureuses. L'homme sauvage, tout à la fois féroce et indolent . . . commande despotiquement à des êtres que la raison fit ses égaux, mais que la foiblesse lui assujettit" (Antoine-Léonard Thomas, *Essai sur le caractère, les moeurs et l'esprit des femmes dans les différens siècles* [Paris: Moutard, 1772], 2–3).

10. "La femme soumise dans les pays policés est dans l'oppression chez les nations sauvages, dans toutes les régions barbares. Tout entier à ses besoins, le sauvage ne s'occupe que de sa sûreté et de sa subsistance" (Denis Diderot, "Sur les femmes," in Diderot, *Oeuvres complètes,* ed. Roger Lewinter [Paris: Le Club français du livre, 1971], 10:46–47).

11. Harris, *The Rise of Anthropological Theory*, 39.

12. "[T]out étranger est admis à participer à ces heureux mystères; c'est même un des devoirs de l'hospitalité que de les y inviter" (Philibert Commerson, "Sur la découverte de la nouvelle Isle de Cythère ou Taïti," *Mercure de France* [November 1769]: 198).

13. C.f., Rousseau's famous contention: "J'ose presque assurer que l'état de réflexion est un état contre nature, et que l'homme qui médite est un animal dépravé" (Rousseau, *Discours sur l'inégalité*, 168).

14. "[C]e droit de propriété est-il dans la nature? Non; il est de pure convention" (Commerson, "Sur la découverte," 204).

15. "Nous avons admiré la simplicité de leurs moeurs, l'honnêteté de leurs

procédés, sur-tout envers leurs femmes qui ne sont nullement subjuguées chez eux comme chez les sauvages" (Commerson, "Sur la découverte," 200).

16. Michèle Duchet, *Anthropologie et histoire au siècle des lumières* (Paris: Librairie François Maspero, 1971), 217.

17. "La jeune fille laissa tomber négligemment une pagne qui la couvrait et parut aux yeux de tous, telle que Vénus se fit voir au berger phrygien" (Louis-Antoine de Bougainville, *Voyage autour du monde par la frégate du Roi "La Boudeuse" et la flûte "L'Etoile,"* ed. Jacques Proust [Paris: Gallimard, 1982], 226).

18. "L'air qu'on respire, les chants, la danse presque toujours accompagnée de postures lascives, tout rappelle à chaque instant les douceurs de l'amour, tout crie de s'y livrer" (Bougainville, *Voyage,* 259).

19. "Législateurs et philosophes, venez voir ici, tout établi, ce que votre imagination n'a pu même rêver. Un peuple nombreux, composé de beaux hommes et de jolies femmes, vivant ensemble dans l'abondance et la santé, avec toutes les marques de la plus grande union, connaissant assez le mien et le tien pour qu'il y ait cette distinction dans les rangs nécessaires au bon ordre, ne le connaissant pas assez pour qu'il y ait des pauvres et des fripons" (Bougainville, *Journal* [unpublished MS.], quoted in Jean-Etienne Martin-Allanic, *Bougainville navigateur et les découvertes de son temps* [Paris: Presses Universitaires de France, 1964], 1:683).

20. Aotourou (also known as Ahutoru, Poutaveri or Boutavéris—Tahitian approximations of "Bougainville") had befriended the French crew from the start, offering his services to the captain of the "Etoile." Bougainville describes his political and linguistic reasons for taking on the islander in his *Voyage,* 244–45; 262–63.

21. Charles de la Roncière, "Le Routier inédit d'un compagnon de Bougainville," *La Géographie* 35, no. 3 (March 1921): 217–50.

22. Patrick O'Reilly and Raoul Teissier, *Tahitiens: Répertoire biographique de la Polynésie française* (Paris: Publications de la Société des Océanistes, 1975), 16.

23. Michael Alexander, *Omai, "Noble Savage"* (London: Collins and Harvill Press, 1977), 92.

24. Aotourou was in Paris for less than a year (April 1769-March 1770). Bougainville sacrificed a third of his personal fortune and Mme la duchesse de Choiseul (wife of the minister of foreign affairs) also donated generously to equip him with a variety of presents (livestock, tools, seeds) before he left for Tahiti on a ship bound for Ile de France. His patrons' dreams were dashed, however, as Aotourou never reached his native isle. He died of smallpox on Ile de la Réunion in 1771.

25. Georges May, *Le Dilemme du roman au XVIIIe siècle* (Paris: Presses Universitaires de France, 1963), 245.

26. Eric Walter details this semantic shift in "Les Auteurs et le champ littéraire," 394–95.

27. Roger Chartier, *The Cultural Uses of Print in Early Modern France,* trans. Lydia G. Cochrane (Princeton, N.J.: Princeton University Press, 1987), 225.

28. Darnton, *The Literary Underground of the Old Regime,* 40.

29. Walter, "Les Auteurs et le champ littéraire," 394.

30. Darnton, *The Literary Underground of the Old Regime,* 22.

31. "Mais je sens que ma main veut s'arrêter; je sens que ma tête s'embarrasse. Qui! moi? oser vous écrire?" (Nicolas Bricaire de La Dixmerie, *Le Sauvage de Taïti aux Français, avec un envoi au philosophe ami des sauvages* [London and Paris: LeJay, 1770], 6). All references to Dixmerie's work refer to this edition.

32. "Il fut un tems où l'on se serait uniquement informé si cette Isle produit beaucoup d'or; il serait possible qu'aujourd'hui cette question n'eût pas même été faite. Je le désire pour l'honneur de la Philosophie. Nous avons encore plus besoin de moeurs que de richesses" (vii–viii).

33. "Je te quitte, ô Peuple affable et dédaigneux . . . Je n'attirai que tes regards; tu fixas mon attention. Tu m'ignores, et je te connais" (3).

34. English Showalter argues that the central difference between novels from the early eighteenth century (1720–1740) and those published late in the century (1770–1780) is this thematic shift from a focus on the individual character's struggle to enter French society to a focus on the repressive laws and institutions of that society. See Showalter, *The Evolution of the French Novel: 1641–1782* (Princeton, N.J.: Princeton University Press, 1972), 262–347.

35. "C'est pour n'avoir point sçu parler que je prends le parti d'écrire. Je n'ai jamais sçu répondre verbalement à une seule de vos questions" (7).

36. "Que ne pouvez-vous entendre la nôtre! Elle ne fatigue point l'attention de ceux qui la parlent; elle flatte l'oreille de ceux qui l'écoutent. Nous passons pour être tous éloquens, et nous lui devons notre éloquence" (6).

37. "Tout cet extérieur n'a pu m'en imposer; il n'a pu tromper les regards d'un homme qui voit par les yeux de la nature" (80).

38. "Quelqu'un dira peut-être: voilà trop d'érudition pour un Sauvage. Comment apprîtes-vous à raisonner?" (61). "Mais un Sauvage qui vous écrit, méritera-t'il d'être lû?" (106).

39. "Voyez nos belles Taïtiennes! Leurs vêtemens légers voltigent au gré des vents. Une gaze industrieuse ne dérobe aux regards que la nudité, et nous laisse appercevoir le nud. Rien ne combat nos désirs, et tout les excite" (46).

40. "On dit que vous n'êtes pas imprenables, et vous vous fortifiez comme si vous vouliez l'être" (46).

41. "Vous marcheriez bien, si vous pouviez marcher. Mais il est du bon ton parmi vous de ne faire presque aucun usage de ses jambes. Vous laissez ce privilège à de petites Bourgeoises qui n'en usent que très-sobrement (47–48).

42. "Nous croyons qu'une belle femme est le plus beau présent que la nature ait fait à l'homme. Nous recevons ce présent avec reconnaissance; nous en usons; mais nous en connaissons toujours le prix" (19).

43. "Nous sommes tous enfans d'une même famille; nous nous traitons en freres" (35).

44. "Tout habitant de notre Isle est un homme à nos yeux. Chaque profession aurait notre estime, s'il était parmi nous des professions" (93).

45. "Je doute qu'il y ait jamais d'Académies à Taïti; en tout cas, je réponds que les femmes n'en seraient point exclues" (84–85).

46. "Epargnez-lui la honte, et je vous garantis du crime. Simplifiez vos loix" (61).

47. "[Vos Loix] semblent vouloir les retrancher de ce que vous nommez l'ordre civil. Je ne vois . . . aucune profession qui ne leur soit interdite. Eh! pourquoi les leur interdire? Il en est dont elles s'acquitteraient mieux que vous" (83).

48. "Cette famille . . . dévouée aux plus durs travaux, n'attend de vous aucun soulagement. Elle a des droits à votre reconnaissance, et ne peut même esquiver vos mépris" (92–93).

49. "Nous parlerons contre les Lois insensées jusqu'à ce qu'on les réforme . . . en attendant nous nous y soumettrons" (Denis Diderot, *Supplément au Voyage de Bougainville,* ed. Gilbert Chinard [Paris: Droz, 1935], 198).

50. "Quoique ce fussent nos rangs, nos privilèges qu'on minait sous nos pas, cette petite guerre nous plaisait; nous n'en éprouvions pas les atteintes, nous n'en avions que le spectacle. Ce n'étaient que combats de plumes et de paroles, qui ne nous paraissaient faire aucun dommage à la supériorité d'existence dont nous jouissions, et qu'une possession de plusieurs siècles nous faisait croire inébranlable" (quoted in Louis Ducros, *La Société française au dix-huitième siècle, d'après les mémoires et les correspondances du temps* [Paris: Librairie A. Hatier, 1922], 363).

51. For more on the ideological context of Condorcet's work and his readers' (lack of) reaction, see Madelyn Gutwirth, "1788: Civil Rights and Wrongs of Women" in *A New History of French Literature,* ed. Denis Hollier (Cambridge, Mass.: Harvard University Press, 1989), 558–66.

52. "J'ai dit en secouant mes chaînes: soyons libre, et allons gouverner un Peuple qui doit se croire libre. Il n'est pas nombreux, mais il est fidèle. Il me respecte et je l'aime. Ce que j'exige est toujours ce qu'il peut desirer de mieux: ce qu'il desire est toujours ce que je puis permettre" (105). The *Encyclopédie* defines the lawmaker's powers thus: "Il n'y a point de climat . . . où le législateur ne puisse établir des moeurs fortes, pures, sublimes, foibles, et barbares" (*Encyclopédie,* 9:358).

53. "Venez nous voir, quand le séjour des forêts vous ennuiera. . . . Vous pourrez habiter un antre; mais laissez-nous nos cabannes. Vous pourrez allez nud; mais souffrez que nous soyons vêtus légérement. . . . vous serez libre; mais trouvez bon que des Chefs protégent votre liberté" (148).

54. "Eh! vous osez vous dire un Peuple humain, un Peuple fait pour en civiliser d'autres? Cruels!" (57).

55. "[Bougainville] apporta à l'Europe étonnée la révélation de Tahiti qui, renouvelant le mythe usé du Bon Sauvage, suscita un branle-bas philosophique et anti-colonialiste. De tous ses appels, l'appel à la colonisation fut donc le moins entendu" (Jean-Paul Faivre, *L'Expansion française dans le Pacifique de 1800 à 1842* [Paris: Nouvelles Editions Latines, 1953], 66).

56. Already in 1771 one of Cook's men denounced the utopian versions of Tahiti publicized by the French: "J'apprends que dans des journaux français on a peint l'île de Tahiti comme le séjour de la paix, de la concorde, du bonheur et de la vertu simple et naturelle: si c'est celle dont je parle, comme il n'y a pas lieu d'en douter, les moeurs de ces insulaires avaient bien dégénéré dans un très court espace de temps" (*Le Journal d'agriculture,* 1771, quoted by Duchet, *Anthropologie et histoire,* 63). For the contributions of Cook, Banks, Forster, et al. to the debate on

Tahiti, consult P.J. Marshall and Glyndwr Williams, *The Great Map of Mankind: British Perceptions of the World in the Age of Enlightenment* (London: J.M. Dent and Sons, Ltd., 1982), 258–98.

57. George Robertson remarked during his 1767 visit that Tahitian men play an active role in pushing the women into prostitution. The male islanders urge the girls to "play a great many wanton tricks" to bring the Englishmen ashore and start the commerce. He also noted the price inflation that quickly followed: "the Young Girls . . . had now rose their price . . . from a twenty to a thirty penny nail, to a forty penny nail, and some was so extravagant as to demand a Seven or nine inch Spick" (quoted in Edward H. Dodd, Jr., *The Rape of Tahiti* [New York: Dodd, Mead and Co., 1983], 60).

58. See Alexander, *Omai*, 58–64, for all the gruesome details of these murders. H. Jacquier details the growing evidence of aggression and French reactions to it in "Le Mirage et l'exotisme tahitiens dans la littérature," *Bulletin de la société des études océaniennes* 7, no. 2 (June 1945): 70–71.

59. The French side of this controversy is presented by Bougainville's surgeon Vivès in Charles de la Roncière, "Le Routier inédit d'un compagnon de Bougainville," 236; and by Bougainville in *Voyage,* 271. The British side is summarized by Hugh Carrington in George Robertson, *The Discovery of Tahiti,* ed. H. Carrington (Cambridge, England: The Hakluyt Society, 1948), 284–87.

60. James Cook, *Journal 1772–1775* (quoted in Marshall and Williams, *The Great Map of Mankind,* 280).

61. "A peine vous êtes-vous montré parmi eux qu'ils sont devenus voleurs; à peine vous êtes-vous descendu dans leur terre qu'elle a été teinte de sang" (Denis Diderot, *Supplément au Voyage de Bougainville* in *Oeuvres complètes,* ed. Jean Assézat [Paris: Garnier frères, 1875], 2:203–4).

62. Marie-Josephine de Lescun de Monbart, *Lettres taïtiennes, suite aux Lettres péruviennes* (Paris: Les Marchands de Nouveautés, n.d.), 1:v. All references to Monbart's work refer to this edition. The *Lettres taïtiennes* was originally published in 1784 (Breslau: Guillaume Théophile Korn), according to *Bibliographie du genre romanesque français 1751–1800,* ed. Angus Martin, Vivienne Mylne and Robert Frautschi (Paris: France Expansion, 1977).

63. "[D]eux jeunes gens simples, qui ne doivent avoir eu d'autre maître que la nature" (1:vi).

64. "Des arbres de toute espèce, couverts d'une multitude d'oiseaux courbent mollement leurs branches enlacées, pour embrasser de riantes cabanes, qu'ils dérobent à la vue et rendent inaccessibles aux raïons du soleil" (1:viii).

65. Michel de Certeau analyzes the symbolism of the body in early voyage literature in *Heterologies: Discourse on the Other,* trans. Brian Massumi (Minneapolis: University of Minnesota Press, 1986), 72–75.

66. "[P]lus l'on s'éloigne de la nature et plus l'on s'égare, voilà le fruit des sévéres leçons que l'on a donné à Julie" (1:67).

67. "Que béni soit à jamais, mon cher Zeïr, l'honnête François qui m'apprit l'art de fixer mes pensées, et de faire passer jusqu'à toi les mouvemens de mon ame" (1:1).

68. Bernard Bray and Isabelle Landy-Houillon discuss the "aesthetic of disorder" as a typically female configuration in their introduction to the *Lettres portugaises* in *Lettres portugaises, Lettres d'une Péruvienne et autres romans d'amour par lettres,* 65–66.

69. "[St. Val] . . . a été étonné qu'une Taïtienne peut s'exprimer aussi facilement dans une langue étrangère . . . il a paru encore plus surpris de la netteté et de la justesse des idées" (1:110–11).

70. Henri Baudet, *Paradise on Earth: Some Thoughts on European Images of Non-European Man,* trans. Elizabeth Wentholt (New Haven, Conn.: Yale University Press, 1965), 58.

71. Ellen Moers, *Literary Women* (New York: Doubleday and Co., 1976), 121–24.

72. "La pluralité des hommes et des femmes est également permise à Taïti," "Mes compagnes pleurent aussi ton absence, mais elles peuvent encore se livrer au plaisir, elles te regrettent, mais elles sont encore heureuses" (1:5).

73. "Pourquoi ces Etrangers aborderent-ils dans notre Isle? Pourquoi les fîmes-nous participer à nos plaisirs? Les cruels! . . . ils ont porté le trouble dans ces paisibles contrées" (1:4).

74. "[C]es fiers et jaloux Etrangers, oubliant les droits sacrés de l'humanité, ont osé violer l'azile que nous leur avions accordé" (1:11–12).

75. "[L]eur chef . . . a voulû s'autoriser des usages de Taïti pour me forcer à me donner à lui: mes larmes, ma repugnance . . . mes continuels et humilians refus, rien n'a pû rebuter sa folle passion" (1:124–25).

76. "[I]l a payé ma liberté d'une partie de ses dangereux trésors et mes lâches compatriotes, séduits par de faux biens, s'applaudissent de leur trahison" (1:127).

77. Peter Brooks, "Gaugin's Tahitian Body," *Yale Journal of Criticism* 3, no. 2 (1990): 58.

78. "Je n'ai plus d'amis, plus de parens, plus de patrie; en un mot je ne m'appartiens plus" (1:126).

79. "Ne reviens plus dans cette île malheureuse, tous les vices des Européens y sont entrés avec eux: la bonne foi, le désinteressement en sont bannis; la debauche a pris la place de l'amour, et nos Dieux irrités en ont retiré les plaisirs" (1:127).

80. "Docile aux mouvemens de mon coeur, j'osai dans cet instant être Taïtien, et la Duchesse ne parut pas s'en offenser" (1:146).

81. "Tous mes amis disent que j'ai fait des progrès merveilleux dans cette *Scéleratesse* si fort de mode à Paris" (2:4). "Eh bien, St. Val, reconnoissez-vous un compatriote, ai-je enfin saisi le caractere national?" (2:7).

82. "Quand l'amour s'éteint, le coeur se corrompt; c'est pour cela qu'il y a si peu de vraie passion dans les grandes villes" (2:4).

83. Chinard, *L'Amérique et le rêve exotique,* 396.

84. "Je suis charmé de savoir qu'il y a un peuple comme les Groënlandais, qui, sans aucune notion de la Divinité, sans principes de morale, sans lois, sans gouvernement, est doux, sociable, humain, vivant dans une égalité et une union parfaite" (Guillaume Raynal, *Nouvelles littéraires* [1754], 2:154; quoted in Anatole

Feugère, *Un Précurseur de la révolution: L'Abbé Raynal (1713–1796)* [1922; reprint, Geneva: Slatkine Reprints, 1970], 101).

85. "[J]e suis peu curieux d'apprendre que ces Groënlandais ne portent pas de chemise, ont l'haleine puante et ne lavent point les plats dans lesquels ils mangent" (Raynal, *Nouvelles littéraires,* quoted in Feugère, *Un Précurseur,* 101–2).

Conclusion

The goal of this study has been to show that relatively canonical male-authored texts, popular novels by women since neglected, and travel writings all imagine the non-European Other in terms of her cultural and sexual difference from French norms. My thematic focus on the preliterate or nonfrancophone outsider goes hand in hand with a historical focus on the forgotten woman writer in that both highlight the unfair distribution of power under the ancien régime and bring up the issue of who may contribute to the French literary or cultural "conversation." Whether identified primarily by their sexuality or cultural background, the heroines of early modern novels must all negotiate their passage through a marginal space on the borders of society to gain membership in the known (French) world. The same journey model applies to women writers trying to find a place in the male-dominated world of literary production. For the novelistic heroine and the woman writer, success is rewarded with the symbolic attributes of social membership: access to speech, writing and the authority to relate one's story to others.

Let us first consider the treatment of cultural difference in ancien régime literature. The novels studied trace an uneven movement toward an increasingly acute depiction of the moral, religious and political differences that divide the world's peoples. Far from being a linear, evolutionary trend, this development nevertheless seems to follow the philosophical shift from the seventeenth-century aesthetic of artistic and social unity to an enlightened stance characterized by greater tolerance for religious differences and political dissent. With its many maxims on female duplicity and male gullibility, Lafayette's novel epitomizes the pessimistic universalist view of human nature that was popularized by the writings of seventeenth-century moralists. The warped perspective of Prévost's fictional memoirs demonstrates the dangers of European ethnocentrism, but without proposing an alternative manner of understanding the oriental Other. Montesquieu claims to serve the cause of enlightened relativistic philosophy in his Persian fiction, although he leaves intact a belief in the universal need for patriarchal control in human societies. While Graffigny tends to blur the distinctions between French and Peruvian by the end of her novel, the foreign heroine nevertheless questions the superiority of French society, protects her autonomy and calls for tolerance of religious and cultural difference. La Dixmerie and Monbart reverse the values of "civilized" and "primitive" completely; in these works the exotic Other is used to demonstrate civilization's dangers, to challenge Eurocentrism and to justify a cultural relativism. But the inconsistency that marks much of eighteenth-century philosophy touches these texts as well, for their polemic relativistic stance privileges the primitive to such an extent that it posits a reversed universalism, and simply replaces one norm with another—the supremacy of European culture with the ideal of primitive nature.

In their portrayal of primitive cultures as viable, morally acceptable social systems and in their condemnation of the European cultural hegemony, the Peruvian and Tahitian fictions foreshadow the development of "expressionist" anthropology in the nineteenth century. This school of thought is exemplified by the work of the German philosopher Johann von Herder, who argued that the role of the anthropologist was to protect non-European peoples from European imperialism and to celebrate the "natural" expression of each ethnic and social group. In his widely read *Ideen zur Philosophie der Geschichte des Menscheit* (*Reflections on the Philosophy of the History of Mankind*, 1784–1791), Herder dismantles the time-honored Eurocentrism of Enlightenment thought by announcing the right of all individuals in all nations—no matter how primitive or backward they may seem to European eyes—to express themselves and to pursue happiness in any way they choose: "It would be the most stupid vanity to imagine, that all the inhabitants of the World must be europeans to live happily [*sic*]." [1]

But the progression I have outlined from seventeenth-century universalism to Herder's late eighteenth-century model of relativism signals the very problem that anthropologists have lately put into question. Instead of resolving the question of relativism and essentialism, Herder creates a new kind of national essentialism, claiming: "Each [nation] bears in itself the standard of its perfection, totally independent of all comparison with that of others" (452). Nations (and individuals) are always already complete and autonomous, he implies, their "purity" should not be contaminated by "outside" influence. While Herder's formula is certainly a helpful way to denounce colonial depredations, the thematic construction of clear insides and outsides upon which it rests is itself the product of a mentality formed by divisive nationalistic boundaries and identities. By valuing nationalistic identities over the notion of a unified human nature, this attitude lays the moral foundations for colonial intervention. If the notion of a degraded Other is a useful support for the first forms of colonization (and commercial exploitation), the notion of simple, better Others is the necessary support for the colonization of tourism. As Stanley Diamond points out, "Relativism is the bad faith of the conqueror, who has become secure enough to become a tourist."[2] Both attitudes make use of the Other in their own rhetorical strategies; and those strategies equally ignore the native voice except as an instrument in their own national scripts.

The non-European characters in the fictions studied here represent some of the different kinds of anthropological "interlocutors" described by Edward Said; their stories are stylized confrontations of Europe and the Other that fill in the gaps in the pre-history of colonialism.[3] Montesquieu's Persian philosophers play the role of the *évolué* or notable Other who is given the extraordinary privilege of becoming Frenchified in return for suppressing his connections with the Orient. La Dixmerie's Tahitian figures as an *évolué* also; after criticizing French society in comparison to his own, he returns to Tahiti as a satellite of European political idealism. The female characters in these fictions all play subaltern roles, though they make enough noise—that is, they challenge the authority of the Western (male) ethnographer/colonist/lover—so as to force the European characters (and readers) to account for their differences.

But these fictions rest on a paradox: claiming to represent the Other, they are written by delegates of French culture. As such they fall prey to a kind of cultural bad faith, plagued by the problems Minnie Bruce Pratt has signaled in literature of Otherness. Given the paucity of actual interaction between the authors and their subjects, the subjectivity of the Other necessarily remains an object of speculation or invention. Given the ontological advantage of writing on/as another person, the European writer holds a privileged position of knowledge over the Other.[4] Some authors, like Prévost and Montesquieu, portray the exotic woman as a degraded commodity, a useful support for French political and colonial ambitions. Others, such as Graffigny and Monbart, play at cultural impersonation and borrow the identity of the Other to enact European dramas of guilt and pain.

Two basic attitudes toward the non-European Other emerge from my readings of fictional and anthropological texts, depending on the exotic locale and ideological intentions of the writer. Narratives of contact with the Turks and Moors of the Orient portray the Other as a cruel and tyrannical barbarian and use this figure to show the evils of irrational, unprogressive (i.e., Muslim) social and political practices. As France was involved in expanding its commercial control over the Levant during the period in question, these fictions were politically instrumental in justifying European intervention in the commerce and politics of the Eastern Mediterranean. When the locale shifts from the Old World to the New, the Other comes across as a glowing symbol of man's innate goodness, an essentially unreal zoo specimen to be preserved for the purposes of European tourism and philosophical speculation. While espousing an anti-colonial agenda, the celebration of difference in these fictions also suggests the authors' reification of the Other as a European possession or spectacle. What emerges in all these texts is a sense of the complex power relations between European observers and non-European Others, whether they be resolved in scenarios of redemption or repression.

The narrative of an Other's entrance into European society, as we have seen, can be used to structure one or another version of national history. As philosopher Dom Deschamps remarked, "The order that we read into the universe is the expression of our own submission to civil laws."[5] The thematic resolution in Lafayette's *Zaïde* of internal political divisions (between a king and his ambitious courtiers) and external military conflicts (between a Christian monarchy and a Muslim despotism) belies the author's dream of a reunited French national community in the difficult years after La Fronde. The tragic encounter between the domineering French ambassador and the elusive oriental woman in *Histoire d'une Grecque moderne* dramatizes the conflicts created by French imperialist initiatives in the Ottoman states. The heroine's futile efforts to assimilate to French custom explode the myth of European moral superiority over the Orient and, by extension, reveal Prévost's skepticism toward the authority of Louis XV's regime. The creation of an exotic "native script" to imagine a better destiny for French women is particularly explicit in the work of Graffigny, as evidenced by the Franco-Peruvian utopia at the end of the *Lettres d'une Péruvienne*.

Men and women authors fictionalize the "woman question" in very different ways. Male-authored fictions tend to portray women as beings conditioned by their sexual or reproductive functions. Prévost and Montesquieu depict the ideal woman as a sexual commodity exchanged among men. In spite of his proto-feminist agenda for French women, La Dixmerie also relies on traditional masculinist fantasies in his image of the Tahitian woman as a gift given to man by nature. Female-authored fictions, on the other hand, tend to perceive women as social beings who struggle against such functionalist notions of women's nature. The heroines invented by Lafayette, Graffigny and Monbart are all seen to oppose the social, religious and parental laws that limit their participation in society to roles prescribed by their biological apparatus or social rank. By structuring my arguments in reading pairs of male- and female-authored texts, I have underlined these thematic variations and suggested the implications that their differential visions of power and social participation might hold for French social history.

The uneven treatment of women's authority and access to voice in these fictions points to the importance of gender in French literary history as well. The practice of reading in pairs has the advantage of demonstrating women's contributions to intellectual and cultural history, but it also raises other questions about their works' reception and place in the literary canon. By reading Lafayette alongside Prévost, Graffigny alongside Montesquieu and Monbart alongside La Dixmerie, I have elevated all these authors to the status of equal participants in French literary history. This may be misleading, however, because despite the popular success of their works during their lifetimes, most of the women writers did not fare half so well as their male partners in the canon as it was formulated and passed down through the years.

The best example of the disparity between the original reception of a female-authored text and its latter-day status in the canon of French literature is Mme de Graffigny's *Lettres d'une Péruvienne*. Translated several times into English and Italian, re-edited thirty times in the thirty years after its first edition of 1747, Graffigny's work was one of the few female-authored best sellers of its time. Although the novel was published continuously up until 1835, it fell into the oblivion of the "no longer read" in the nineteenth century (thanks in part to the dismissive comments of the influential critic Sainte-Beuve).[6] It was not until the novel was re-edited again, in the late 1960s, that readers began rediscovering the *Lettres d'une Péruvienne*. Graffigny's reading "partner" and contemporary, Montesquieu, however, had quite a different future in store. His *Lettres persanes* was an overnight sensation when it first appeared and has since become a veritable icon of eighteenth-century literature, inspiring scores of sequels, translations, critical editions and scholarly studies from the eighteenth century to the present.

Why has Graffigny's best seller been classified as a dead novel, while Montesquieu's work has remained popular until the present day? The answer lies (partly, at least) in the forces that conspired to create a single, unified French canon of national literature. The notion of literary history is an eighteenth-century invention, product of the many compilations, dictionaries and encyclopedias of cultural literacy written for the growing readership of ancien régime society. The anthologies of French literature published in the late seventeenth and the early eighteenth centuries were what Joan DeJean terms "worldly anthologies" designed for the continuing education of an adult public.[7] While their pedagogical qualities vary greatly, these collections are striking in their inclusion of the many female writers of the day. The "worldly anthology," however, was soon superseded by the development of pedagogical anthologies designed for use in French *collèges* and aimed at forming model Frenchmen, that is, "good Christians" "useful to civil society."[8] It is this later model that laid the groundwork for the French canon as we know it today. Women writers were largely omitted from these collections. Those that were included were cited as examples of "dangerous" morals capable of undermining the nation's male fiber or summarily dismissed as "boring" or "no longer read." We know from publishing data that many female-authored works enjoyed great popularity throughout the eighteenth century, but it seems that these texts were "so threatening to the ideology of the developing pedagogical canon," as DeJean argues, "that their elimination had to be reimposed until the new curriculum was firmly established" (37).

As a genre favored by women writers, the novel was believed by many to carry those dangerous, effeminate morals that threatened to infect the virile French spirit. In his "Harangue sur les romans" (1738), Père Porée warns against the novel as a seditious form of writing, harmful to the national virtues of the French republic, for it encourages women to overstep the boundaries of their natural roles in society:

> In civil society what are women? One part of society, but a subordinate part which must receive laws and not make them. . . . Novels upset the order of nature, they make women independent of men, they make them the supreme arbiters of everything, they deify women, how can a woman preserve her modesty in the midst of such honors?[9]

Porée's vision of women's subaltern role in civil society prefigures the Rousseauean model of domestic virtue that was to gain such currency in the late years of the eighteenth century. His remarks on the novel's danger to public morals reinforce DeJean's claim on the eighteenth-century pedagogue/critic's adversarial relationship with the products of female literary creation.

The anthropological strategy of excluding an exotic Other from "civilized" status or absorbing her under the category of token European resides on a similar understanding of power and voice as the critical act of excluding women writers from "citizenship" in the French republic of letters or assimilating them into the category of the "no longer read." In both cases the ultimate decision to accept or deny acceptance seems to be made by an invincible master narrative of French culture. As my comparison of women's and men's writings has shown, however, the master tropes of French social propriety, morality and aesthetic value are not ethical absolutes but products of a particular historical and national context, often informed by specific gender politics. Stories of an outsider's intrusion on the known world reveal the local conflicts and power struggles at stake in the relationships between "us" and "them," be it the political relationship between a European power and a non-European country or the pragmatic relationship between the male literary tradition and the woman writer.

Notes

1. Johann Gottfried von Herder, *Outlines of a Philosophy of the History of Man,* trans. T. Churchill (1800; reprint, New York: Bergman Publishers, 1966), 218.
2. Stanley Diamond, *In Search of the Primitive: A Critique of Civilization* (New Brunswick, N.J.: Transaction Books, 1974), 110.
3. Said, "Representing the Colonized," 209–10.
4. Minnie Bruce Pratt, "Identity: Skin Blood Heart" in Elly Bulkin, Minnie Bruce Pratt and Barbara Smith, *Yours in Struggle: Three Feminist Perspectives on Anti-Semitism and Racism* (Brooklyn, N.Y.: Long Haul Press, 1984), 11–68.
5. Quoted by Lionel Gossman, *French Society and Culture: Background for Eighteenth-Century Literature* (Englewood Cliffs, N.J.: Prentice-Hall, 1972), 88–89.
6. In his periodical *Causerie* of Monday, June 17, 1850, Sainte-Beuve announces, "On peut être tranquille, je viens parler ici ni du drame de Cénie, ni même des *Lettres péruviennes,* de ces ouvrages plus ou moins agréables à leur moment, et aujourd'hui tout à fait passés" (Charles-Augustin Sainte-Beuve, *Causeries du lundi,* 7th ed. [Paris: Garnier frères, (1924–25)], 2:208).
7. Joan DeJean, "Classical Reeducation," 28–29.
8. Goujet, *Bibliothèque française; ou Histoire de la littérature française* (Paris, 1740–56), quoted by DeJean, "Classical Reeducation," 31.
9. "Dans la société civile que sont [les femmes]? Une partie de la société, mais une partie subalterne qui doit recevoir la loi et non pas la donner. . . . Les Romans renversent l'ordre de la nature, ils rendent la femme indépendante de l'homme, ils la font arbitre suprême de tout, ils la divinisent; comment une femme au milieu de tant d'honneurs conserverait-elle la modestie?" (Père Porée, "Harangue sur les romans," quoted by François Granet, *Réflexions sur les ouvrages de littérature* [1737–1741; reprint, Geneva: Slatkine Reprints, 1968], 1:33).

Bibliography

Abensour, Léon. *La Femme et le féminisme avant la révolution*. 1923. Reprint. Geneva: Slatkine-Megariotis Reprints, 1977.

Adams, Percy G. *Travel Literature and the Evolution of the Novel*. Lexington: University Press of Kentucky, 1983.

Aïssé, Charlotte-Elisabeth. *Lettres de Mademoiselle Aïssé à Madame C. . . .* Paris: La Grange, 1787.

Alexander, Michael. *Omai, "Noble Savage."* London: Collins and Harvill Press, 1977.

Almansi, G. and D. A. Warren. "Roman épistolaire et analyse historique: 'L'Espion turc' de G. P. Marana." *Dix-septième siècle* 110–11 (1976): 57–73.

Altman, Janet Gurkin. "Graffigny's Epistemology and the Emergence of Third-World Ideology." In *Writing the Female Voice: Essays on Epistolary Literature*, edited by Elizabeth C. Goldsmith, 172–202. Boston, Mass.: Northeastern University Press, 1989.

Anderson, Benedict. *Imagined Communities: Reflections on the Origin and Spread of Nationalism*. London: Verso Editions, 1983.

Asad, Talal, ed. *Anthropology and the Colonial Encounter*. New York: Humanities Press, 1973.

Asad, Talal. "Two Images of Non-European Rule." In *Anthropology and the Colonial Encounter*, edited by Talal Asad, 103–18. New York: Humanities Press, 1973.

Atkinson, Geoffroy. *Les Relations de voyages du XVIIe siècle et l'évolution des idées*. Paris: Edouard Champion, 1924.

Bachaumont, Louis Petit de. *Mémoires secrets pour servir à l'histoire de la république des lettres en France*. London: John Adamsohn, 1777.

Balmas, Enea. "Introduction." In *Les Lettres iroquoises*, by J.-H. Maubert de Gouvest, 7–65. Paris: G. Nizet, 1962.

Baré, Jean-François. *Tahiti, le temps et les pouvoirs: Pour une anthropologie historique du Tahiti post-européen*. Paris: Editions de l'ORSTOM, 1987.

Barthes, Roland. "Image, raison, déraison." In *L'Univers de l'Encyclopédie*, by Roland Barthes, Robert Mauzi and Jean-Pierre Seguin, 11–16. Paris: Les Libraires Associés, 1964.

———. *S/Z*. Paris: Editions du Seuil, 1970.

Bassy, Alain-Marie. "Le Texte et l'image." In *Histoire de l'édition française*. Vol. 2, *Le Livre triomphant 1660–1830*, edited by Roger Chartier, Henri-Jean Martin and Jean-Pierre Vivet, 140–61. Paris: Promodis, 1984.

———. "Typographie, topographie, 'outopo-graphie': L'illustration scientifique et technique au XVIIIe siècle." In *Die Buchillustration im 18. Jahrhundert*, 206–33. Heidelberg: Carl Winter, Universitätsverlag, 1980.

Baudet, Henri. *Paradise on Earth: Some Thoughts on European Images of Non-European Man.* Translated by Elizabeth Wentholt. New Haven, Conn.: Yale University Press, 1965.

Bayle, Pierre. *Dictionnaire historique et critique.* 3d ed. Rotterdam: Michel Bohm, 1720.

———. *Pensées sur la comète.* Edited by A. Prat. Paris: E. Cornély, 1911–12.

Behdad, Ali. "The Eroticized Orient: Images of the Harem in Montesquieu and His Precursors." *Stanford French Review* 13, nos. 2–3 (Fall–Winter 1989): 109–26.

Bérenger, Jean Pierre. *Collection de tous les voyages faits autour du monde par les différentes nations de l'Europe.* Vol. 8. Lausanne: J.P. Heubach et cie., 1789.

Beyer, Charles-Jacques. "Montesquieu et la censure religieuse de 'L'Esprit des lois'." *Revue des sciences humaines* 70 (April–June 1953): 105–31.

Blet, Henri. *Histoire de la colonisation française: Naissance et déclin d'un empire.* Paris: B. Arthaud, 1946.

Boileau-Despréaux, Nicolas. *L'Art poétique.* Edited by Guillaume Picot. Paris: Bordas, 1972.

Boisrobert, M. *Histoire indienne d'Anaxandre et d'Orasie.* Paris: Frères Pomeray, 1629.

Boon, James. "Comparative De-enlightenment: Paradox and Limits in the History of Ethnology." *Daedalus* 109, no. 2 (Spring 1980): 73–91.

Bougainville, Louis-Antoine de. *Voyage autour du monde par la frégate du Roi "La Boudeuse" et la flûte "L'Etoile."* Edited by Jacques Proust. Paris: Gallimard, 1982.

Bouvier, Emile. "La Genèse de 'L'Histoire d'une Grecque moderne'." *Revue d'histoire littéraire de la France* 48 (1948): 113–30.

Bray, Bernard, and Isabelle Landy-Houillon. "Introduction." In *Lettres portugaises, Lettres d'une Péruvienne et autres romans d'amour par lettres,* edited by Bernard Bray and Isabelle Landy-Houillon, 15–56. Paris: Flammarion, 1983.

Breuil, Yves. "Une Lettre inédite relative à 'L'Histoire d'une Grecque moderne' de l'abbé Prévost." *Revue des sciences humaines* 33, no. 131 (July–September 1968): 391–400.

Broc, Numa. *La Géographie des philosophes: Géographes et voyageurs français au XVIIIe siècle.* Paris: Editions Ophrys, 1974.

Brooks, Peter. "Gauguin's Tahitian Body." *Yale Journal of Criticism* 3, no. 2 (1990): 51–90.

———. *The Novel of Worldliness.* Princeton, N.J.: Princeton University Press, 1969.

Bruner, Edward M. "Ethnography as Narrative." In *The Anthropology of Experience,* edited by Victor W. Turner and Edward M. Bruner, 3–30. Chicago, Ill.: University of Chicago Press, 1986.

Burke, Carolyn. "Psychoanalysis and Feminism in France: Rethinking the Maternal." In *The Future of Difference,* edited by Hester Eisenstein and Alice Jardine, 107–14. New Brunswick, N.J.: Rutgers University Press, 1985.

Campbell, Leon G. "Racism Without Race: Ethnic Group Relations in Late Colonial Peru." In *Studies in Eighteenth-Century Culture.* Vol. 3, *Racism in the Eighteenth Century,* edited by Harold E. Pagliaro, 323–33. Cleveland, Ohio: Press of Case Western Reserve University, 1973.

Campbell, Mary B. *The Witness and the Other World: Exotic European Travel Writing, 400–1600*. Ithaca, N.Y.: Cornell University Press, 1988.

Carcassonne, Elie. "Introduction." In *Lettres persanes*, by Charles Louis de Montesquieu, 1:vii–xxxvi. Paris: Editions Fernand Roches, 1929.

Cassirer, Ernst. *The Philosophy of the Enlightenment*. Translated by Fritz C.A. Koelln and James P. Pettegrove. Princeton, N.J.: Princeton University Press, 1951.

Cazenave, Jean. "Le Roman hispano-mauresque en France." *Revue de la littérature comparée* (October–December 1925): 594–640.

Certeau, Michel de. *Heterologies: Discourse on the Other*. Translated by Brian Massumi. Minneapolis: University of Minnesota Press, 1986.

Chardin, Jean. *Voyages de Monsieur le Chevalier Chardin, en Perse, et autres lieux de l'Orient*. Amsterdam: Jean Louis de Lorme, 1711.

Charnes, Abbé de. *Conversations sur la critique de la "Princesse de Clèves."* Paris: Barbin, 1679.

Chartier, Roger. *The Cultural Uses of Print in Early Modern France*. Translated by Lydia G. Cochrane. Princeton, N.J.: Princeton University Press, 1987.

Chartier, Roger, Dominique Julia and Marie Madeleine Compère, *L'Education en France du XVIe au XVIIIe siècle*. Paris: S.E.D.E.S., 1979.

Chartier, Roger, Henri-Jean Martin and Jean-Pierre Vivet, eds. *Histoire de l'édition française*. Vol. 2, *Le Livre triomphant 1660–1830*. Paris: Promodis, 1984.

Chartier, Roger, and Daniel Roche. "Les Pratiques urbaines de l'imprimé." In *Histoire de l'édition française*. Vol. 2, *Le Livre triomphant 1660–1830*, edited by Roger Chartier, Henri-Jean Martin and Jean-Pierre Vivet, 403–29. Paris: Promodis, 1984.

Chinard, Gilbert. *L'Amérique et le rêve exotique dans la littérature française au XVIIe et au XVIIIe siècle*. 1913. Reprint. Geneva: Slatkine Reprints, 1970.

Cixous, Hélène, Madeleine Gagnon and Annie Leclerc. *La Venue à l'écriture*. Paris: Union Générale d'Editions, 1977.

Clifford, James. "Introduction: Partial Truths." In *Writing Culture: The Poetics and Politics of Ethnography*, edited by James Clifford and George E. Marcus, 1–26. Berkeley and Los Angeles: University of California Press, 1986.

———. *The Predicament of Culture: Twentieth-Century Ethnography, Literature, and Art*. Cambridge, Mass.: Harvard University Press, 1988.

Commerson, Philibert. "Sur la découverte de la nouvelle Isle de Cythère ou Taïti." *Mercure de France* (November 1769): 196–207.

Conant, Martha Pike. *The Oriental Tale in England in the Eighteenth Century*. New York: Columbia University Press, 1908.

Constantine, David. *Early Greek Travellers and the Hellenic Ideal*. Cambridge: Cambridge University Press, 1984.

Cook, James. *A Collection of Voyages Round the World Performed by Royal Authority. Containing a Complete Historical Account of Captain Cook's First, Second, Third and Last Voyages*. London: A. Millar, W. Law and R. Cater, 1790.

Crisafulli, Alessandro S. "L'Observateur oriental avant les 'Lettres persanes'." *Lettres romanes* 8, no. 2 (1954): 91–113.

Dallas, Dorothy Frances. *Le Roman français de 1660 à 1680*. 1932. Reprint. Geneva: Slatkine Reprints, 1977.

Daniel, Norman. *Islam, Europe and Empire*. Edinburgh: Edinburgh University Press, 1966.

Darnton, Robert. *The Literary Underground of the Old Regime*. Cambridge, Mass.: Harvard University Press, 1982.

De Brosses, Charles. *Histoire des navigations aux terres australes*. 1756. Reprint. New York: DaCapo Press, "Bibliotheca Australiana #1," 1967.

DeJean, Joan. "Classical Reeducation: Decanonizing the Feminine." *Yale French Studies* 75 (1988): 26–39.

———. "The Female Tradition." *L'Esprit créateur* 23, no. 2 (Summer 1983): 3–8.

———. "Lafayette's Ellipses: The Privileges of Anonymity." *PMLA* 99, no. 5 (October 1984): 884–902.

———. "No Man's Land: The Novel's First Geography." *Yale French Studies* 73 (1987): 175–89.

De la Porte, Joseph, and J.-F. Lacroix, eds. *Histoire littéraire des femmes françaises*. Paris: Librairie Lacombe, 1769.

Démoris, René. *Le Roman à la première personne: Du Classicisme aux Lumières*. Paris: Armand Colin, 1975.

Deschamps, Léon. *Histoire de la question coloniale en France*. Paris: Librairie Plon, 1891.

D'Herbelot, Barthélemy. *Bibliothèque orientale ou Dictionnaire universel, contenant généralement tout ce qui regarde la connoissance des Peuples de l'Orient*. Paris: Par la compagnie des Libraires, 1697.

Diamond, Stanley. *In Search of the Primitive: A Critique of Civilization*. New Brunswick, N.J.: Transaction Books, 1974.

Diderot, Denis. *Supplément au Voyage de Bougainville*, edited by Gilbert Chinard. Paris: Droz, 1935.

———. *Supplément au Voyage de Bougainville*. In *Oeuvres complètes*, edited by Jean Assézat. Vol. 2. Paris: Garnier frères, 1875.

———. "Sur les femmes." In *Oeuvres complètes*, edited by Roger Lewinter, 10:31–53. Paris: Le Club français du livre, 1971.

Diderot, Denis, Jean le Rond d'Alembert, Louis de Jaucourt et al., eds. *Encyclopédie ou dictionnaire raisonné des sciences, des arts et des métiers*. Vols. 8, 9, 12. Neuchâtel: Chez Samuel Faulche (Fauche) et cie, 1765.

Dodd, Edward H., Jr. *The Rape of Tahiti*. New York: Dodd, Mead and Co., 1983.

Douglas, Mary. *Natural Symbols*. New York: Pantheon Books, 1973.

Duchêne, Albert. *La Politique coloniale de la France*. Paris: Payot, 1928.

Duchet, Michèle. *Anthropologie et histoire au siècle des lumières*. Paris: Librairie François Maspero, 1971.

Ducros, Louis. *La Société française au dix-huitième siècle, d'après les mémoires et les correspondances du temps*. Paris: Librairie A. Hatier, 1922.

Dufrenoy, Marie-Louise. *L'Orient romanesque en France 1704–1789*. Montreal: Editions Beauchemin, 1946.

Engel, Claire-Eliane. *Figures et aventures du XVIIIe siècle: Voyages et découvertes de l'Abbé Prévost*. Paris: Editions "Je sers," 1939.

———. *Le Véritable Abbé Prévost*. Monaco: Editions du Rocher, 1957.

Evans-Pritchard, E. E. *Social Anthropology and Other Essays*. New York: The Free Press of Glencoe, 1962.

Fabian, Johannes. *Time and the Other: How Anthropology Makes Its Object*. New York: Columbia University Press, 1983.

Faivre, Jean-Paul. *L'Expansion française dans le Pacifique de 1800 à 1842*. Paris: Nouvelles Editions Latines, 1953.

Fauchery, Pierre. *La Destinée féminine dans le roman européen du dix-huitième siècle (1713–1807)*. Paris: Librairie Armand Colin, 1972.

Fénelon, François de Salignac de la Mothe-. "Lettre à M. Dacier, secrétaire perpétuel de l'Académie française, sur les occupations de l'Académie." In *Oeuvres de Fénelon, archevêque de Cambrai*, 21: 156–261. Paris: Imprimerie de J.-A. Lebel, 1824.

Féral, Josette. "The Powers of Difference." In *The Future of Difference*, edited by Hester Eisenstein and Alice Jardine, 88–94. Boston: G. K. Hall and Co., 1980.

Feugère, Anatole. *Un Précurseur de la révolution: L'Abbé Raynal (1713–1796)*. 1922. Reprint. Geneva: Slatkine Reprints, 1970.

Foucault, Michel. *Discipline and Punish: The Birth of the Prison*. Translated by Alan Sheridan. New York: Vintage Books, 1979.

———. *The Order of Things: An Archaeology of the Human Sciences*. New York: Vintage Books, 1973.

Frye, Northrop. *Secular Scriptures: A Study of the Structure of Romance*. Cambridge, Mass.: Harvard University Press, 1976.

Furetière, Antoine. *Dictionnaire universel*. La Haye and Rotterdam: Arnout and Reinier Leers, 1691.

Furman, Nelly. "The Politics of Language: Beyond the Gender Principle?" In *Making a Difference: Feminist Literary Criticism*, edited by Gayle Greene and Coppélia Kahn, 59–79. New York: Methuen, 1985.

Galland, Antoine. "Discours pour servir de Préface à la 'Bibliothèque orientale'." In *Bibliothèque orientale ou Dictionnaire universel . . .* , by Barthélemy d'Herbelot, unnumbered. Paris: Par la compagnie des Librairies, 1697.

———. *Les Paroles remarquables, les bons mots et les maximes des Orientaux*. Paris: Simon Bernard, 1694.

Garcilaso de la Vega. *Histoire des Incas, Rois du Pérou*. Translated by Jean Baudoin. Amsterdam: Gerard Kuyper, 1704.

Gauthier, Xavière. "Is There Such a Thing as Women's Writing?" In *New French Feminisms*, edited by Elaine Marks and Isabelle de Courtivron, 161–64. New York: Schocken Books, 1981.

Gelfand, Elissa, and Margaret Switten. "Gender and the Rise of the Novel." *French Review* 61, no. 3 (February 1988): 443–53.

Genette, Gérard. *Figures II*. Paris: Editions du Seuil, "Tel Quel," 1969.

———. *Figures III*. Paris: Editions du Seuil, "Poétique," 1972.

Gerbi, Antonello. *The Dispute of the New World: The History of a Polemic, 1750–1900*. Translated by Jeremy Moyle. Pittsburgh, Pa.: University of Pittsburgh Press, 1973.

Girard, René. *Mensonge romantique et vérité romanesque*. Paris: Bernard Grasset, 1961.

Göçek, Fatma Müge. *East Encounters West: France and the Ottoman Empire in the Eighteenth Century*. New York: Oxford University Press, 1987.

Gomberville, Marin le Roy, sieur de. *Polexandre.* 1641. Reprint. Geneva: Slatkine Reprints, 1978.

Gossman, Lionel. *French Society and Culture: Background for Eighteenth-Century Literature.* Englewood Cliffs, N.J.: Prentice-Hall, Inc., 1972.

——. "Male and Female in Two Short Novels by Prévost." *Modern Language Review* 77, no. 1 (January 1982): 29–37.

Graffigny, Françoise-Paule d'Issembourg d'Happoncourt de. *Lettres d'une Péruvienne.* In *Lettres portugaises, Lettres d'une Péruvienne et autres romans d'amour par lettres,* edited by Bernard Bray and Isabelle Landy-Houillon, 249–362. Paris: Flammarion, 1983.

——. [Morel de Vindé, Mme.] *Lettres d'une Péruvienne par Madame de Grafigny. Nouvelle édition, augmentée d'une suite qui n'a point encore été imprimée.* Paris: P. Didot l'aîné, 1797.

Granet, François. *Réflexions sur les ouvrages de littérature.* 1737–1741. Reprint. Geneva: Slatkine Reprints, 1968.

Greenblatt, Stephen. *Renaissance Self-Fashioning: From More to Shakespeare.* Chicago, Ill.: University of Chicago Press, 1980.

——. "Towards a Poetics of Culture." In *The New Historicism,* edited by H. Aram Veeser, 1–14. New York: Routledge, 1989.

Grosrichard, Alain. *Structure du sérail.* Paris: Editions du Seuil, 1979.

Gudin de la Brenellerie, M. *Aux Manes de Louis XV, et des grands hommes qui ont vécu sous son règne.* Lausanne: n.p., 1777.

Gueulette, Thomas Simon. *Peruvian Tales.* Translated by Samuel Humphreys. In *The Novelist's Magazine.* Vol. 21. London: Harrison and Co., 1786.

Gutwirth, Madelyn. "1788: Civil Rights and Wrongs of Women." In *A New History of French Literature,* edited by Denis Hollier, 558–66. Cambridge, Mass.: Harvard University Press, 1989.

Guyot, Chamfort et al., eds. *Le Grand Vocabulaire françois.* Vol. 12. Paris: Hôtel de Thou, 1762.

Hanley, Sarah. "Family and State in Early Modern France: The Marriage Pact." In *Connecting Spheres: Women in the Western World, 1500 to the Present,* edited by Marilyn J. Boxer and Jean H. Quataert, 53–63. New York: Oxford University Press, 1987.

Hanse, Joseph. "Rocroi, 'Le Grand Cyrus', 'Zayde' et Bossuet." *Lettres romanes* 8, no. 2 (1954): 115–38.

Harari, Josué V. *Scenarios of the Imaginary: Theorizing the French Enlightenment.* Ithaca, N.Y.: Cornell University Press, 1987.

Harris, Marvin. *The Rise of Anthropological Theory.* New York: Thomas Y. Crowell Co., 1968.

Harth, Erica. *Ideology and Culture in Seventeenth-Century France.* Ithaca, N.Y.: Cornell University Press, 1983.

Hartzog, François. *The Mirror of Herodotus: The Representation of the Other in the Writing of History.* Translated by Janet Lloyd. Berkeley and Los Angeles: University of California Press, 1988.

Hauser, Arnold. *The Social History of Art.* Translated by Stanley Godman. New York: Vintage Books, 1951.

Hazard, Paul. *La Crise de la conscience européenne 1680–1715.* Paris: Fayard, "Les Grandes études littéraires," 1961.

———. *La Pensée européenne au XVIIIe siècle de Montesquieu à Lessing.* Paris: Boivin et cie, 1946.

Heilbrun, Carolyn G., and Margaret R. Higonnet, eds. *The Representation of Women in Fiction.* Baltimore, Md.: Johns Hopkins University Press, 1983.

Herbette, Maurice. *Une Ambassade persane sous Louis XIV.* Paris: Perrin et cie, 1907.

Herder, Johann Gottfried von. *Outlines of a Philosophy of the History of Man.* Translated by T. Churchill. 1800. Reprint. New York: Bergman Publishers, 1966.

Herrmann, Claudine. *Les Voleuses de langue.* Paris: Editions des Femmes, 1976.

Hill, Emita B. "Virtue on Trial: A Defense of Prévost's Théophé." *Studies on Voltaire and the Eighteenth Century* 67 (1969): 191–209.

Hodgen, Margaret T. *Early Anthropology in the Sixteenth and Seventeenth Centuries.* Philadelphia: University of Pennsylvania Press, 1964.

Hubert, René. "Essai sur l'histoire des origines et des progrès de la sociologie en France." *Revue d'histoire de la philosophie et d'histoire générale de la civilisation* 22 (April 1938): 111–55.

———. "Essai sur l'histoire des origines et des progrès de la sociologie en France (2e partie)." *Revue d'histoire de la philosophie et d'histoire générale de la civilisation* 24 (October 1938): 281–310.

Huet, Pierre-Daniel. "Lettre de Monsieur Huet à Monsieur de Segrais. De l'origine des romans." In *Zayde, Histoire espagnole,* by Monsieur de Segrais [Mme de Lafayette], 1:3–99. Paris: Claude Barbin, 1670.

Hugary de Lamarche-Courmont, Ignace. *Lettres d'Aza, ou d'un Péruvien.* In *Lettres d'une Péruvienne,* by Mme de Graffigny. Amsterdam: Aux Dépens du Délaissé, 1755.

Ivanoff, Nicola. *La Marquise de Sablé et son salon.* Paris: Les Presses modernes, 1927.

Jacquier, H. "Le Mirage et l'exotisme tahitiens dans la littérature." *Bulletin de la société des études océaniennes* 7, no. 2 (June 1945): 50–76.

Jones, Ann Rosalind. "Writing the Body: Towards an Understanding of *L'Ecriture féminine.*" *Feminist Studies* 7, no. 2 (1981): 247–63.

Kamuf, Peggy. *Fictions of Feminine Desire: Disclosures of Héloïse.* Lincoln: University of Nebraska Press, 1982.

Kerber, Linda K. "The Republican Ideology of the Revolutionary Generation." *American Quarterly* 37, no. 4 (Fall 1985): 474–95.

Kirsop, Wallace. "Nouveautés: théâtre et roman." In *Histoire de l'édition française.* Vol. 2, *Le Livre triomphant 1660–1830,* edited by Roger Chartier, Henri-Jean Martin and Jean-Pierre Vivet, 218–29. Paris: Promodis, 1984.

Kristeva, Julia. *Polylogue.* Paris: Editions du Seuil, 1977.

La Dixmerie, Nicolas Bricaire de. *Le Sauvage de Taïti aux Français, avec un envoi au philosophe ami des sauvages.* London and Paris: LeJay, 1770.

Lafayette, Marie-Madeleine Pioche de la Vergne, comtesse de. *Zaïde, Histoire espagnole.* In *Romans et nouvelles.* Edited by Emile Magne, 37–235. Paris: Editions Garnier, 1970.

Lambert, Anne Thérèse, marquise de. *Avis d'une mère à sa fille.* In *Oeuvres,* 55–116. Amsterdam: Par la Compagnie, 1766.

Landes, Joan B. *Woman and the Public Sphere in the Age of the French Revolution.*
    Ithaca, N.Y.: Cornell University Press, 1988.
Larnac, Jean. *Histoire de la littérature féminine en France.* Paris: Editions KRA,
    "Les Documentaires," 1929.
Lassalle-Maraval, Thérèse, and Christiane Faliu. "'Zaïde': du poncif mauresque à
    'l'incommunicabilité'." *Littératures (Annales de l'Université de Toulouse-Le Mi-
    rail)* 21 (1974): 149–64.
Laugaa, Maurice. *Lectures de Madame de Lafayette.* Paris: Librairie Armand Colin,
    1971.
LeBreton, André. *Le Roman du dix-huitième siècle.* 1898. Reprint. Geneva: Slatkine
    Reprints, 1970.
Leclerc, Gérard. *Anthropologie et colonialisme: Essai sur l'histoire de l'africanisme.* Paris:
    Librairie Arthème Fayard, 1972.
Lever, Maurice. *Le Roman français au XVIIe siècle.* Paris: Presses Universitaires de
    France, "Littératures modernes," 1981.
Lévi-Strauss, Claude. *Le Regard éloigné.* Paris: Plon, 1983.
Levy, Anita. "Blood, Kinship, and Gender." *Genders* 5 (Summer 1989): 70–85.
Locke, L. Leland. *The Ancient Quipu or Peruvian Knot Record.* New York: The
    American Museum of Natural History, 1923.
Lougee, Carolyn C. *Le Paradis des femmes: Women, Salons, and Social Stratification
    in Seventeenth-Century France.* Princeton, N.J.: Princeton University Press,
    1976.
Lovejoy, Arthur O. "The Supposed Primitivism of Rousseau's 'Discourse on In-
    equality.'" *Modern Philology* 21 (1923–24): 165–86.
Lussan, Marguerite de. *Les Veillées de Thessalie.* In *Le Cabinet des fées,* Vols. 26–27.
    Geneva: Barde, Manget et cie., 1787.
Lyons, John. "The Dead Center: Desire and Mediation in Lafayette's 'Zayde'."
    L'Esprit créateur 23, no. 2 (Summer 1983): 58–69.
MacArthur, Elizabeth J. "Devious Narratives: Refusal of Closure in Two Eigh-
    teenth-Century Novels." *Eighteenth-Century Studies* 21, no. 1 (Fall 1987):
    1–20.
MacKinnon, Catharine A. "Feminism, Marxism, Method, and the State: An
    Agenda for Theory." *Signs* 7, no. 3 (Spring 1982): 515–44.
Magendie, Maurice. *Le Roman français au XVIIe siècle: De "L'Astrée" au "Grand
    Cyrus."* Paris: Librairie E. Droz, 1932.
Marana, Giovanni P. *L'Espion dans les cours des princes chrétiens.* Cologne: Erasme
    Kinkius, 1700.
Marcus, George E., and Michael M. J. Fischer. *Anthropology as Cultural Critique:
    An Experimental Moment in the Human Sciences.* Chicago, Ill.: University of
    Chicago Press, 1986.
Marmontel, Jean-François. *Les Incas, ou la destruction de l'empire du Pérou.* Paris:
    Verdière, 1824.
Marshall, P. J., and Glyndwr Williams. *The Great Map of Mankind: British Per-
    ceptions of the World in the Age of Enlightenment.* London: J. M. Dent and
    Sons, Ltd., 1982.
Martin, Angus, Vivienne Mylne and Robert Frautschi, eds. *Bibliographie du genre
    romanesque français 1751–1800.* Paris: France Expansion, 1977.

Martin-Allanic, Jean-Etienne. *Bougainville navigateur et les découvertes de son temps.* Paris: Presses Universitaires de France, 1964.

Martino, Pierre. *L'Orient dans la littérature française au XVIIe et au XVIIIe siècle.* 1906. Reprint. New York: Lenox Hill, "Burt Franklin," 1971.

Masson, Paul. *Histoire du commerce français dans le Levant au XVIIIe siècle.* 1896. Reprint. New York: Burt Franklin, 1967.

Maupertuis, Pierre Louis Moreau de. *Oeuvres.* 1768. Reprint. Hildesheim, RFA: Georg Olms Verlagsbuchhandlung, 1965.

May, Georges. *Le Dilemme du roman au XVIIIe siècle.* Paris: Presses Universitaires de France, 1963.

Mercier, Paul. *Histoire de l'anthropologie.* Paris: Presses Universitaires de France, 1966.

Mesnardière, H.-J. Pilet de la. *La Poétique.* 1640. Reprint. Geneva: Slatkine Reprints, 1972.

Miller, Nancy K. "Emphasis Added: Plots and Plausibilities in Women's Fiction." *PMLA* 96, no. 1 (January 1981): 36–48.

———. *The Heroine's Text: Readings in the French and English Novel, 1722–1782.* New York: Columbia University Press, 1980.

———. "'L'Histoire d'une Grecque moderne': No-Win Hermeneutics." *Forum* (Houston) 16, no. 11 (1978): 2–10.

———. *Subject to Change: Reading Feminist Writing.* New York: Columbia University Press, 1988.

Moers, Ellen. *Literary Women.* New York: Doubleday and Co., 1976.

Monbart, Marie-Josephine de Lescun de. *Lettres taïtiennes, suite aux Lettres péruviennes.* Paris: Les Marchands de Nouveautés, [1786].

Montesquieu, Charles Louis de Secondat, baron de la Brède et de. *Lettres persanes.* In *Oeuvres complètes,* edited by Roger Caillois. Vol. 1. Paris: Gallimard, "Bibliothèque de la Pléiade," 1949.

———. *Persian Letters.* Translated by John Davidson. London: Privately Printed, 1892.

Mornet, Daniel. "Le Roman français de 1741 à 1760." In *La Nouvelle Héloïse,* by Jean-Jacques Rousseau, 7–75. Paris: Librairie Hachette, 1925.

———. "Les Enseignements des bibliothèques privées (1750–1780)." *Revue d'histoire littéraire de la France* 17 (1910): 449–96.

Mouligneau, Geneviève. *Madame de Lafayette, romancière?* Brussels: Editions de l'Université de Bruxelles, 1980.

Mylne, Vivienne. *The Eighteenth-Century French Novel: Techniques of Illusion.* New York: Barnes and Noble, 1965.

Newton, Judith Lowder. "History as Usual? Feminism and the 'New Historicism'." In *The New Historicism,* edited by H. Aram Veeser, 152–67. New York: Routledge, 1989.

Nicoletti, Gianni. "Introduzione." In *Lettres d'une Péruvienne,* by Mme de Graffigny, 11–46. Bari: Adriatica Editrice, 1967.

Niderst, Alain. "Introduction." In *Romans et nouvelles,* by Mme de Lafayette, vii–xliv. Paris: Editions Garnier, 1970.

Okin, Susan Moller. *Women in Western Political Thought.* Princeton, N.J.: Princeton University Press, 1979.

O'Reilly, Patrick, and Raoul Teissier. *Tahitiens: Répertoire biographique de la Polynésie française*. Paris: Publications de la Société des Océanistes, 1975.

Pagden, Anthony. *The Fall of Natural Man: The American Indian and the Origins of Comparative Ethnology*. Cambridge: Cambridge University Press, 1982.

Perry, Ruth. *Women, Letters and the Novel*. New York: AMS Press, 1980.

Pollack, Ellen. "Feminism and the New Historicism: A Tale of Difference or the Same Old Story?" *The Eighteenth Century* 29, no. 3 (1988): 281–86.

Popkin, Richard H. "The Philosophical Basis of Eighteenth-Century Racism." In *Studies in Eighteenth-Century Culture*. Vol. 3, *Racism in the Eighteenth Century*, ed. Harold E. Pagliaro, 245–62. Cleveland, Ohio: Press of Case Western Reserve University, 1973.

Pratt, Mary Louise. "Scratches on the Face of the Country; or, What Mr. Barrow Saw in the Land of the Bushmen." In *"Race," Writing and Difference*, edited by Henry Louis Gates, Jr., 138–62. Chicago, Ill.: University of Chicago Press, 1986.

Pratt, Minnie Bruce. "Identity: Skin Blood Heart." In *Yours in Struggle: Three Feminist Perspectives on Anti-Semitism and Racism*, by Elly Bulkin, Minnie Bruce Pratt and Barbara Smith, 11–68. Brooklyn, N.Y.: Long Haul Press, 1984.

Prévost, Antoine François, abbé. *Histoire d'une Grecque moderne*. Edited by Robert Mauzi. Paris: Union Générale d'Editions, "Bibliothèque 10/18," 1965.

———. *Manuel lexique, ou Dictionnaire portatif des mots françois dont la signification n'est pas familière à tout le monde*. Paris: Didot, 1755.

———. *The Story of a Fair Greek of Yesteryear*. Translated by James F. Jones, Jr. Potomac, Md.: Scripta Humanistica, 1984.

———. ed. *Histoire générale des voyages ou Nouvelle collection de toutes les relations de voyages par mer et par terre qui ont été publiées jusqu'à présent dans les différentes langues de toutes les Nations connues*. Vols. 1, 19 and 20. Amsterdam: E. Van Harrevelt and J. Changuion, 1773.

Pucci, Suzanne L. "Orientalism and Representations of Exteriority in Montesquieu's 'Lettres persanes'." *The Eighteenth Century* 26, no. 3 (1985): 263–79.

Rabasa, José. "Dialogue as Conquest: Mapping Spaces for Counter-Discourse." *Cultural Critique* 6 (Spring 1987): 131–59.

Ratner, Moses. *Theory and Criticism of the Novel in France From "L'Astrée" to 1750*. New York: De Palma Printing Co., 1937.

Raynal, Guillaume Thomas François, abbé. *Histoire philosophique et politique des établissemens et du commerce des Européens dans les deux Indes*. La Haye: Gosse fils, 1776.

———. *Histoire philosophique et politique des établissemens et du commerce des Européens dans les deux Indes*. Geneva: Jean-Léonard Pellet, 1781.

Rich, Adrienne. *On Lies, Secrets, and Silence: Selected Prose 1966–1978*. New York: W. W. Norton and Co., 1979.

Robertson, George. *The Discovery of Tahiti*. Edited by Hugh Carrington. Cambridge, England: The Hakluyt Society, 1948.

Rogers, Katharine M. "Subversion of Patriarchy in 'Les Lettres persanes'." *Philological Quarterly* 65, no. 1 (Winter 1986): 61–78.

Roncière, Charles de la. "Le Routier inédit d'un compagnon de Bougainville." *La Géographie* 35, no. 3 (March 1921): 217–50.

Rosso, Jeannette Geffriaud. *Etudes sur la féminité au XVIIe et XVIIIe siècles.* Pisa: Editrice Libreria Goliardica, 1984.

———. *Montesquieu et la féminité.* Pisa: Libreria Goliardica Editrice, 1977.

Rousseau, Jean-Jacques. *Discours sur l'origine de l'inégalité.* Edited by Jacques Roger. Paris: Garnier-Flammarion, 1971.

Rousselot, Paul. *Histoire de l'éducation des femmes.* 1883. Reprint. New York: Lenox Hill, "Burt Franklin," 1971.

Rousset, Jean. *Forme et signification: Essai sur les structures littéraires de Corneille à Claudel.* Paris: Librairie José Corti, 1962.

Ryan, Michael T. "Assimilating New Worlds in the Sixteenth and Seventeenth Centuries." *Comparative Studies in Society and History* 23, no. 4 (October 1981): 519–38.

Said, Edward W. *Orientalism.* New York: Vintage Books, 1978.

———. "Representing the Colonized: Anthropology's Interlocutors." *Critical Inquiry* 15, no. 2 (Winter 1989): 205–25.

Sainte-Beuve, Charles Augustin. *Causeries du lundi,* 7th ed. Vol. 2. Paris: Garnier frères, [1924–25].

———. *Portraits littéraires.* Paris: Garnier, 1864.

Schroeder, V. *L'Abbé Prévost: Sa vie, ses romans.* Paris: Hachette, 1898.

Schweitzer, Jerome W. *Georges de Scudéry's "Almahide": Authorship, Analysis, Sources and Structure.* Baltimore, Md.: Johns Hopkins University Press, 1939.

Scott, Joan Wallach. *Gender and the Politics of History.* New York: Columbia University Press, 1988.

Scudéry, Georges de. *Almahide ou l'esclave reine.* Paris: Augustin Courbé, 1660.

Scudéry, Madeleine de. *Ibrahim, ou l'illustre Bassa.* Paris: Antoine de Sommaville, 1644.

Sédillot, René. *Histoire des colonisations.* Paris: Librairie Arthème Fayard, 1958.

Segalen, Victor. *Essai sur l'exotisme: Une esthétique du divers.* Paris: Fata Morgana, 1978.

Segrais, Jean Regnault de. "Mémoires-Anecdotes." In *Oeuvres,* Vol. 2. Paris: Durand, 1755.

Sermain, Jean-Paul. "'L'Histoire d'une Grecque moderne': Une Rhétorique de l'exemple." *Dix-huitième siècle* 16 (1984): 357–67.

Serres, Michel. *The Parasite.* Translated by Lawrence R. Schehr. Baltimore, Md.: Johns Hopkins University Press, 1982.

Sewell, William. *Work and Revolution in France: The Language of Labor from the Old Regime to 1848.* Cambridge: Cambridge University Press, 1980.

Sgard, Jean. *Prévost romancier.* Paris: Librairie José Corti, 1968.

Showalter, English, Jr. *The Evolution of the French Novel, 1641–1782.* Princeton, N.J.: Princeton University Press, 1972.

———. "Les 'Lettres d'une Péruvienne': Composition, Publication, Suites." *Archives et Bibliothèques de Belgique* 54, nos. 1–4 (1983): 14–28.

Singerman, Alan J. "Réflexions sur une métaphore: le sérail dans les 'Lettres persanes'." *Studies on Voltaire and the Eighteenth Century* 185 (1980): 181–98.

Snyders, Georges. *La Pédagogie en France aux XVIIe et XVIIIe siècles.* Paris: Presses Universitaires de France, 1965.

Sontag, Susan. *Styles of Radical Will.* New York: Farrar, Straus and Giroux, 1966.

Spivak, Gayatri Chakravorty. *In Other Worlds: Essays in Cultural Politics.* New York: Routledge, 1988.

Stewart, Joan Hinde. "The Novelists and Their Fictions." In *French Women and the Age of Enlightenment,* edited by Samia I. Spencer, 197–211. Bloomington: Indiana University Press, 1984.

Stewart, Philip. *Imitation and Illusion in the French Memoir-Novel, 1700–1750: The Art of Make-Believe.* New Haven, Conn.: Yale University Press, 1969.

———. "On the 'Iconology' of Literary Illustration." In *Dilemmes du roman: Essays in Honor of Georges May,* edited by Catherine Lafarge, 251–67. Saratoga, Cal.: Anma Libri and Co., 1989.

Stone, Harriet. "Reading the Orient: Lafayette's 'Zaïde.'" *Romanic Review* 81, no. 2 (March 1990): 145–59.

Strong, Susan C. "Why a *Secret* Chain? Oriental Topoi and the Essential Mystery of the 'Lettres persanes.'" *Studies on Voltaire and the Eighteenth Century* 230 (1985): 167–79.

Tavernier, Jean Baptiste. *Les Six Voyages de Jean Baptiste Tavernier, Ecuyer Baron d'Aubonne en Turquie, en Perse, et aux Indes.* Paris: n.p., 1678.

Terdiman, Richard. "Is There Class in This Class?" In *The New Historicism,* edited by H. Aram Veeser, 225–30. New York: Routledge, 1989.

Thomas, Antoine-Léonard. *Essai sur le caractère, les moeurs et l'esprit des femmes dans les différens siècles.* Paris: Moutard, 1772.

Todorov, Tzvetan. *Nous et les autres: La Réflexion française sur la diversité humaine.* Paris: Editions du Seuil, "La Couleur des idées," 1989.

Toldo, Pietro. "Dell' Espion di Giovanni Paolo Marana e delle sue attinenze con le 'Lettres persanes' de Montesquieu." *Giornale storico della letteratura italiana* 29 (1897): 46–79.

Tomaselli, Sylvana. "The Enlightenment Debate on Women." *History Workshop* 20 (Autumn 1985): 101–24.

Torgovnick, Marianna. *Gone Primitive: Savage Intellects, Modern Lives.* Chicago, Ill.: University of Chicago Press, 1990.

Tournefort, Joseph Pitton de. *Relation d'un voyage du Levant fait par ordre du roy.* Paris: Imprimerie royale, 1717.

Turk, Edward Baron. *Baroque Fiction-Making: A Study of Gomberville's "Polexandre."* Chapel Hill, N.C.: North Carolina Studies in the Romance Languages and Literatures, 1978.

Undank, Jack. "Grafigny's Room of Her Own." *French Forum* 13, no. 3 (September 1988): 297–318.

Vandal, Albert. *Une Ambassade française en Orient sous Louis XV: La Mission du Marquis de Villeneuve 1728–1741.* Paris: Librairie Plon, 1887.

Van Roosbroeck, G. L. *Persian Letters Before Montesquieu.* New York: Lenox Hill, "Burt Franklin," 1972.

Vartanian, Aram. "Eroticism and Politics in the 'Lettres persanes'." *Romanic Review* 60, no. 1 (February 1969): 23–33.

Versini, Laurent. *Laclos et la tradition: Essai sur les sources et la technique des "Liaisons dangereuses."* Paris: Librairie Klincksieck, 1968.

Villedieu, Marie Catherine [Desjardins] de. *Carmente, Histoire grecque.* In *Oeuvres.* Vol. 3. Paris: Par la compagnie des Libraires, 1740.

Voltaire [François Marie Arouet]. *Alzire ou les Américains, tragédie.* Avignon: Louis Chambeau, 1764.

Walter, Eric. "Les Auteurs et le champ littéraire." In *Histoire de l'edition française.* Vol. 2, *Le Livre triomphant 1660–1830,* edited by Roger Chartier, Henri-Jean Martin and Jean-Pierre Vivet, 383–99. Paris: Promodis, 1984.

White, Hayden. "The Noble Savage Theme as Fetish." In *First Images of America,* edited by Fredi Chiapelli, 2:121–35. Berkeley and Los Angeles: University of California Press, 1976.

Wokler, Robert. "Perfectible Apes in Decadent Cultures: Rousseau's Anthropology Revisited." *Daedalus* 107, no. 3 (1978): 107–34.

Zurowski, Maciej. "L'Illustration du livre au XVIIIe siècle et l'histoire littéraire: Quelques questions de méthode." In *Illustration du livre et la littérature au XVIIIe siècle en France et en Pologne,* edited by Zdzislaw Libera, 105–18. Warsaw: Editions de l'Université de Varsovie, 1982.

Index

University of Pennsylvania Press
NEW CULTURAL STUDIES
Joan DeJean, Carroll Smith-Rosenberg, and Peter Stallybrass, Editors

Barbara J. Eckstein. *The Language of Fiction in a World of Pain: Reading Politics as Paradox.* 1990

Alex Owen. *The Darkened Room: Women, Power and Spiritualism in Late Victorian England.* 1990

Jonathan Arac and Harriet Ritvo, editors. *Macropolitics of Nineteenth-Century Literature: Nationalism, Exoticism, Imperialism.* 1991

Kathryn Gravdal. *Ravishing Maidens: Writing Rape in Medieval French Literature and Law.* 1991

Karma Lochrie. *Margery Kempe and Translations of the Flesh.* 1991

Julia V. Douthwaite. *Exotic Women: Literary Heroines and Cultural Strategies in Ancien Régime France.* 1992

John Barrell. *The Birth of Pandora and the Division of Knowledge.* 1992

Bruce Thomas Boehrer. *Monarchy and Incest in Renaissance England: Literature, Culture, Kinship, and Kingship.* 1992

This book has been set in Linotron Galliard. Galliard was designed for Mergenthaler in 1978 by Matthew Carter. Galliard retains many of the features of a sixteenth century typeface cut by Robert Granjon but has some modifications that give it a more contemporary look.

Printed on acid-free paper.